Christian Science in the Age of Mary Baker Eddy

Recent titles in
Contributions in American History

Christian Science in the Age of Mary Baker Eddy

Stuart E. Knee

Contributions in American History, Number 154
Jon L. Wakelyn, *Series Editor*

GREENWOOD PRESS
Westport, Connecticut
London

Library of Congress Cataloging-in-Publication Data

Knee, Stuart E.
      Christian Science in the age of Mary Baker Eddy / Stuart E. Knee.
          p.   cm—(Contributions in American history, ISSN 0084-9219
   ; no. 154)
      Includes bibliographical references and index.
      ISBN 0-313-28360-5 (alk. paper)
      1. Christian Science—United States—History—19th century.
   2. United States—Church history—19th century.   3. Eddy, Mary
   Baker, 1821–1910. 4. Christian Scientists—United States—
   Biography.   I. Title.   II. Series.
   BX6931.K54 1994
   289.5′09′034—dc20   93–37506

British Library Cataloguing in Publication Data is available.

Library of Congress Catalog Card Number: 93–37506
ISBN: 0-313-28360-5
ISSN: 0084–9219

First published in 1994

Greenwood Press, 88 Post Road West, Westport, CT 06881
An imprint of Greenwood Publishing Group, Inc.

Printed in the United States of America

The paper used in this book complies with the
Permanent Paper Standard issued by the National
Information Standards Organization (Z39.48–1984).

10 9 8 7 6 5 4 3 2 1

Copyright Acknowledgments

The author and publisher gratefully acknowledge permission to quote from the
following sources:

Streeter, Frank Sherwin. Mary Baker Eddy Litigation Papers, 1907, 1912, at the
New Hampshire Historical Society, Concord, New Hampshire.

Personal Miscellaneous—Mary Baker Eddy. Rare Books and Manuscripts Division,
The New York Public Library. Astor, Lenox and Tilden Foundations.

Every reasonable effort has been made to trace the owners of copyright materials
in this book, but in some cases this has proven impossible. The author and publisher
will be glad to receive information leading to more complete acknowledgments in
subsequent printings of the book and in the meantime extend their apologies for
any omissions.

For my father, Harold E. Knee,
and his youngest grandson, Eric

Contents

Preface

Christian Science was a manifestation of the unrest gripping the United States after the Civil War. The age in which the movement flowered was, at once, sordid and gilded, commercial and idealistic, disillusioned and optimistic. The "stormy way"[1] through which the ostensibly new religion passed was, in a sense, the road upon which many ideas and schemes are tried.

After a monumental surge of reaction against the institutions and ideology of the South, the myth of a united America vanished. Transcendental optimism, rugged individualism and unfettered democracy were old beliefs, withered and fading: they did not seem to suit a different age of conservatism, consolidation and business opportunism. Drawing on a combination of ideas gleaned from ancient Christian faith and antebellum New England popular culture and tradition was Christian Science, the formulation of a fragile, impressionable matron of forty-four, who slipped on the ice of Lynn, Massachusetts, and was "miraculously" healed of her physical injuries several days later.

Mary Baker Eddy's loss of "balance" may have gone unnoticed had it not occurred in 1866. That was a year, and in the latter third of the nineteenth century a generation, in which the Christian Science doctrine found an especially receptive audience. Intuitively, the belief in a spiritual presence capable of healing the body was more attractive than the selective, patrician Social Darwinist doctrine of Herbert Spencer. But the faith, apparently idealistic, emerged from a prophetic but deeply ambivalent intellect. It was not unusual, then, for Christian Science to project, at times, the narrow and uncompromising personality of its founder. At other times, Eddy's religion echoed the pragmatists' defense of individual worth against an entrenched order and, by its spiritual credo, heralded an age of optimism. But to her detractors, who felt threatened by her "strident cries," ruthless actions and uninvolving personality, Christian Science merely anaesthetized a society wallowing in its own laxity and self-contentment.

Eddy's vision was subjected to reasoned and irrational scrutiny until her death in 1910. In truth, Christian Science belonged only tenuously to a modern era. It reflected the prevailing optimism, feminism and utopianism of the Gilded Age—even a sense of order consonant with the Progressive period—but did not illuminate the stage with a unique light of its own. In a wider sense, its failure lay in its inability to overcome denominationalism and, perhaps, this was its major shortcoming. Rather than a radical movement to revivify sagging Protestantism, Christian Science remained the highly personal, occasionally untranslatable, extremely intense vision of one individual. Consequently, much of her disciples' force was spent in rationalizing a personal prophecy rather than creating a vital social consciousness.

NOTE

1. "Christian Science," *Current Opinion* 66 (June 1919): 382–83.

Acknowledgments

When I was a graduate student at Queens College of the City University of New York, I became interested in researching the topic of Christian Science in American culture. Perhaps it was a youthful fascination with alternative faiths bred by my personal experiences in the late 1960s or a generalized urge to research and write on religion; perhaps it was a subject that was just underwritten, especially by scholars who are not Christian Scientists. In any event, I am indebted to Professor Stanley P. Hirshson, who offered unstinting encouragement and enthusiasm.

More recently, when I decided that all my thoughts could and should properly coalesce into a book, I received the support of Greenwood Press series adviser Jon Wakelyn and editors Cynthia Harris and Dan Eades. I obtained primary materials from Ms. Melanie Yolles, Manuscript Specialist, Rare Books and Manuscripts Division, New York Public Library, and Ms. Elizabeth Hamlin-Morin, Manuscripts Curator, New Hampshire Historical Society. The documents arrived quickly and were processed efficiently by C. Michael Phillips, Reference Librarian and Coordinator of Interlibrary Loans at the College of Charleston's Robert Scott Small Library. Special thanks go to Library Director David Cohen, whose office absorbed all acquisition and duplication charges, and History Department secretary, Patricia Johnson, who prepared the manuscript for publication. To say I express my gratitude to Pat is simply inadequate. I couldn't have done it without her.

During the many months of preparation, research and writing, Professors Lee Drago, Malcolm Clark, Vincent Lannie, Jung-Fang Tsai, Clark Reynolds, Alpha Bah and James Vincent, all of the University of Charleston's History Department, and graduate student William Manning, listened to my endless discussions on Christian Science without being bored. I would like to offer warm words of appreciation to my wife Sonya, who remained enthusiastic in good times and bad. Last, but never least, I would like to thank my children, Karen, Mark and Ricky, for just being themselves. Their reward is that they get to see their names in print. Of course, I stand alone in accepting responsibility for any errors of fact or interpretive deficiencies recorded herein.

Christian Science
in the Age of
Mary Baker Eddy

Born in Belief

Mary Baker Eddy's life was neatly halved by the Civil War. Nondescript and aimless before 1866, her life became purposeful and powerful thereafter. Doubtlessly, the American cultural environment had a shaping influence on Eddy, but the founder of the Christian Science movement needed no particular milieu to solve what had become, by her middle age, an identity crisis of personal rather than national dimension. Very much like the founders of major Western faiths, her actions were not always consistent, her commitments not originally universal and the facts of her life far less intriguing than her perceived aura. It all adds up to a two-tiered existence. One layer is easily discernible because it can be documented; a second is more impressionistic and in some respects impenetrable. It is just at that impasse that the historian takes a leap of faith, utilizes more speculative and imaginative tools and occasionally departs from fact to explain the apparently unexplainable. If he or she does a creditable job, formidable oaks may sprout from little acorns. Perhaps that, too, was the desire of Mary Baker Eddy.

The environment of Eddy's youth was common for New England but the times were changing. The advent of Thomas Jefferson's Republican party and controversy surrounding participation in the War of 1812 uprooted Federalism in New Hampshire, although Portsmouth remained a proud seaport and a pocket of past glory. Native son Daniel Webster continued to think as a Federalist[1] but he could no longer speak for the party after 1816 because, in that presidential election year, it disintegrated. The interior played an increasingly central role in the life of the state, and fast replacing the word "commerce" were those defining industrialization: the mill, the "factory girl," entrepreneurialism and the Jacksonian Democratic party. In only two ways did New Hampshire remain unchanged: in the power of its religious faith, despite the disestablishment of the Congregational Church in 1817; and the status of its women, who were notably better off as spinsters or widows. Not so strangely, since it is a usual human trait, the negatives of New Hampshire life impressed Mary Baker Eddy more than the positives, though she rarely attempted to articulate a reason. Long on ideas but short on formal education, she sometimes wrote poetry but internalized much of her discontent. This made admirable sense, since it was not yet the season for women to reveal their grievances publicly or to participate actively to redress them.

As a matter of fact, Eddy was outwardly conventional in her youth and remained so into old age. By conventional, I mean the conforming fashion in which a nineteenth-century woman might approach her personal or societal difficulties. For example, Eddy would, in all likelihood, not be demonstrative since that wouldn't be consonant with the proprieties of Victorian culture. Her option, acceptable in a way that would doubtlessly confound Seneca Falls conventioneers, was to act obliquely, indirectly but nevertheless compellingly. In several revealing situations, Mary Baker Eddy developed this response to a high art.

The memories she had of her parents, Mark and Abigail, were respectful and loving but commonplace, with greater significance attached to the relationship she maintained with her father, a forbidding patriarch. In a recent interpretive biography of Mary Baker Eddy, Julius Silberger offered a description of Mark Baker that recalls Hans Luther, father of Martin: aggressive, driven, ambitious, irritable and authoritarian.[2] It would be a remarkable coincidence if this particular sketch didn't fit about one-third of the fathers in the Western world between the sixteenth and twentieth centuries! Since one normally debated one's father on important Calvinist matters, like the concept of predestination, Mary did so, while poor mother receded to a corner of her mind, nurturing and tender to be sure, but also passive, shadowy and wraithlike. It seemed a man's world where an insubstantial woman was dramatically overpowered by the decisive male. Mary Baker Eddy was impressed but not overwhelmed by this truth. She admired her father, she was thrice married and relied on male leadership within the Christian Science hierarchy, but she did make a subtle change in male-dominated faith during the creative phase of her spiritual life. If not precisely "mother," womanhood prevailed in Christian Science doctrine since the belief was founded on what was known as a maternal rather than a paternal principle.

Mary Baker Eddy had one natural child, George Glover, the product of her abbreviated first marriage to a man who died of yellow fever in June 1844, about three months before his son was born. George called Mary "mother" but only from a distance, since she rarely saw him after 1856.[3] This may be unusual for mothers of the nineteenth century, but it is even more so for a religious leader who enjoyed her adherents referring to her as "mother."

It is this relationship that is most difficult to explain. Until George was in his mid-thirties, Mary Baker Eddy could best be described as an absent mother, with a tie to her son that existed more in theory than in fact. As a young widow with a delicate constitution and no employment prospects, she relinquished her son, first to relatives and then to a trusted woman who had once worked for her grandmother. Before 1866 she dealt with this dilemma by rationalization.[4] After 1866 she did so by an interesting twist: she became the "mother" to a community that she could not be or was not capable of being individually.

Ostensibly the conventional daughter in a masculine environment and the conventional mother in a world where motherhood was a prevailing feminine value, Eddy demonstrated that appearances could be deceiving. And developing unconventional responses extended beyond personal relationships into medical practice.

When Mary Baker Eddy took a teenage interest in healing at her Sanbornton Bridge, New Hampshire, home, the medical profession in America was in its infancy, in both research and application. Real treatment competed with snake oil, states were just a half dozen years from repealing laws requiring licensing and education to practice medicine and treatment was often a local village art rather than an exact science. According to testimony she offered as an octogenarian, Eddy's chronic ailments helped sharpen her curiosity.[5]

A homeopathic physician experienced some success in alleviating her weakness and dyspepsia. "I got well under his treatment . . . and I studied homeopathy." Then, Eddy accepted a case that local physicians considered hopeless "and I cured" it. She actually used drugs but diluted them until they became mere placebos; a Boston chemist to whom she had sent a sample of what she called "attenuated medicine" assured her that it was nothing but "common table salt." Still, her patient gained. "There was my first discovery of the science of the mind." From that time, she rejected mediums and spiritualists as agents of recovery but not prayer, "since she was of a religious turn of mind."[6]

Crude discoveries like this, restless energy, transition and movement characterized American proletarian society in the antebellum era. For those seeking a more elite form of enlightenment, transcendentalism was an important intellectual orientation of formally educated Protestant Americans, including clergymen, authors, feminists and utopians. It influenced abolitionists in its insistence on moral perfectionism, human progress and humanity's triumph over illusory evil. It was optimistic, as was its founder, Ralph Waldo Emerson, about America's potential to master its future, harness its resources and lead civilization, but was cool to *The Scarlet Letter* and *Moby Dick*, romantic, almost Shakespearean works that were less sanguine about the fate of the human spirit and the elimination of evil.

Removed from its center, both intellectually and emotionally, Mary Baker Eddy's creative spark approached but never embraced transcendentalism.

The Civil War altered America's intellectual and philosophic orientation. Transcendentalism died as did its abolitionist offshoot. Both were buried at Bull Run, Antietam, Shiloh, Gettysburg, Atlanta, Spotsylvania, the Wilderness and Cold Harbor. In their stead, Reconstruction and the Gilded Age flourished, with their attendant characteristics of calculated opportunism, random perverse indecency and a pervasive callousness.[7] For observers like Mark Twain, who idealized the naivete of young lives once lived along the Mississippi, those years were tragic but also nostalgic. Indeed, the ebb tide following Appomattox offered opportunities of a different sort for Americans.

Naturalism, the study of man and his environment, replaced Jacksonian idealism. What counted between 1865 and 1890 was not where you hoped to be but where you were and there were two yardsticks by which to measure progress. Social Darwinism was the first and pragmatism was the second.

Social Darwinism, whose chief proponents were Herbert Spencer, William Graham Sumner, David Wells and E. A. Godkin, was a philosophy diverging from that of the "self-made man," prevalent in the United States before the Civil War. The latter signified that man was unique. Social Darwinism reflected the opposite: man was compelled to submit to natural law, which he must not and could not question. This philosophy supported extreme Calvinism in the religious sphere, with the rich being the elect, the Protestant ethic and status quo socially and a laissez-faire attitude economically. It was unnatural for the federal government to interfere with the activities of John D. Rockefeller, Andrew Carnegie and George Pullman. A Social Darwinist might evince a real distaste for "do-gooding" social workers who interfered with the natural order.

Around 1890 an intellectual shift got underway. Studied by philosophers Charles Peirce and William James, it challenged both social passivity and America's upper class. It was called pragmatism and was a necessary departure from rigid Spencerian dogma; it bridged the gap between nineteenth-century vision and twentieth-century achievement.

Pragmatism was the philosophy of experimentation and a departure from inflexible, Spencerian naturalism. According to its proponents there were universal laws, but human beings could comprehend and cope with them; it was optimistic about the ability of Americans to reconstruct society and solve collectively pressing social and economic problems. In brief, industrialization and self-development could go hand-in-hand, reason developed its own truth and relativism was a part of natural law.

The reasons for the shift in ideas were clear. Vast consolidation of business, the widening gap between the rich and the poor, great industrial strikes between 1877 and 1910, the depressions of 1873 and 1893, the

Populist revolt and unrelenting immigration caused what Richard Hofstadter called a "psychic crisis" of the 1890s.[8] Political reformers like Robert La Follette, Samuel "Golden Rule" Jones and Theodore Roosevelt concluded that citizens could stop those problems that consolidation and urbanization started. Positive action via government intervention was introduced at the state level by 1900; between 1901 and 1917, the managerial revolution became a national quest under three Progressive presidents: Theodore Roosevelt, William Howard Taft and Woodrow Wilson.

The social component of political Progressivism was called Reform Darwinism—the idea that every man was responsible for his fellow. Sociology, education, law, criminology, history and social work were disciplines taking an activist, environmentalist point of view. In protecting the rights of women in the workplace, jurist Louis D. Brandeis suggested that to be beneficial, law must spring from human need fostered by contemporary concerns. Oddly enough, the one ambivalent discipline was religion and the concept of organic law would encourage serious Protestant debate.

Theoretically, all Protestant denominations could agree on responsibility; fewer would aver that salvation was attainable by all and fewer still that society was improvable. Fundamentalists cared only for personal salvation and those called Radical Social Gospelers believed that a basic change from capitalism to socialism was necessary for the Kingdom of God to arrive. The middle-of-the-roaders are most interesting, however, because they made the greatest impact on the direction of social consciousness within the Protestant faith.

Led by Congregationalist minister Washington Gladden of Columbus, Ohio, those in the middle were known as advocates of the Social Gospel. Like most clerics of the day, they were interested in individual movements—temperance, alcoholism, prostitution—but their rhetoric furthered the cause of general societal reform. In denying survival of the fittest and reinterpreting original sin to mean bad environment rather than bad genes, they leaned toward positions favoring labor unions, welfare legislation and government action. If this was an urban phenomenon, a middle-class revolt of the early twentieth century whose purpose was to relieve the tension of being squeezed by big business, big labor and immigrants, what was the position of Christian Science, whose vital years (1850–1910), were shaped by the Mary Baker Eddy vision?

Some striking features of Mary Baker Eddy's life, both before and after 1850, are her diminished political consciousness, lack of interest in societal reform and intellectual banality. Having been reared in a Democratic household, whose opinion on slavery was ambiguous, much like that of doughface Franklin Pierce, she shared none of the guilt of Cambridge School transcendentalists for the Peculiar Institution. When it was convenient for her to do so, and perhaps politically correct, she spoke of an antislavery attitude but never felt any deep commitment toward it. Though she mentioned the greatness of Charles Sumner and "the martyrdom of John Brown,"[9] Eddy's attitude toward these men and their philosophies was impersonal. What seemed to enthrall her were heroism, honor and the battle for an ideal. She spoke favorably of America's war with Mexico in 1846,[10] not for the carnage but for the glory of triumph against an evil foe; she viewed the Civil War as a moral rather than a political struggle, pitting the force of darkness (the Confederacy) against the force of light (the Union). As a matriarch of Christian Science during the progressive period, war was still honorable, and she supported, at least verbally, the Caribbean and Latin American "Big Stick" policy of Theodore Roosevelt. Though she protested against the trinity of "imperialism, monopoly and a lax system of religion,"[11] she was a defender of William McKinley's foreign policy and the general policy of military preparedness.[12]

However, positions on American involvement abroad did not concern her primarily, nor did social reform at home. Insofar as social legislation was morally justifiable, she favored it. Monopoly crushed the spirit of the downtrodden: the workingman's salvation was just as important as the bank president's; the moral evil in "industrial slavery . . . insufficient freedoms and trusts" was undesirable. She upheld the "Declaration of Labor Unions" (1902) on purely humanitarian grounds.[13]

But these were only moral sanctions—wishes—with no activist mechanism and essentially no teeth. Closer to the mark on these issues are the pronouncements of Eddy's chief disciple and leader of New York City's Christian Science movement until 1909, Augusta E. Stetson. Her only concern with strikes were that they might inhibit church work. On unions, there was only one: that between God and man. If people were hungry, depressed, ill or jobless, she recommended "the teachings of our beloved leader, Mrs. Eddy. . . . our text-book, *Science and Health* will feed the . . . multitude . . . the bread of Life."[14]

Eddy's contribution to American reform must be understood in a different context. Indeed, historians would like to understand that the roots of this indigenous American Christian denomination somehow reflect the country's heritage and commitment. In some respects, they do, but only tenuously. Christian Scientists and Eddy biographer Robert Peel claim that the germ of Eddy's idea was transcendental, a natural outgrowth of that philosophy and 1830s religious revivals in New England villages.[15] According to Raymond J. Cunningham, it is also possible to link Christian Science to pragmatism, since its credo heralded an age of optimism by defending individual worth against an entrenched order.[16] Actually it is also possible that Christian Science is not antithetical to a pair of seemingly disparate movements, Social Darwinism and Progressivism; nor is it uncomfortable with post-Napoleonic Romanticism, first- and second-century Platonism or modern feminism. How can this be? Simply because Christian Science is the product not of social need, although it may have filled such a need in its maturity. As is the case with religions of Western civilization, personal quest preceded social fulfillment by at least a generation.

Eddy was reared in a Congregational, "predestined" home with a domineering father complementing the forbidding faith. Whether she liked or disliked being judged is unknown, but she structured her life in a way that might indicate a need to be mentally, if not physically, free. She utilized her family position—the youngest of six children—as a shield between herself and her father. Not much was expected from her and she didn't deliver much either—perhaps a smattering of classical knowledge that she obtained from her Dartmouth-educated brother Albert and those limited social graces appropriate for the Merrimack River environment of which she was a part. Perhaps she recognized something was amiss in her life because she was usually ill, with one chronic disorder or another. After all, the way to escape a controlling environment, even minimally, is to control it yourself. She may not have been successful at this time, but the effort was all. "I was born in belief . . . born not of God but of the flesh. . . . I was an invalid from . . . birth."[17] Even if she didn't know it or didn't care about it, the malady for which she sought a cure, powerlessnes and dependence, was a common one for nineteenth-century women.

Had she been a successful Victorian, Eddy might have well remained what she was. There is no evidence to substantiate any displeasure she might have had with the relatively uneventful life she led. She enjoyed small crises, ever-present suitors, family life in a small town, a little gossip and dabbling. Over the long run, however, she was unsuccessful in maintaining this rather placid existence, not through any fault of her own but just by the press of circumstance.

At age twenty-three she left her parents for marriage with George Glover. Following his sudden death she returned to New Hampshire from Wilmington, North Carolina, and remained with her mother and father for five more years. Following her mother's death in 1849, Mary, feeling that the texture of life had indeed altered, moved in with her sister Abigail, who lived a few miles north at Tilton. In 1853, nearly a decade after Glover's death, she married Daniel Patterson, an itinerant dentist. Wedded to him for twenty years in name, but only for the first ten in fact, they lost interest in each other after he returned from nine months of captivity in a Confederate prison. In 1862 she sought therapy from a Portland, Maine, mental healer named Phineas P. Quimby, possibly to ease her mental as well as her physical stress. She came to rely on him as she could not on her husband or father, but he died on 16 January 1866. Her father had died on 13 October 1865, leaving his estate to Mary's brother George Sullivan Baker, and $1.00 to each of his three daughters. Though it wasn't unusual for a father to pass his assets to a sole, surviving male heir,[18] it would be safe to assume that his action distanced Mary from the security she craved. At this point, she was a woman of reduced means, with the men she relied on unreliable, unavailable or deceased. If she disliked the Calvinist God of predestination as a girl and had "resisted her father on the matter of 'unconditional election,' "[19] she would be ill-disposed to accept divine judgment as an adult. It was, in the words of Edgar Allan Poe, her most "immemorial year."

On 1 February 1866, Eddy slipped on the ice of Lynn, Massachusetts, fell and suffered some sort of injury. Accounts vary as to what happened subsequently. According to Mary Baker Eddy, she was miraculously healed of her life-threatening wounds by the immediate curative powers of Scripture and Christ. Once she had activated the process, it took three days. Forty years after the event, attending physician Alvin Cushing claimed a two-week recuperation for Eddy from minor discomfort incurred from her fall. The active agencies in her recovery were an eighth of a grain of morphine to induce sleep and bedrest thereafter.[20]

Whether the claims of Eddy were true or not is beside the point. At the time of her accident, she was a self-involved wanderer; afterwards, she changed, not so much in content but in intent. As the years went on, she offered her adherents, women and men, the benefit of that change. It was a sense of mission, one for which a social conscience was unnecessary, only a religious one. In a way, then, followers of Christian Science did manifest a group awareness appropriate for the early twentieth century, albeit a more conservative one than that of the social reformers. Its followers were from the middle class; they may have looked content or serene to reporters but they were not, simply because the post-1865 world had left them powerless, squeezed in a vice between big business, big labor, immigration and urbanization. Mary Baker Eddy's sense of purpose offered them a path, though their work was far less tangible than that of the political Progressives.

Incidentally, to say that Mary Baker Eddy was a wanderer or self-centered is not meant to be critical; nor should it be taken negatively to portray her as a loner, an individual with many acquaintances, even an impressive array of disciples, but few if any intimate friends. Keeping a safe distance, remaining aloof or even acting and speaking as if one is bereft, a martyr, may not inhibit ideas. Strangely enough, this sort of withdrawal into the self might even enhance them. These characteristics were part of Eddy's persona and, without drawing too overconfident an analogy, one might suggest that she shared some qualities common to religious personalities of the Western tradition.

A wilderness is not uncommon for prophetic figures, whether it is physical or mental, real or imagined. Moses had a shaping experience at the burning bush, Jesus had his at the Last Supper and Luther experienced what Erik Erikson has called an "identity crisis" in a thunderstorm and a monastery.[21] Eddy had hers in more prosaic surroundings but the mechanism is identical. Unable to resolve a deeply personal conflict—in the case of Moses, what is monotheism; in the case of Jesus, what is history; in the case of Luther, what is salvation; in the case of Eddy, what is dependence—creative religious thinkers withdraw into a mental or physical desert, sometimes both. When such a person emerges, he or she has invented nothing. Rather, the individual has been inspired to use, discard and recast those forms that are best suited for conflict resolution. However, original thinkers are not always applauded for reworking the past. Sometimes they are so self-involved, they are not even aware of the debt they owe to previous minds and civilizations. Essentially, it is not for them to assess their contribution but for those who succeed to edit, interpret and widen the vision for the clarification and benefit of larger communities. Remember that every Moses has his Aaron, every Jesus his Paul, every Luther his Calvin. So the issue shifts from one of creativity—there is nothing new under the sun—to one of durability. Was Eddy's highly individualized, innovative, eccentric vision capable of being perpetuated? Under the proper circumstances, others were. Did she have or lack an editor? Was her work glacial—frozen in time—or malleable, flexible, adaptable?

Critical to her in 1866 was that her life lacked a focus or center. This was a wider issue, perhaps, for women of the nineteenth century who lacked men, means and faith in judgmental, patriarchal deities, but Eddy was not in any way concerned with relieving any human being's distress save her own. Between the years 1866 and 1873, she sought refuge in the homes of several different people, virtually oblivious to everything and everyone save her writing project which, in completion, revealed less about the human condition than it did the quest of a single person to free herself from many of the vows and promises of her immediate past. She apparently hit a societal nerve, since she was domiciled with people like herself who sought inner peace from a world out of control, or, more precisely, out of their control. For Mary Baker Eddy, the answers were Biblical, Scriptural and revelational; for others, peace lay in Eastern philosophies, forms of mysticism, parapsychology or psychotherapy. One thing was assured: the search was on.

Mary Baker Eddy surfaced in 1875 as the author of *Science and Health with Key to the Scriptures*, a text seven years in preparation and published with a subvention from her small circle of students.[22] Though several other Christian Science books were published between 1875 and 1910, as were newspapers and periodicals, none would ever replace *Science and Health* as the formulator of those principles always associated with Christian Science.

In the Christian Science system, as conceived by its founder, there are two types of thought, human and divine. The former is undesirable since physical or mortal perception is illusory, deceitful, even evil. The latter is of God, the true stuff of creation, and is scientific law—hence the name Christian Science. It is absolute, unchangeable, virtuous, principled, heavenly and unfailingly demonstrable, like a mathematical formula.[23]

"God thought" emanates from the only real thought source, a feminine and masculine wellspring of spirit called the Father-Mother God, and is eternal truth. Any other thought, specifically that emanating from the human mind and called "mortal," is pernicious and has to be overcome. If one learns to "transcend" mortal thought, as Christian Science metaphysicians or practitioners claim to do, one banishes mortal perception of disease, suffering and death. Having been overcome, the three vanish because their nature is insubstantial. What remains for those who perceive it is "real," indeed the only reality: eternal, spiritual, truthful, verifiable "God life," or what existed for Jesus in his resurrected state, after he had shed his mortal illusion. Christian Science posits that there is no actual organic disease, physical suffering or absolute death, only the shadowy fears they project upon humanity. Ridding people of fear will rid them of physical maladies, which exist only in fearful minds. Thus, replacing "wrong" thoughts with "right" thoughts is the medicine and curative of Christian Science.

The characteristics of Christian Science tend to shed some light on its varied provenance. In the face of tragedy, sorrow or illness, the way of the faith is "cool," detached, impersonal rather than "hot," personally compelling or involved. Perfectionist, Platonic,[24] serene and passive, the Scientist responds in ways equally suitable for some nineteenth-century Victorians, some first- and second-century Christians and some twentieth-century communitarians. In short, its public image closely corresponds to the personality of Mary Baker Eddy.

Prior to her seven-year departure for Boston from Lynn, beginning the summer of 1882, and the introduction of Christian Science into a large, urban environment, Mary Baker Eddy was again widowed, this time from Asa Eddy, a former pupil whom she wed in 1877. She had also become pastor to the tiny sect she had founded, was the sole instructor at a school she had created, the Massachusetts Metaphysical College, founded the Christian Science Association and chartered, with twenty-six students, the Church of Christ, Scientist. To Eddy, the truth she taught was neither Protestant nor social: it was an exact science. As she perceived it, Christian Science "truth, independent of doctrines and time-honored systems," had begun to "twist the knife . . . into the fleshy conventionality of materialism." It was "no transcendental philosophy for the occasional visionary; it must work in the . . . face of small minds, petty, personal spites, deep-lying resistance and malice."[25] But it did have a tacit agenda: it had to work personally to justify the image Eddy shaped of herself in the cauldron of a quarter-century struggle to achieve dignity, self-reliance, control and independence, which was a difficult task for a woman of the 1870s. With tenacity and single-mindedness, she sought freedom from want, freedom from unreliable males (though she married three times) and freedom from the burden of the Congregational faith, which she left in 1875. There was bound to be, and always was, a conflict between personal realization and group interests. This conflict, usually resolved in mainstream Western faith by a socially conscious religious disciple and systematizer, was never dealt with conclusively. But in the movement's formative phase, such tension proved creative.

To achieve resolution, it was essential that Christian Science obtain a public forum and debate social or religious issues. Broadening the founder's vision by applying it to a variety of situations was a way to attract a wider membership. In Boston, Mary Baker Eddy made notable appearances in defense of her truth at wealthy, impressive Protestant churches; in 1893 Christian Science was represented at a congress of international religion convened at the Chicago World's Fair.[26] To observers and supporters, Science assumed a burden that traditional religion and Social Darwinism were unable to shoulder: that of supplying solutions to problems confounding other systems of thought. Its experimental nature seemed to confirm its affinity to pragmatism; its system of spiritual perfectibility appeared more realizable than failed, intensely guilt-ridden, hopelessly utopian, outmoded transcendentalism. Also, the leader herself was pastor and the mere fact of her leadership offered a promise of feminine achievement that would outstrip the accomplishments of social reformers like Jane Addams, Elizabeth Cady Stanton and Susan B. Anthony, none of whom corresponded significantly with Mary Baker Eddy, though all were her contemporaries.

Truthfully, the connection between Christian Science and reform was moot. Its commitment to women's physical benefit was not what it appeared to be. While it is so that middle-class women were represented in the movement's membership to an extraordinary degree, that women were trained as Christian Science practitioners and the elevation of a woman to First Reader or pastor in the Church was possible, women were, in 1909, unrepresented on the Mother Church Board of Directors[27] and the Christian Science Publication Society. At the time of her death, Mary Baker Eddy was attended by a large administrative staff, the most notable of whom were men. With regard to an appointment to the Publication Committee at the large New York City Christian Science church, Eddy considered the role that "females" should play but advised that "a male must be the one."[28]

It is a contradiction, but a resolvable one in terms of Victorian mentalities in general and Eddy's view of male dependability in particular. One notes that Christian Science leans heavily on the concept of divine Love, a feminine manifestation of God coequal with the spiritual, healing Christ and combined in an all-embracing Father-Mother God.[29] This God, representative of maternal instinct, curbed the judgmental qualities of Congregationalism, which probably troubled Eddy for so long, while incorporating a contemporary view that woman was "a higher idea of God" than man.

No less a feminist than Charlotte Perkins Gilman, certainly not a defender of Victorian matriology, was sympathetic to the idea that women were representative of "life and love" in religion while a masculine emphasis focused on "death and punishment."[30] With the incorporation of such a belief into Christian Science, Mary Baker Eddy may have been attempting to find her self-worth, though she continued to depend on men, however disappointing they were, for support and legitimacy. Traditional feminist concepts, grounded in human concerns, did not move Eddy as much as imagery. After all, one need not defend the flesh if reality was spiritual.

Her relation to transcendentalism and pragmatism was equally ambiguous. While Christian Science could be construed as defending individual worth against an entrenched order, Eddy had no faith in institutions or people. She once said that the times she lived in engendered "the disease of moral insanity and idiocy,"[31] and the way to cure it was the exercise of an unyielding, universal spiritual law. Within this context, chameleon Science had a Darwinist thread, of which Eddy may have been aware. "Religions may waste away," she intoned, "but the fittest survives."[32]

It should be clear by now that Christian Science utilized certain historical elements but it is difficult to contend that it drew inspiration from any of them since the foundations of the belief—Gospel healing, revelation, immediacy—deny historical processes. "Mere historic incidents and personal events are frivolous . . . unless they illustrate the ethics of Truth. . . . [H]uman history needs to be revised, and the material record expunged."[33] In its place, Eddy empowered ahistorical trends and impersonal principles that always worked and couldn't disappoint, as fallible humanity often did.

Historian Stephen Gottschalk correctly avers that Christian Science is not Protestant.[34] Its rudiment is drawn from a form of Christianity which, in the first few centuries before Christ through the first few centuries following him, derived its strength from the sort of apocalyptic Judaism practiced by the Dead Sea sect of Essenes. Both the ancient and modern beliefs rushed to precipitate a kingdom of the spirit by passivity, withdrawal and, generally, ending human involvement in the historical process. Both also incorporated a dualistic system pitting good against evil, mind against matter and, in the case of Christian Science, spiritual truth against Malicious Animal Magnetism (MAM). The latter, an uncomfortable construct for some Christian Science leaders at the time of Eddy's death,[35] was a sort of dogma incorporated into *Science and Health* never emphasized but always an undercurrent. Malicious Animal Magnetism was a form of thought capable of existing only in the absence of "God-thought." It was at once intangible, illusory, carnal and mortal; it could be projected upon Scientists engaged in healing for the purpose of either injuring or assassinating them. Yet it had no substance. Like a black hole in the universe, its existence was entirely dependent on invisible, negative forces. Banishing MAM was a preoccupation of Eddy, Augusta E. Stetson (her chief disciple until 1909) [36] and lesser-known Scientists. To confront it meant to enter a spiritual combat in which concentration on Love, healing, truth and Life rearranged, turned, overcame and annihilated the minions of darkness. Christian Scientists had no need to attack social issues if their battlefield existed on another plane, a higher one, withdrawn from the vacuous human struggle. Nevertheless, they did see themselves as reformers, [37] not in the urban, political sense but in their expression of satyagraha, or passive resistance, as a method of triumph. Powerless individuals and groups, or those who feel that way, from Nazarenes to Hindus to American Victorian women to Christian Scientists do not meliorate the flesh because they feel helpless to do so; they overcome it,[38] thus crowning an earthly defeat with the garland of spiritual triumph. Unfortunately, this sort of activity did not make pleasant reading in newspapers in the late nineteenth and early twentieth centuries, when a male leadership anticipating the future sought respectability.

Finally, it is hard to say how Mary Baker Eddy viewed herself. "Soulful-eyed,"[39] grandmotherly, reclusive twice in her career (1866–1873; 1889–1910), she wanted privacy. Seeking seclusion can be understood within the wider scheme of religious history as a prophetic style and within the Victorian framework as suitable for women. In the latter instance, it can be called exercising power behind the scenes. Eddy often said that her calling demanded privacy since one could not serve two masters, the crowd and Christian Science. She was at ease in a role in which she could receive male support: in matters of schism, bad publicity and worldly challenge, she entrusted a male staff or a male Board of Directors with adjudicating the issue. She taught, offered guidance to and received gifts from students but rarely defended them in crises relating to doctrinal change; moreover, she was aloof to those of her followers who sought to exercise individuality. Invariably she left them to the mercies of the Mother Church Board of Directors. Her motivations are obscure. She normally said that she had no time for mundane matters, since she was fully engaged in realizing a higher purpose,[40] but the effect was to preserve her unchallenged vision and the revelational, concretized version of her faith.

Since prophets tend to interpret visions, it may not be absolutely correct to call Eddy a prophet. A "way-shower," a spiritual incarnation of feminine Principle, divine Love, and Gospel healing put us closer to the mark. "Jesus was not Christ," Eddy wrote in 1900. "Christ is spiritual. . . . Jesus was a Godlike man. I am . . . a Godlike woman. . . . Jesus was not understood at the time [he] demonstrated . . . so I am not."[41] Her frequent allusions to abandonment, friendlessness, loneliness, suffering, martyrdom and spiri-tual—not bodily—resurrection[42] indicate that she reserved a position for herself at the heart of the drama rather than at its periphery. On 3 October 1904, she invited her "dearest Student . . . Augusta to be my Mary."[43]

Aside from all this, there was a plethora of trends unfavorable for universalizing the faith. Among them were the petrification of the Eddy vision within the 1895 Mother Church *Manual*, the founder's failure to entertain suggestions for change from students, many of whom were content with preservation rather than interpretation, Eddy's mandate that Christian Science and the Mother Church be acknowledged as only "hers"[44] and a medical practice based entirely on the application of the Gospel's universal healing law to physical and mental disease. The movement acquired an impressive but one-dimensional membership, drawn from those who found liberation in an eternal, timeless spiritual law. Nevertheless, those who did labored tirelessly on behalf of Science and remained loyally pro-Eddy, even within the larger, decentralized post-1889 Church framework. In that year, at age sixty-eight, Eddy withdrew to Pleasant View, her Concord, New Hampshire, estate, where she was attended by a retinue of former students, mostly men, who assumed the day-to-day responsibilities for—but not primacy in—the Christian Science movement. These men, or their types, were represented on the Board of Directors of the Boston Mother Church, a key governing body, and the Board of the Christian Science Publication Society, founded in 1898. Intensely supportive, the sort of men Eddy sought in her youthful maturity, they followed her back to Boston in January 1908, where she died nearly three years later at Chestnut Hill. "God is my life"[45] were her final words, but men remained her protectors.

During her active years in Boston, (1882–89), she taught, wrote and publicized on the illusory qualities of matter, the reality of divine Love and the relevance of Christ's law, which was immediately and unconditionally available for those who sought its spiritual, healing qualities. She made inroads among the anxious—professionals, civil servants, merchants, their wives and single women—who regarded social action for the dispossessed as inimical to their status aspirations but viewed personal assurance and reassurance in a more favorable light. Most assuredly, they lacked the resources of an Armour, Swift and Westinghouse but, in the 1890s and early 1900s, they had sufficient capital to finance the construction of two tremendous institutions, the Mother Church in Boston and the First Church of Christ, Scientist, on New York's upper West Side. They lacked reforming zeal but the *Christian Science Monitor*, founded in November 1908, was the perfect vehicle for expressing spiritual concerns.

What did these middle-class citizens desire from America? Obviously, it was something they were not getting: a dream, a desire, a memory, an identity (that was not quite tangible and not redeemable), something fading in the grass that could not be regained but could also not be articulated. Much as the closing of the frontier, it was more a state of mind than a piece of territory.

What they wanted was a "forever young, forever old"feeling of security offered them by Christian Science. Though it seemed a heavenly philosophy, it mentioned no afterlife. What it promised in spiritual perfection would be delivered here and now.[46] One did not have to queue up behind Afro-Americans, labor leaders, Italian and East European ethnics, billionaires or suffragettes; one, of course, could sympathize with the urban proletariat, but theirs was not the struggle of the Scientist. It was altogether too mundane. On the other hand, here was Mary Baker Eddy, a formerly afflicted woman, similar to others of her class, but now "well" and fashioning a response suitable for others who were neither rich nor poor—just "needy." To those who followed Science, the belief was appropriate because it was "modern": like Theodore Roosevelt, it searched for order, but obtained a moral high ground uniquely appropriate for those adrift with no particular champion. If the membership of Science was circumscribed— permanently set in the low six figures from the time of its greatest growth to the present—there is a good reason. It has a socially limited but not socially deprived following, all of whom attest in greater ways to the tenacity rather than the universality of Christian Science. The members' arena is one of divine demonstration (for which they need assume no responsibility) rather than human performance (where there is much room for error).

As divorced as they wished to be from the theater of human action, Scientists nevertheless became involved in positive and negative ways. Positively, Christian Science practitioners were to be found, by 1900, in Brazil, England, France, Germany, Scotland and the four Canadian provinces of Nova Scotia, Quebec, Ontario and Manitoba. Shortly thereafter, Christian Science churches were founded in Africa, China, the Philippines, Australia, Iceland, Wales, Holland, Norway, Sweden, Panama and Argentina. Christian Science, therefore, was active in spreading Christianity via the means of "missionary" imperialism during the Progressive era. A contradiction arose when Science declined to enter the field of social reform in these countries as well as the United States.[47] But it couldn't and wouldn't. The limits of Christian Science participation were to project Mary Baker Eddy as a role model for Victorian womanhood, assure salvation as an immediate spiritual possibility rather than a remote physical one and scotch the collective egos of those urban managers who assumed that tinkering with technology, big business and big labor would ensure societal betterment. Perhaps the best of Eddy's message, the part that would endure beyond her death, is that social reform was only a part of national faith.[48] Real confidence would have to be purchased with right states of mind as well as federal legislation. One day, in the not too distant future, the medical profession and mainstream Protestantism would take heed.

In 1910, though, Eddy was an icon to her followers rather than a heroic human being capable of emulation. Ironically, it really didn't matter whether she was personally inconsistent[49] in her spiritual practice. She retained forms within the Church with which she was comfortable, like christening and communion,[50] either because she found them appealing or her congregants did. Schism, sundry and diverse litigation, exploitive yellow journalists, critical Protestant ministers of both conservative and liberal bent and an abusive medical establishment ill at ease with its somatic orientation heightened her charisma. "Christian Science was born out of a materialist age which regarded man as a machine . . . his diseases were disorders of the machine. It was born out of a nationalistic age: an age which confounded dogma with faith, which refused to look at things unseen and eternal . . . which condemned mysticism and glorified the scientific method."[51] One might add that it had been conceived eighteen centuries before by apocalyptic Jews, Essenes, Nazarenes and new Christians, who banked their future on "amazing grace" rather than human agencies, of which they had despaired, and historic processes.

As for Mary Baker Eddy, she was, remained and in a sense still is the sole unassailable Christian Science leader, the single memorable name among tens of thousands of adherents. She was adored and despised in her lifetime, but never ignored; she was feared and detested by an elite who wished to preserve its prerogatives from a middle-class challenge. Yet she herself was elite, a supreme individual whose movement left little room for the socially disadvantaged.

Christian Science was the subject of wide controversy during the lifetime of Mary Baker Eddy. Her accusers judged her harshly but the verdict was turned back upon them. Science survived the Gilded Age and the Progressive era.

NOTES

1. Merrill D. Peterson, *The Great Triumvirate: Webster, Clay and Calhoun* (New York: Oxford University Press, 1987), 33–37, 97.

2. Julius Silberger, Jr., *Mary Baker Eddy: An Interpretive Biography of the Founder of Christian Science* (Boston: Little, Brown, 1980), 18–19.

3. Ibid., 54, 135.

4. Ibid., 54.

5. Mary Baker Eddy's interview before Hon. Edgar Aldrich, Hon. Hosea W. Parker and Dr. George F. Jelly at Concord, N.H., 14 August 1907. Mary Baker Eddy Litigation Papers, 1907, 1912. Steno Records, 1907, Folder 1, 104 under Frank Sherwin Streeter, New Hampshire Historical Society, Concord, N.H.

6. Steno Records, 1907, Folder 1, 106, Streeter, Eddy Litigation Papers.

7. *Editorial Comments on the Life and Work of Mary Baker Eddy* (Boston: Christian Science, 1911), 19–20; Lloyd Morris, *Postscript to Yesterday: America, The Last Fifty Years* (New York: Random House, 1947), 430.

8. Richard Hofstadter, *The Age of Reform* (New York: Vintage Books, 1955), 17, 93, 166.

9. Robert Peel, *Mary Baker Eddy: The Years of Discovery* (New York: Holt, Rinehart and Winston, 1966), 143, 277–78.

10. Ibid., 85.

11. "Christian Scientists' Annual Communion Service at the Mother Church," *New York Times*, 5 June 1899.

12. "$100,000 for Missionaries," *New York Times*, 22 August 1898.

13. Erwin D. Canham, *Commitment to Freedom* (Boston: Houghton Mifflin, 1958), 13.

14. Augusta E. Stetson, *Reminiscences, Sermons and Correspondence Proving Adherence to the Principle of Christian Science as Taught by Mary Baker Eddy* (New York: G. P. Putnam's Sons, 1913), 266, 587, 623.

15. Robert Peel, *Christian Science: Its Encounter with American Culture* (New York: Henry Holt, 1958), xi. A similar theme may be found in I. Woodbridge Riley, "The Personal Sources of Christian Science," *Psychological Review* 10 (November 1903): 606. A few years later, Riley tried to show that Eddy plagiarized from Bronson Alcott and "borrowed" from the writings of the spiritualist Emanuel Swedenborg. See B. R. Wilson, "The Origins of Christian Science: A Survey," *Hibbert Journal* 57 (January 1959): 164.

16. Raymond J. Cunningham, "The Impact of Christian Science on American Churches 1880–1910," *American Historical Review*, 72 (April 1967): 886.

17. Steno Records, 1907, Folder 1, 103, Streeter, Eddy Litigation Papers.

18. Silberger, *Mary Baker Eddy*, Chaps. 2–3.

19. Ibid., 25.

20. Briefs for the case of Eddy, by Next Friends, against Frye, et al. in the Superior Court of the State of New Hampshire, April 1907, 16–19, Streeter, Eddy Litigation Papers.

21. Erik H. Erikson, *Young Man Luther: A Study in Psychoanalysis and History* (New York: W. W. Norton, 1962), Chap. 2 and 91–93.

22. Silberger, *Mary Baker Eddy*, 119.

23. Mary Baker Glover (Eddy) to W. W. Wright, ca. 10 March 1871, Personal Miscellaneous Papers—Mary Baker Eddy, Rare Books and Manuscripts Division, The New York Public Library, Astor, Lenox and Tilden Foundations, New York City.

24. Stetson, *Reminiscences, Sermons and Correspondence*, 279, 304.

25. Peel, *Christian Science*, 67.

26. *Letters of Mary Baker Eddy to Augusta E. Stetson, C.S.D. 1889–1909*, reproduced from the manuscript collection in the Huntington Library, San Marino, Calif. (Cuyahoga Falls, Ohio: Emma, 1990), 40; Stephen Gottschalk, *The Emergence of Christian Science in American Religious Life* (Berkeley: University of California Press, 1975), prologue and 193.

27. Stetson, *Reminiscences, Sermons and Correspondence*, 1196.

28. *Letters of Mary Baker Eddy to Augusta E. Stetson*, 66–67.

29. Stetson, *Reminiscences, Sermons and Correspondence*, 250–51, 253–54, 264, 266, 284–85, 287, 289, 300, 302–3, 306, 335, 360–61, 382, 387, 398, 404, 408–9, 415, 424, 434, 480, 483, 505, 578, 581, 609, 619, 621, 625, 638, 692, 706, 719, 722, 724, 753, 773, 777, 878, 1105, 1107, 1110, 1155, 1164, 1181; *Letters of Mary Baker Eddy to Augusta E. Stetson*, 97.

30. Gayle Kimball, *The Religious Ideas of Harriet Beecher Stowe: Her Gospel of Womanhood* (New York: Edwin Mellen, 1982), 81.

31. Mary Baker Eddy to Ebenezer J. Foster Eddy, 17 March 1897, Steno Records, 1907, Folder 2, 256, Streeter, Eddy Litigation Papers.

32. *Letters of Mary Baker Eddy to Augusta E. Stetson*, 8.

33. Stetson, *Reminiscences, Sermons and Correspondence*, 1085.

34. Gottschalk, *Emergence of Christian Science*, 46, 89, 96–97, 286.

35. R. Laurence Moore, *Religious Outsiders and the Making of Americans* (New York: Oxford University Press, 1986), 113.

36. Legal discussion of Frank S. Streeter, William E. Chandler and John W. Kelley before the Hon. Edgar Aldrich, Steno Records, 1907, Folder 3, 323–32; Mary Baker Eddy to William G. Nixon, 3 November 1890, Steno Records, 1907, Folder 2, 226, Streeter, Eddy Litigation Papers; *Letters of Mary Baker Eddy to Augusta E. Stetson*, 13, 15, 24, 31–32, 34, 39, 48, 50, 61, 66, 71, 79–80, 84, 92, 94–95, 102–3, 110; Stetson, *Reminiscences, Sermons and Correspondence*, 29, 267, 276, 339, 347, 471, 492, 497–99, 564–65, 590, 595, 645, 864–65, 1022–36, 1163; Gottschalk, *Emergence of Christian Science*, 92–93, 124–28.

37. Stetson, *Reminiscences, Sermons and Correspondence*, 608, 668; Gottschalk, *Emergence of Christian Science*, 265, 268, 270–72.

38. Donald Meyer, *The Positive Thinkers: A Study of the American Quest for Health, Wealth and Personal Power from Mary Baker Eddy to Norman Vincent Peale* (New York: Doubleday, 1965), 58; Stetson, *Reminiscences, Sermons and Correspondence*, 740, 786, 788, 790.

39. Stetson, *Reminiscences, Sermons and Correspondence*, 854.

40. Streeter Testimony, 23 May 1907, 36, Streeter, Eddy Litigation Papers; Stetson, *Reminiscences, Sermons and Correspondence*, 730; *Letters of Mary Baker Eddy to Augusta E. Stetson*, 73, 82–83, 85, 88–90, 93, 100, 108, 111.

41. *Letters of Mary Baker Eddy to Augusta E. Stetson*, 72.

42. Mary Baker Eddy to George Washington Glover, 27 April 1898, Steno Records, 1907, Folder 2, 269–71, Streeter, Eddy Litigation Papers; *Letters of Mary Baker Eddy to Augusta E. Stetson*, 25, 30–31, 38, 41, 81, 85; Stetson, *Reminiscences, Sermons and Correspondence*, 256, 754, 756.

43. *Letters of Mary Baker Eddy to Augusta E. Stetson*, 82.

44. Ibid., 74, 76.

45. Stetson, *Reminiscences, Sermons and Correspondence*, 931, 984, 1073–74, 1099.

46. Gottschalk, *Emergence of Christian Science*, 95, 291.

47. Georgine Milmine, "Literary Activities," *McClure's Magazine* 29 (October 1907): 695; Norman Beasley, *The Cross and the Crown* (New York: Duell, Sloan and Pearce, 1953), 348; E. Mary Ramsay, *Christian Science and Its Discoverer* (Boston: Christian Science, 1935), 43; "Mary Baker Eddy's Immense Achievement," *Current Literature* 50 (January 1911): 58; "Christian Science Angers the Kaiser," *New York Times*, 9 February 1902.

48. Morris, *Postscript to Yesterday*, 431.

49. Gottschalk, *Emergence of Christian Science*, 224.

50. Ibid., 191.

51. "Truth and Error in Christian Science," *Outlook* 83 (23 June 1906): 404–5.

2

Disciples and Dissidents

"Richard," said Mrs. Eddy to her young, ambitious convert, Richard Kennedy, "I was born an unwelcome child but I mean to have the whole world at my feet before I die."[1] Defiant words, honored more in the breach than in their fulfillment, Mary Baker Eddy brooked defeat on a regular basis until 1892, when a formal infrastructure for the Christian Science Church replaced a quarter-century of jerry-built leadership. Far from being deliberate or conniving, she stumbled from relationship to relationship, misjudging her followers' intents as they misjudged hers. She made poor choices for associates, partly attributable to the limited and limiting range of lower middle-class life she moved with; partly due, as well, to her personal, emotional, sporadically ruthless method of dealing with oppositional elements. When the spirit moved her, she could be a very attractive individual but was often the reverse. She fared well only in the final phase of her career, when a bureaucracy that she claimed was unnecessary for perpetuating Christian Science shielded her consistently, if unimaginatively, from direct onslaughts. Ironically, the bureaucracy survived her but today, after eighty years, it too is breaking down.[2]

Those who drew close to Mary Baker Eddy arrived in waves, following a distinct pattern of ebb and flow suitable to her needs. From 1866 to 1870 she gravitated toward couples of the Massachusetts working class; from 1870 to 1881 she relied on a series of men, strong or otherwise, for counsel, partnership and support. When she was ready to leave Lynn for Boston in 1882, many of these alliances were dissolved in courtrooms but "divorce" of this kind left permanent scars. In the 1880s she located loyal and apparently stable men, but the focus of discontent was an array of independent women, based in the urban East and Midwest who, for various reasons, "loved" and then lost their leader. As a rule, Eddy was less driven and less dominated by feminine influences since her reaction to the women, in all cases, was to dismiss them from her thought after short, painful episodes. The men lingered long after their material threat waned, in the shadow their personae cast on Christian Science—a shadow, incidentally, that the new Church organization would have to deal with as the movement's membership neared one hundred thousand.[3] Between 1892 and 1910 Mary Baker Eddy presided over the edifice she had constructed but was neither responsible for its decisions nor obligated to enforce them. At this point, when she dealt with none of the everyday operations of the Church, when a loyal clique served her in retirement and she was, in fact, answerable for very little, she was the most influential of women. Like Queen Victoria, she came to symbolize achievement[4] in a world where women desired "election" and self-fulfillment even if they were often wary of or uninvolved in social justice.

It is difficult to tell whether Eddy chose her first companions or they chose her, but for four years after the Civil War she was on the move, traveling from boardinghouse to boardinghouse, private home to private home, seeking a harbor with people who, very much like herself, lacked that and an anchor as well. They lived, and so did she, in villages and towns with enchanting names—Swampscott, Stoughton, Taunton—but her two favorites, the places she returned to in those early years, were Lynn and Amesbury. A manufacturing town located along the Merrimack, nearly at the New Hampshire border, Amesbury resembled Bow, Mary Baker Eddy's 1821 birthplace. Lynn, Eddy's residence with her husband, Daniel Patterson, from June 1864 to the summer of 1866 was the site of two things: a thriving shoe factory and an interest in Christian Science. Lynn was only ten or eleven miles from Boston, so cheap labor from that big city greased the industrial wheels there; it is not coincidental that shoe factory employees at Lynn were among the first to gravitate toward Mary Baker Eddy.

Hat, carriage and shoe manufacture may have been the vocations of those interested in Christian Science, but spiritualism was their avocation. A popular diversion since the Fox sisters, Kate and Margaret, allegedly "rapped" with the departed in 1848, spiritualism was fashionable among those who were dissatisfied or disillusioned with conventional responses to social change, especially those given by the Protestant faith.[5] In small towns, where hopes and dreams die fastest and citizens are caught in the backwash of rising expectations, dignity is a hard commodity to come by as are definitive answers for humanity's drift. Seeking shelter from the same storm was Mary Baker Eddy, who lived and worked for five years in family settings that recalled that of her parents; perhaps that's why she chose them. Until she alienated all her hosts, was compelled to leave at each instance and change her source of stability, Hiram and Mary Crafts, Mr. and Mrs. Nathaniel Webster and the Wentworths, Horace and Sally, provided a roof and sustenance but in Eddy's opinion, very little to slake a personal thirst.

The spiritualists who took Mary Baker Eddy in were not religious in a conventional sense, were not profound thinkers but were generous and of the "live and let live" school of thought. She was not, mixed too much into household affairs and regularly overstepped those tacit bounds separating guest and boarder from host.[6] In a basic way she wasn't like them, at least not like the women, who could afford a spiritual fad because their husbands were employed. Sarah Bagley of Amesbury was the only person Eddy resided with twice, not because Bagley was unmarried or a spiritualist, but probably because she was somehow more substantial, rather like a male provider, and had once had a career as organizer of the Lowell Female Labour Reform Association.[7]

Whether Eddy actually wanted a career or needed to be accepted by spiritualists is debatable, since Christian Science is not spiritualism and careers were not the way she was reared. Nevertheless, she did respect what might be termed "Yankee entrepreneurialism" among nineteenth-century men she had known, including her own father and those she had seen, proudly independent, at Amesbury and Lynn. It was not the position of foreman or mill owner that interested her; rather, it was the assurance of respectability such positions offered. To her, spiritualism was a mere diversion, a dalliance, for those whose husbands provided security and stability. Frustrated and impatient with herself, more determined and motivated to be free than the women she met, attracted and repelled by the many husband-wife bonds she was not a party to, she wrote to relieve her anxiety, justify her travail and teach something useful. And that was the key: teaching. It was a profession, it could be lucrative, it could make her independent, and she could work with the ambitious men she respected. Furthermore, what she taught, what she knew to be Biblical, truthful, precise, unyielding and unalterable, was in sharp contrast to soft, unreliable spiritualism. It was Christian Science and, by 1870, she was prepared to discourse upon it, professionalize it and propagate it. No longer a writer, a student or an enthusiast, she entered into a teaching partnership with Richard Kennedy, a young man of twenty-one whom she had met at the Websters' in Amesbury three years before.[8]

In March 1871 she explained her system to a potential student and Unitarian minister from Amesbury, Wallace W. Wright. He required that she give answers to nine weighty questions in twenty-four hours, since he had to catch a train home. Upon what principle is your science founded? Is a knowledge of anatomy necessary to the success of the student or practitioner? Will it meet the demands of extreme, acute cases? Is a knowledge of disease necessary to effect cures? Is it always applicable regardless of the disorder? Does it always work? Does it replace surgery in the case of fractures? Has anyone practiced it recently? What is the cost and duration of instruction?[9]

The reply is fascinating since Christian Science remained faithful, in a literal, absolute sense, to the early vision. The principle on which Science was founded Eddy termed "God, the principle of man." As the letter progresses the definition clarifies as precise, mathematical, universal, divine healing that re-creates Gospel healing in the manner of Christ rather than the physical being of Jesus, in which there is little interest. As for surgery, medical cure and requisite knowledge of the body and organic disease, there was no need for it: "this knowledge is what science came to destroy." A three-week term of instruction was prescribed to master the law of healing and constant practice made perfect. If rendered correctly, the Christian Science principle of spiritual cure might be successfully applied "to raising or restoring those called dead. I have witnessed this myself," she wrote, "therefore I testify to what I have seen."

What appears to be an extreme claim for people was not so for God, although it would be impossible to conceive in humanistic terminology. Since Christ was the catalyst, miracles were everyday affairs—not even miracles, in fact, but divine demonstrations, quite ordinary and repeatable. "It belongs not to mystery, to mediums, so called, to . . . theology [or] physiology but a . . . principle that harmonizes all it controls." Control, then, a keystone for Eddy, is asserted at three points in this letter.[10] Nothing organic or physical and especially nothing derived of man, his actions, his personal history, his mind or his mortality "controlled" as well as God's calculus, which was at hand, immediately available. Control was not to be compromised and it certainly didn't exist in nineteenth-century scientific and occult phenomena. Those who confused divine with human wisdom were not merely mistaken or in error: they were out of control—purveyors of a disintegrating, disruptive, erroneous and evil projection called MAM. If one was a student of Eddy's, had altered, misconstrued or strayed from the two thousand year old principle, as conceived by Jesus and his disciples, there would be no conciliatory bridge; the small Christian Science band and, four decades hence, the larger movement would maintain its homogeneity by repeatedly casting out traitors. But that is to be expected since judgment is the way of the prophet. It seemed, though, that some traitors wouldn't retreat, no matter how concerted the Eddy counteroffensive. The men she lost in the 1870s grew to legendary proportions, not in deed, but in malicious intent. They did not merit the memory Eddy lent them but were not forgotten until her death.

In 1867 Eddy was hard at work on a manuscript entitled *The Science of Man* when she first met Richard Kennedy at the Amesbury home of Mrs. Nathaniel Webster. He was eighteen, she forty-five, and the lesson she taught was very much in keeping with the contents of the 1871 Wright letter. It is hard to say whether Kennedy was impressed with or interested in Eddy's view of Christianity: after all, she lived with spiritualists and it is nowhere indicated, except in the cases of Hiram Crafts and Sally Wentworth, that any were moved to study with her. However, from 1868 Kennedy was interested in the system of therapeutics she mastered. It was eminently marketable in a working-class society in which tired faith no longer addressed the pressing problems of the day. Others were drawn into her orbit, too, both women and men of the same social milieu as Eddy. Finally, she became a teacher and, via her partnership with Kennedy, hoped to free herself from dependence: more than a physician's cure, teaching would make her "well." In February 1870 she agreed to enter a working partnership with Kennedy while simultaneously instructing him in the science of healing. He would pay her $1,000 and half his earnings from the practice they would jointly establish.[11] That summer she held her initial class at Lynn, using *The Science of Man*, shortly to become *Science and Health*, as a text; in December, her second session included none of those she lived with. There were factory people, accountants, businessmen and women; one of her first converts wandered, just as she had done, but not from house to house. He was a sailor, just home from the sea. His name, George Tuttle, is not quite as important as the lessons she taught him and others at Lynn. A sailor of sorts herself, Mary Baker Eddy began making waves. In a January 1872 issue of the Lynn *Transcript*, would-be student Wallace W. Wright claimed Christian Science to be moral but useless as a healing art. He thought that man, God's noblest creation, was the center of the universe and the instrument of progress. He labeled Eddy a mesmerist. On 20 January 1872 Eddy replied in the *Transcript* that Wright was merely being vindictive because she refused to refund his $200 tuition fee.[12]

At the time of Eddy's rejoinder, she was set to break with Kennedy and did so in the spring. He strayed from the teachings of his mentor and, as his practice grew, stressed manipulation of the limbs and several other physical treatments. The homogeneity of her small following was threatened by a Judas. Eddy's reaction to this situation became typical. Jettisoning him would not be sufficient; he would have to be broken as well. The partnership was dissolved but Eddy sued her former student to recover $750 she alleged he owed her.[13] She lost the case—and a number of similar ones.

If this would have been the end of it, Kennedy might have deservedly faded from Christian Science, but he didn't. Instead of disappearing, he became the focus of Malicious Animal Magnetism (MAM), the foe of Science generally and Eddy particularly. In ensuing years, she attributed some of Science's failures and prominent defections to a man's thought, a man she had not seen since the 1872 break, who was destined to die in an insane asylum but grew in stature once he was physically removed from her presence.[14] Twenty years after the partnership's dissolution he was still wandering across the Christian Science landscape as a malignant presence[15] for which Eddy, as victim, was not responsible.

Perhaps Kennedy's real mistake, and that of others who ran afoul of Mary Baker Eddy, was not to take her literally, at her word. She was what she claimed, regardless of incidental, modern trappings: a representative of the New Testament, closely akin to the thought and inspiration conveyed in John's Gospel. Unfortunately, though, she did have modern trappings that Kennedy and others confused with her Biblical foundation. Phineas Parkhurst Quimby was one of those trappings. Eddy was initially unsure of how and to what extent he fit into her vision. He was a mental healer she had consulted in Portland, Maine, between 1862 and 1865; she saw him first when she was alone but continued her correspondence with him after Daniel Patterson had returned from the Civil War and they both resided at Lynn. Quimby triggered Mary Baker Eddy's religious consciousness, though he invoked no creed in his mental treatment of psychosomatic and bodily ailments. More will be said about Quimby's role in the next chapter, but Eddy did convey a feeling of indebtedness to him and his work at the time of her association with Kennedy. Consequently, it may not have been Kennedy's fault or responsibility for confusing a minor current in Christian Science for a major one, especially if his interest lay in contemporary healing as an art rather than revelation.

Nevertheless, he became a disembodied phantom, an icon of sorts, that Eddy was unable and unwilling to expel as Christian, woman or leader. Ironically, Kennedy, or his essence, remained a part of the movement in absentia, a force rather than a physical presence, incorporated into Christian Science as an emanation of MAM. Cast in the role of a pariah, Kennedy became what Eddy needed him to be: a source of external opposition upon which she could exert her Christian, religious creativity. If successful, she would destroy the devil—hopefully, even her devil. Such destruction has been a recurrent Christian theme and so it was with Eddy, in both her writing and her actions. Except she did it with a twist in attempting a noncorporeal, solely spiritual exorcism on Kennedy and a number of those who followed.

Whether by lawsuit or malign accusation during the years 1872–81, favorite after favorite assumed his place near Mary Baker Eddy, only to be removed a year or two later.[16] The young seaman George Tuttle, who had been one of her first converts, was sued by Eddy to recover tuition fees; George Barry, a devoted student who helped subsidize the first edition of *Science and Health*, broke with her after she married Asa Gilbert Eddy. Barry then sued his benefactress when he was not paid for preparing a number of her manuscripts for the press, but won only $350.[17]

In 1878 Eddy accused one of her disciples of witchcraft. She had known Daniel Spofford since 1875, when he was one of her six students. He was employed as a foreman in the local shoe factory and he proved to have some business ability. He quickly established a Christian Science practice once he had completed the course of study and Eddy entrusted him to manage the publication process of, distribute and seek reviews for *Science and Health*. She admired his dynamism and determination and he had also introduced her to Asa Eddy, who was soon to become her third husband. He had become what Richard Kennedy had been just a few years before: indispensable.

Spofford's fall from grace was as precipitous as his rise. Eddy's public complaint against him, brought in court at Salem, Massachusetts, on 14 May 1878, was that Spofford claimed to but in reality did not employ the Christian Science method of healing; instead he exerted undue "mental influence" on patients for injurious purposes. Eddy and a new male convert, Edward J. Arens, petitioned the judge for an injunction, restraining the defendant from doing this "evil." Since courts in Salem preferred to prosecute an action rather than an injurious thought, the case was dismissed.[18]

Until she became comfortable in Boston, Eddy tended to rely on the court for adjudication of disputes. This tactic, perhaps a necessary adaptation for a woman alone among potentially overpowering males, embarrassed Christian Scientists and caused mass desertions. It probably factored into her departure from Lynn because she had difficulty balancing income against expenditures and student converts against student departures. Mary Baker Eddy did not rely on her husband for practical support though he was a Christian Scientist and ten years her junior. But this follows a pattern, too: she never relied on her first husband because he died, nor the second because he lacked character, nor the third because he lacked ability. Those she cared for in a practical sense were the Phineas Quimbys of New England: speculative, adventurous types who were a little unsafe. She never married them but, unlike the husbands left far behind, she could never separate from them either. The last of the entrepreneurs, Edward Arens, stayed on her mind as well. Once loyal, then disaffected, he engaged Eddy in an 1883 court battle over copyright. This was her only victory since Arens, indeed, had plagiarized some twenty pages of *Science and Health*, incorporating them into his own pamphlets.[19]

The cumulative effect upon Christian Science of the Kennedy, Spofford and Arens years was negative. Following the Spofford decision, Mary and Asa Eddy found their Lynn home attached by their lawyer until his fee was paid, and so they moved temporarily to Boston and Washington, D.C. Meanwhile, Christian Scientists had begun meeting for Sunday services, followed Eddy from city to city to hear her lectures, formed an association reflective of serious intent and, within a short period, chartered a Church of Christ, Scientist, and a Massachusetts Metaphysical College for the training of practitioners. It was a small undertaking of dedicated students who sufficiently revered their leader to name her College and Church president, but eight of them resigned from the Church on 21 October 1881, accusing Eddy of "departure from the straight and narrow road . . . ebullitions of temper, love of money and the appearance of hypocrisy."[20] Unfortunately, Mary Baker Eddy couldn't refrain from creating that appearance in public, no matter the cost, as her husband played the tragic male lead in the staging of an all too familiar drama.

Having recently returned to Boston from Washington, D.C., Asa Eddy died of heart disease. An autopsy was performed for the purpose of ascertaining the cause of death, since Eddy had written to the Boston press that MAM, which took the form of arsenic, had entered her husband's body and killed him. No evidence of arsenic was uncovered, but Eddy persisted in her allegation that her husband had been mentally assassinated by Arens, with whom she was currently involved, Spofford, whom she hadn't seen in four years and Kennedy, who had been gone for a decade.[21]

The natural—or, as some would say "unnatural"—unfolding of events surrounding Asa Eddy's death defined his wife's future course in Boston. Mary Baker Eddy certainly could not have thought about what she did—taking a public stand against "mental" or "magnetic" killers—but the situation left her with no alternative but to remain in Boston and she did so, making as permanent a move as she could commit to in August 1882. Evidently she had no plan as the incidents of the previous year attest to, but for a number of reasons Boston was a good place to regroup: it was convenient, relatively anonymous (or could be) and offered a viable alternative to the movement at Lynn that had become moribund via schism, unpleasant publicity and embarrassing displays of Eddy's troubling and troubled spirituality. She required associates to be fully engaged with her own well-being and that was never really possible at Lynn where wage earners were always preoccupied with personal struggles—very immediate, practical struggles—for economic survival. Also, converts were few, interest was waning and, once again, Mary Baker Eddy was faced with declining resources. At this point her path led away from the "peasantry," of whom she was not a natural ally, and toward the "princes" or "princesses" of the middle class who harbored and succored her because she offered them something of utilitarian value.

Eddy maintained a tiny following from Lynn, but Boston had a vast, untapped citizenry with time, emotional sympathy, wherewithal and stamina to help her; additionally—and this was good for her—they lacked those sharp, working-class edges that had grown tiresome and unresponsive. There, the membership of Christian Science would change and, with it, the character, potential and needs of the movement. Middle-class women, in search of a cause, occasionally bored, better educated and with the potential to be as independent and as highly motivated as Kennedy, Spofford and Arens, sought purpose, direction and opportunity within Christian Science. Whether they would realize their quest was not yet as pressing as having the potential to do so. Indeed, the 1880s was Science's "feminine" period, a time when it gained a reputation, however imperfectly and inaccurately understood, as prowoman. Mary Baker Eddy would again face an insurgent tide: if the 1870s were used as a barometer, one might guess that she could probably weather the storm, but only for a while. She definitely had her limits.

The Boston atmosphere seemed right for Christian Science. Competition for the interest and sympathies of the white urban population was the order of the day as diverse groups sought social champions. Mediterranean and East European ethnics attempted to find fraternity within the established Catholic Church, labor unions and local political organizations; white Protestant men opted for the exclusive, restricted country club, the corporate board room, the ivy league or investment banking. White Protestant women, however, were anchorless, having discovered that the city's new privilege had its price. With changes in the family pointing in the direction of the individual rather than joint enterprise and leisure time a given, these women were "all dressed up with no place to go." Christian Science promised to redeem them from a sense of marginality while, at the same time, leaving their sense of election undiminished. At first, it welcomed and invigorated independent women but, by 1889, the tide turned.

Despite the continued interest of Mary Baker Eddy in maintaining a Christian Science Association with a national focus, her good instinct in founding the *Christian Science Journal* to better explain the faith and to answer critics and an expanded forum in Chicago and New York City, her movement had not taken off. In a very decisive sense, the 1880s demonstrated that, on the whole, she could not command long-term loyalty, especially if lieutenants lived out of her purview; she was too old to joust with younger women whose ideas were more contemporary and less oriented to the Gospel. Christian Science required something more to bind it than Eddy's personality, and prophets do not make naturally adept administrators. No matter how popular she was, the audience seemed to vary little—95 percent women by one 1889 estimate—but, with the exception of Eddy, it was addressed by male speakers.[22] In sum, never having journeyed more than a few hours from one's birthplace, having no intimate friends, taking no vacations and abjuring responsibility for one's statements and actions may provide some rationale for being prophetic but absolutely none for being sage, respectable or respected. The revolt of the middle-class women tested Eddy's direct leadership skills and resulted in her retirement from visible participation in the Christian Science movement at age sixty-nine.

The impressive women of the 1880s were Clara Choate, Emma Hopkins, Mary H. Plunkett, Sarah Crosse, Ursula Gestefeld, Josephine Curtis Woodbury and Augusta E. Stetson. All of them were students of Eddy, all of them were "Mrs.," all of them were younger and all dropped out or were pushed out of the movement. Choate was the least troublesome since she returned in 1884 to the mainstream after having established a rival institute to the

Massachusetts Metaphysical College. Sarah Crosse founded her own church distinct from Science;[23] some, however, remained too close for comfort, using the Christian Science name to underwrite more contemporary modes of thought.

Augusta Stetson built the New York City movement and the grand church that was its monument, but she is more properly placed where she provided the most controversy: at the end of Mary Baker Eddy's career. Ursula Gestefeld was no longer a factor in Christian Science after 1888, though she appropriated the name of the faith for a book she wrote as did Emma Hopkins for a magazine she edited; both became affiliated after their secession with a metaphysical, moral movement called New Thought.[24] Accusations bounced back and forth from Chicago to Boston and, suffice it to say, they did not reveal any particular truth about Eddy, Gestefeld or Hopkins. They did reveal, however, the soft underbelly of an organizational vacuum within Christian Science.

Once an important Scientist in New York City, Mary Plunkett found herself associated with Emma Hopkins in 1887 as president of the Chicago-based Hopkins College of Christian Science. "Odd," "interesting," and "inspired," Plunkett was excommunicated from Christian Science when she announced that she was divorcing her husband in favor of a "spiritual" marriage with A. Bentley Worthington, a gigolo she supposedly reformed. The powerful New York press denounced her, editorializing on Christian Science and its immoral advocacy of free love.[25]

As a result of the "Chicago women" and a tragic incident in the Boston area, a dissident group conspired to unseat Eddy and assume control of the movement. Malden, Massachusetts, was the scene of an April 1888 occurrence that would be reenacted many times in the coming decades. Abby H. Corner, a Christian Scientist, was acquitted of manslaughter in the death of her daughter, Mrs. Lottie James. The charge was failure to provide proper medical assistance for the latter during her pregnancy. A hemorrhage occurred, and the daughter and infant died. Natural childbirth was a good idea, but the failure to consult licensed physicians in complex cases brought it into disrepute.[26] Mrs. G. W. Adams, Mrs. J. H. Bell, the Reverend George P. Day, first reader at the Christian Science Church in Chicago, Mrs. Hannah Laramie, Mr. and Mrs. John Linscott, Mr. and Mrs. Bradford Sherman and Mrs. Elizabeth Webster seceded with more than two dozen others.[27] Eddy's trusted nucleus, thirty-six in all, was shortly to be replaced by men—some trustworthy and some not, who would compose Christian Science along more orderly lines.

Shocked and dispirited by the totality of events, Eddy closed the Massachusetts Metaphysical College where her obstetrics course had been taught and, temporarily, retired to her Pleasant View home in Concord, New Hampshire. Her introspective hiatus lasted three years. She erred in some of her choices for associates but on the whole made the best decision she could have for her personal adjustment. Nevertheless, her flirtation with women ended: she relied nearly entirely on male support until her death. Interestingly, men were always more lingering and threatening to her than women, since the MAM charge was somehow masculine, having risen during the Kennedy–Spofford–Arens years. It was laid only infrequently at the feet of women in the movement, but, once eliminated, the women in question faded from memory like a summer shower or the wicked witch in *The Wizard of Oz*.

One such woman was Josephine Curtis Woodbury, who had been with Eddy since 1879 and, for a brief period, acted as editor for the *Christian Science Journal*. Melodramatic and romantic, she took literally the assertions in Eddy's *Science and Health* and *Miscellaneous Writings* that marriage was a necessary evil and that propagation of the race could be asexual and entirely mental. The theory of agamogenesis was fine for insects but humans were loath to accept it. For this reason, Woodbury became the Christian Science curiosity of the United States when she announced, in June 1890, that her newly born son had been conceived immaculately and was therefore to be named the Prince of Peace. Eddy disclaimed any responsibility for the "evil . . . wicked" miscarriage of her philosophy which, in the area of sexual relations, followed and was derived from Pauline doctrine. Six years after Prince's birth—he was probably the child of Woodbury and an infatuated student, since she abstained from marital intercourse—Woodbury's story had not changed. She, like Plunkett, was excommunicated, branded "that Babylonish woman." Immediately, the fallen angel wrote a long essay scorning the systematizer of Science rather than the system. Eddy was not content with exiling the enemy; following the excommunication, Woodbury was accused of being a mesmerist, and influenced by Richard Kennedy.[28]

In 1899 Frederick Peabody, a Boston lawyer, was retained by Woodbury, who decided to bring Eddy up on charges of slander and defamation of character. Eddy tried and failed to stop the *Arena*, a journal of Progressive opinion, from publishing an article of Woodbury's which, to that date, was the most complete exposé on the Christian Science founder yet written. In uncompromising terms, Eddy was indicted as a plagiarist, criticized for grammatical errors in *Science and Health*, ridiculed for inordinate greed and "trafficking in the Temple," accused of demonophobia and falling victim to superstitions, witchcraft and MAM. Eddy, averred Woodbury, claimed to have ministered to the mortally wounded President Garfield and King Edward VII when he was Prince of Wales through the use of "absent treatment," a spiritual cure administered at a great distance from the subject. She failed with Garfield only because Kennedy and Arens "cast a spell" on her. Attempting to manufacture a smokescreen behind which she could obscure the extraordinary claims she had made a half-dozen years before, Woodbury attacked Eddy's theory of mental generation. The suit received much newspaper coverage through the year. For lack of evidence the case against Eddy was dismissed in 1901[29] and Woodbury disappeared from view, a casualty of a different and more penetrating Christian Science leadership.

When Mary Baker Eddy secluded herself at Concord, the old machinery of Christian Science was disbanded, apparently with her consent. What emerged in 1892, and was refined until Eddy's death, was a centralized body at Boston that spoke authoritatively for the leader but shielded her from the public eye. It modeled its actions on the American Constitution and its relation to the individual states; it delegated to individual Christian Science churches the right to choose pastors, admit and drop members, treat the sick and deal with family affairs (for example, marriage and divorce). The official organ of the movement, the *Christian Science Journal*, would be free to list any practitioners it saw fit and control its editorial policy. Although it sounded democratic, religion by its nature isn't, nor was Christian Science. All privileges would be exercised in keeping with the precise word of Mary Baker Eddy, as laid down in the 1895 Mother Church *Manual*, which was edited on many occasions until 1910, but was not open to interpretation.[30] Perhaps it would be more apt to call the bond between Church, leadership, founder and members a covenant and not a constitution since it spelled out the terms by which an unbreakable spiritual promise might be realized. The *Manual* also seated Mary Baker Eddy as reigning leader protected by a loyal male court, a role much more amenable to her inclination than the one she played her whole life, that of exposed, vulnerable, erratic seer. With more sophisticated, educated, balanced and elegant trustees, directors and Board members, it is no wonder that Christian Science attracted middle-class urbanites in ever increasing numbers as the Gay Nineties drew to a close.

Quantifying the success of the new leadership hinges on asking the right questions. For instance, did it oversee a membership surge by making the Church more visible in a positive sense? Did it encourage the donation of large sums of money to the movement? Did it win court cases and conduct itself when under fire in a more composed fashion than had Eddy? Did it end perceived challenges to its hegemony while permanently relieving Eddy of that responsibility? As a woman in her eighties, she required such relief, having reached that point in her life where she didn't have or want to deal with very public issues, withdrew into her household, and let others handle her inconsistencies. If the leadership succeeded, Eddy could end her days as a powerful, if not lighthearted, Victorian. In sum, preserving her legacy but not her eccentricity was the Mother Church's and Publication Society's priority and they did it reasonably well.

Forty thousand members of the Boston Mother Church,[31] constructed in 1894 and extended in 1906, a like number in Augusta Stetson's tremendous New York City temple on West 96th Street, dedicated on 29 November 1903, and an additional twenty thousand or so Christian Scientists scattered as far west as California indicate that the Publication Society and trustees were doing something right. They were well-positioned on a high, irresistible wave of civilization since the years just prior to World War I lent themselves to universal solutions and universal applicability. Throughout the Western world philosophers, writers and artists became increasingly critical of mechanistic, formal human-centered values, relying instead on diverse forms of impressionism; among the well-known exponents of this sort of value system were Dewey, Bergson, Freud, James,[32] Gauguin, van Gogh, Munch, Thomas Hardy, Matthew Arnold and Henrik Ibsen. Christian Science cannot be omitted from the list, although its quest appeared to be more local, more intense, more extreme and, because of this, more bitter.

Helen Brush was a Christian Scientist who died young and left $75,000 to Stetson's First Church of Christ, Scientist, New York City. Her relatives contested the will in court, claiming that a belief in Christian Science healing through spiritual law rather than medicine or surgery constituted an "insane delusion." Dr. Allan McLane Hamilton, called an "alienist" then but a forensic psychiatrist or insanity expert today, testified on behalf of the plaintiffs that any cure for disease that discounted the germ theory constituted a delusion. Since he was not an expert on religions and their belief constellations, he declined to comment on their relevance to the case but he said that Helen Brush —"Notwithstanding the fact that she was a French and German scholar . . . a skilled musician and a lover of art"—and people like her, who thought "Divine Mind" could cure organic disease, were "insane" and therefore incompetent to dispose of their estates.[33]

Countertestimony by another expert, physiologist Austin Flint, and intelligent questioning, penetrating cross-examination and vigorous summation by counsel brought victory, dignity and a large sum of money into the Christian Science church in New York City. The movement had come a long way since Mary Baker Eddy stood before the bar pressing accusations of mental coercion from afar and MAM. The verdict, passed down in February 1901, several months after Brush died of tuberculosis while refusing conventional medical assistance, vindicated Christian Science. Letters to the editor of the *New York Journal* heralded those "mental" actions, which if not overzealously practiced and regulated accordingly, served to relieve pain and comfort patients. "Is not that the substance of Christian Science?"[34]

In 1898 about one-half of Mary Baker Eddy's estate was devoted to the cause of Christian Science and, increasingly, she permitted Church trustees to manage her property and finances. About nine years later, she formalized this arrangement in a trusteeship, wherein $913,000 would be administered by three individuals: her banker in Concord; her politically active cousin from New Hampshire, Henry Baker; and one Christian Scientist, publications editor and Mother Church Board member Archibald McLellan;

$125,000 was designated as the inheritance of Eddy's natural child, George Glover.[35] Events preceding the trusteeship and the nature of this February 1907 arrangement provided a ready-made series of occurrences and cast of characters for muckraking newspapers to exploit. Such a newspaper was Joseph Pulitzer's *New York World*, owned by "Robber Baron" Jay Gould until 1883. The *World* tradition, if one could call it that, was one of "horror" story, "frenzy," "exaggeration" and falsehood.[36]

Mary Baker Eddy was, at first, a curiosity and then a commodity. She was conspicuously absent from the June 1906 dedication of the Mother Church extension; reporters tried to see her at Concord but were rebuffed by her personal attendant of a quarter century, Calvin Frye. More to the point, she hadn't been seen in public nor granted any interviews in three years. Rumors reached the press that the woman whose followers thronged the dedication and contributed $2 million to the construction of the "Excelsior Extension" was dead or infirm. In either case, "others"—her personal staff at Concord in collusion with major Church officials—controlled her fortune, disinherited George Glover from all but the $125,000 that would act as a sop to keep him quiet, and pocketed vast sums for their own use.[37]

Actually, all of this had happened but not in the fashion described by the *Sun*. Eddy was definitely a phenomenon, the story was enticing, but for the sake of newspaper sales it was embellished until distortion was hopelessly ensnared with reality. The truth is that she was old, was intermittently indisposed with kidney stones and enjoyed the seclusion and personal attention she received at Pleasant View. She didn't give interviews or entertain because she had earned the right not to. Christian Scientists managed her estate via a legal trusteeship drawn on 25 February 1907 but reciprocally agreed upon and entered into only on 6 March 1907, five days after blood relatives with influential legal counsel moved to declare Eddy incompetent to manage her own affairs. Under the terms of the agreement, the trustees would pay Eddy sums out of her net income as were needed to pay her expenses, run her household, donate to charity and advance Christian Science. Upon her death, the trust would terminate, and an executor would dispose of her property in accordance with her written will. In the meantime, the trustees would be "my attorneys in fact, and . . . are . . . invested with full power for me . . . and . . . my . . . estate." The sum set apart for George Glover, $125,000 in bonds for his and his family's benefit, was offered to ensure that the will would not be contested; if it was, this sum "would . . . terminate."[38] It really didn't matter whether one approved of the document or not, approved of Eddy or not, approved of Christian Scientists or not: the act was thoughtfully taken, the trust deed was binding, and this "Mother" bequeathed most of her estate to the children of her choice.

The *Sun* made this legal process necessary after breaking a story on 28 October 1906, in what were called "public disclosures." In that and future articles, Eddy disappeared, replaced by an impersonator or human dummy with malevolent intent. Those who initiated the "suit in equity" on her behalf, but without her permission, against ten supposedly conspiratorial male members of the Church, were designated Eddy's "Next Friends," and, therefore, the affair has been called the "Next Friends Suit." The real plaintiffs, however, were not the "Next Friends," acting to protect Eddy from herself and her assets from unscrupulous Christian Scientists but the *New York World*, which laid the foundation for litigation by actively locating the "Friends," interviewing them in a way creatively suited for yellow journalism, retaining talented counsel and encouraging the institution during the entire proceeding.[39]

There were five "Friends" in all, but the most significant was Eddy's natural son, George. A close reading of the extant correspondence between Glover and his mother indicates the existence of a chasm of silence that was never bridged. In some ways she acted the role of concerned mother and grandmother but always from a distance; she couldn't resist meddling and alternated that with devastating criticism of her son's rough-hewn, unrefined character. For his part, he accepted the money she gave him, modest sums when compared to her larger estate, not because he was venal but because this is the sort of love he—and perhaps she too—felt most comfortable with after 1879. In that year she contacted him for the first time in nearly a quarter-century, only when she felt overwhelmed by ruinous court cases and MAM. He actually came to Boston from Dakota territory to threaten Richard Kennedy.[40] Thereafter he sometimes visited, kept up correspondence but rarely displayed an intimate, friendly or loving feeling for his mother. That must have died in 1856, when Eddy, then Mrs. Patterson, chose between her itinerant dentist-husband and her twelve-year-old son. She sent young George to live with her former housekeeper and her husband, and all three moved to Wisconsin and then Minnesota.

George Glover led an adventurous life, but not one his mother, striving for gentility, could comprehend. With little formal schooling and no advantages, he read and wrote haltingly and became a Civil War casualty when he was wounded in the neck. After the peace, he took off on his own to the Dakota territory where he served as a United States marshal. But he was most notably a miner, with "miner's luck." At times he was poor, at times well-off, but in 1906 he owned eighty acres with big payoff potential underground, "if he could only" obtain the funds to "get it out."[41] He also had a wife and three children and, from extant documentary evidence regarding them, a good deal can be learned about the odd family relationship of mother and son.

Eddy had planned to educate her grandchildren in Boston, and Glover consented to this. Frankly, Eddy was ashamed of her son's educational shortcomings and was not embarrassed to tell him so. Granddaughter Mary's letters to her were so misspelled "that I blush to read them. You pronounce your words so wrongly and then she spells them accordingly. I am even yet too proud to have you come among my society." When in Boston, her other granddaughter Evelyn was regarded "as somewhat like me, and that she would be a scholar." However, she was chronically ill, missed school in Dakota and, according to Eddy, was the victim of MAM and mesmerism, none of which she deigned to treat. She was asked to do so by George, who was not a Christian Scientist, but she left it to a Dr. Easterman, a practitioner of absent treatment. Nevertheless, she persevered with grandson Gersham and the two girls with regard to their conversion. Aside from the classical education she so desired for them, she wanted her grandchildren to familiarize themselves with Christian Science by entering "a class of mine. I will send for them to come to me and . . . teach them."[42]

After weighing and measuring this plan over a period of eleven years, it was finally shelved. Instead of permitting Eddy "sole charge" of her grandchildren's education and "contrary to" her "orders," Mary, the eldest, was sent to St. Joseph, Missouri. Apparently related to this was Eddy's refusal to grant the Glovers an additional $1,100. "I have given you in money . . . land and houses over $20,000 and now I have resolved to throw away no more on you and your family and receive in return for it only disrespect, ingratitude and requests for more money." At other times, she claimed that Calvin Frye, her personal servant and bookkeeper, hoarded her money and she was not free to give it. By 1906 she saw George Glover only by appointment, even at Christmas, as she might any other petitioner. No wonder he was swayed by the *Sun* to litigate his mother.[43] He was not necessarily greedy, but he was desperate. He could be convinced that Eddy was somehow imprisoned at Pleasant View, unbalanced or both.

Washington, D.C., was the place where George Glover spent the holidays of 1906.[44] Reports from Concord to the effect that an imposter rode in his mother's carriage and that Eddy had not been seen in a healthy state for months drew him to the offices of William E. Chandler, whose varied career in the Republican party included service as Secretary of the Navy under President Chester A. Arthur, publisher of the Washington *National Republican*, stalwart senator from New Hampshire and waver of the "Bloody Shirt" until 1890, when he would wave it no more.[45] As an old campaigner and legendary name from Mary Baker Eddy's native state, he was the *World*'s choice for counsel. He agreed to represent the "Next Friends," if any could be found, since the season was conducive to anti-Eddy rhetoric. *McClure's Magazine* had initiated a series of articles that constituted an exposé on the pecuniary and pleasure-seeking principles of Christian Science. Eddy responded, but only to "gross" misstatements concerning her father and his family.[46]

Fearful lest her life and intent be further misconstrued, Eddy wrote her son, imploring him to return "by express all the letters of mine which I have written to you." In attempting to have him act with haste, she sometimes offered gifts ("I . . . will reward you . . . generously") and sometimes invoked MAM ("The enemy of Christian Science is by the wickedest Powers of Hypnotism trying to do me all the harm possible by acting on the minds of people to make them lie about me"), but Glover was unpersuaded. On 26 January 1907 Eddy asked Glover to trust Mother Church President Alfred Farlow—"take his advice and he will be honest; he knows what is best for you"[47]—but by that time Christian Scientists couldn't reach him. He had returned with his daughter Mary to Lead City, South Dakota.

"Why do you treat your mother thus! Have I not helped you in . . . and out of need. . . . tell me what your business is that detains you in Washington or . . . New York?" Eddy arranged to have Christian Science reader Irving Tomlinson go to Lead City to get the letters and if they were delivered to him "I will reward you with some presents." No letters were delivered[48] by the 1 March deadline and, needless to say, Eddy withdrew her offer. She earnestly hoped that MAM had not taken possession of her son, but on 25 February she changed her will and effective 1 March established the trusteeship.

Shortly after the institution of the suit against her by George Glover, his daughter Mary and George Baker, her nephew and her deceased brother George Sullivan's son—his grievance was Eddy's supposed parsimoniousness toward him and his mother—two more plaintiffs joined in: a nephew, Fred W. Baker, and an adopted son who had been deposed after a meteoric rise two decades before, Ebenezer J. Foster Eddy. It wasn't a coincidence that he was adopted in October 1888, at the precise time of a secessionist movement within Christian Science. He was a man to lean on, unlike her own son, an impressive, refined and masterful homeopathic physician. He taught obstetrics, that is, natural childbirth, at the Massachusetts Metaphysical College; after it closed he was president of the Mother Church and chairman of the Publishing Committee. Seemingly, he was not undone by Mary Baker Eddy, although she finally accused him of hypnotism, but by the Boston directors who sought stability rather than the favoritism cum rivalry that beset Christian Science in its pre-1890 generative period. He called himself out of retirement in 1907 to offer a story worthy of Maria Monk's anti-Catholic diatribe of 1836, *Awful Disclosures of the Hotel Dieu Nunnery of Montreal*. In that gothic horror tale readers learned that the nuns were compelled to obey priests in *all* things; in this one, a "pathetic . . . enfeebled . . . palsied . . . pitiable dupe . . . tortured by mental disease" and the "helpless plaything of rival cliques" was traduced, terrorized and manipulated in the Pleasant View "house of mystery."[49] As he had been unable to do in Christian Science, Foster Eddy now became a paragon.

Chandler brought the suit before the New Hampshire Superior Court during its April 1907 term and it was not fully resolved until 21 August. The plaintiffs, George Glover, Mary Glover, Ebenezer J. Foster Eddy, George and Fred Baker all claimed to represent Mary Baker Eddy's interests and were thus called her "Next Friends." Eddy was therefore a symbolic and unwilling plaintiff against the Christian Science leadership who were the defendants. Charges were brought against ten male Scientists in various authoritative posts, among them Calvin Frye, Mother Church President Alfred Farlow, Christian Science Publication Society director Joseph Armstrong and Concord Church readers Hermann S. Hering and Irving C. Tomlinson. The trustees themselves were not the issue and therefore were not charged. At issue was the ability of Eddy to conduct her business affairs properly since the post-1889 Church reorganization. Depositions were collected from a variety of people who had known Eddy in 1866; since Chandler empowered Frederick W. Peabody, once the attorney of banished Josephine C. Woodbury, to take them, one might assume that their content would be unfavorable to Eddy.[50]

Counsel for the Scientists was as distinguished as Chandler. Entirely above reproach, well-known in New Hampshire political circles and noted for his rectitude, Frank S. Streeter was an influential and highly regarded member of the Concord establishment.[51] He believed as did the "Masters" or judges hearing the case that MAM might be a delusion but it ought not to be introduced in testimony, depositions or otherwise if it did not impair Eddy's business judgment. On the other hand, Chandler tried to prove that Eddy, obsessed and deluded her whole life by MAM, was easily controlled by a small, powerful, sinister bloc of Christian Scientists. If this was provable, control of Eddy's estate would undoubtedly be transferred to the "Next Friends"; if not, the trusteeship of 1 March would be validated and, with it, Eddy's control over her own destiny.[52]

The decisive encounter arrived after several months on 14 August 1907, when the Masters and the two contending attorneys suspended the paperwork and endless courtroom procedures; all of them took a trip to Pleasant View to interview Eddy, observe her surroundings and assess her intellectual acumen. She was queried concerning her early life, the foundations of Christian Science, her civic-mindedness as a citizen of Concord and her formation of the trusteeship. She disarmed Chandler, charmed the Masters and, as an octogenarian, triumphed over them with youthful, vigorous clear-headed repartee. If she entertained "grotesque" religious beliefs bordering on "insanity" they were, according to the Masters, inadmissible because her ability to do business and make informed, noncoercive, rational financial decisions was unimpaired. On 21 August 1907 Chandler withdrew the plaintiffs' case, no matter how "altruistic" he claimed it to be.[53] Congratulations were due Eddy all around, and none were more valued than those received from Augusta E. Stetson, First Church of Christ, Scientist, New York City. "Love is enthroned," she telegrammed, "Love has fulfilled Her law. My heart's deepest love to you, my beloved Leader and Teacher."[54]

Twenty-three years had come and gone since Augusta Stetson first studied with Mary Baker Eddy. She had three class terms of instruction, a total of twelve lessons, but she was never quite able to relieve her husband of the intense pain he incurred from rheumatism and curvature of the spine. But her record with a series of other people, young and old, in various states of mental disorder, paralysis and malignancy was astounding. "Many cases of . . . serious diseases were healed by the application of Truth. . . . the lame the halt and the blind rushed to me for help, until I was overwhelmed with patients."[55]

Stetson was also overwhelmed by a sense of mission and acquired honor and station along the way. Charged by Eddy to pioneer Christian Science in New York City, she did so in November 1886, with fourteen adherents, some of whom she healed in the months after her arrival. After the autumn of 1887 she stayed in New York City permanently and was an unusual woman even for that metropolis. Moving from building to building and from rental hall to rental hall for the purpose of holding services did not deter her. Ordained by Eddy as pastor in 1890, she was First Reader of New York City's First Church of Christ, Scientist, until 1902 and a trustee of the church until 1909. Although a decline in status might be inferred from the successive positions she held, they merely reflect her deference to consti-tuted Boston Church authority after 1890 and, especially after 1895, when the Mother Church *Manual* defined *Science and Health*, Eddy's text, as the true pastor of Christian Science. According to the directors at Boston, knowledgeable on the roots and rise of Christian Science, "personality" was not desirable and Stetson might well curb hers for the good of the move-ment. She was encouraged to do so on several occasions and, regardless of ambition and strength of character—both of which she had—she retreated, at least publicly. In two editions of correspondence—one of which features letters written by Stetson to Eddy, the other, letters from Eddy to Stetson over the course of two decades—there is ample room for carp, complaint, corrosive dislike and envy to have taken root, and even if it is not obvious, a researcher can read between the lines. Except for three letters, of 11 and 23 July and 30 August 1909, which are typewritten and signed in a shaky Eddy hand, a display of pique at an 1897 Stetson initiative to consolidate three Christian Science churches in New York City into one and the 1904 elevation of an Eddy favorite to the readership at the West 96th Street church,[56] evidence of clashing personalities, even mild irritation, is absent.

Stetson's approach to Eddy, but not to the Boston directorship, was overly solicitous, even when her New York choir's scheduled performance at the 1895 Mother Church dedication was whimsically cancelled; even when Eddy troubled her for clothing, jewelry and personal favors over a period of two decades; even when *Broadway Magazine* praised the vitality of the New York movement and her own congregation honored her for twenty-five years of service in 1909. She apologized, backed off, pacified and, by all indications, remained subservient to the leader. As the first author of a letter concerning Christian Science published in the *New York Sun*, as the author of a "grand" essay on Science appearing in the *Cyclopedia Britannica*, as a well-developed, focused feminine personality of the 1890s and 1900s, she was compelling. Even if one doesn't necessarily agree with her she was, doubtlessly, the most significant woman in Christian Science save Eddy. She was the one Mary Baker Eddy wished to be her "Mary." However, Stetson saw herself in relation to the founder as Paul[57] and, even in her talk resembled that sort of spiritual dedication reminiscent of pre-Church Christianity. For a bureaucracy in search of order rather than personality or individuality she was more a Judas; she never was permitted to assume the role of an Aaron, Paul or Calvin. Unlike the aforementioned three, she was a little too late in arriving. The hierarchy had strengthened over fifteen years and declared for the ostensible sake of the Christian Science future that there would be no bridge between Boston and New York City.

Stetson's accomplishments in Christian Science were both visible and tangible. As Eddy aged, leading an insular, protected and, for her, a satisfying life at Pleasant View and after January 1908 at Chestnut Hill near Boston, the Mother Church directors naturally assumed more authority. Meanwhile, Stetson operated a successful Sunday school, persuaded Helen Brush and other Scientists to endow the New York City church in their wills and, despite her status of mere trustee, was regarded by practitioners as a leading teacher and spiritual head of the First Church of Christ, Scientist, dedicated in 1903 and built at a cost to the membership of $1.25 million.[58] She had her theology in common with Eddy but was considerably younger, imposing, energetic, dominating and tireless. Had there not been a firmly entrenched institutional bureaucracy, she was positioned to succeed Eddy, widen the framework of the faith and interpret the feminine spiritual incarnation of Christian principle in the same fashion, perhaps, as Paul interpreted Jesus' parables.

But none of this happened. It came to institutional notice that Stetson maintained a theology which, in essential outline, was agreeable with the post-1890 pronouncements of Mary Baker Eddy. When she retired and regrouped after 1889, left for Concord, disbanded the Massachusetts Metaphysical College and disestablished the original Christian Science Church, Eddy proclaimed material organization as unnecessary for proliferating the faith. Henceforward, a "spiritual foundation" whose primary feature was the immediate demonstration of the Gospel healing principle would take precedence. Supposedly, all of the spirituality and none of the chaos was laid out in the Mother Church *Manual*. But, practically, the directors opted for the reality of present and imperfect physical being with the possibility of spiritual perfection at some future date. It seemed a more rational concept for an orderly, improvable Progressive age.

This was not Stetson's understanding of Eddy or Christian Science; nowhere in correspondence was the Stetson concept challenged before June 1907, or about the time of the laudatory *Broadway Magazine* article. And even then it wasn't questioned by Eddy, who wrote to Stetson with cordial regularity, but by a handful of "my [Stetson's] disloyal students" and a "former member of the Mother Church . . . who was very bitter against me." The Mother Church Board of Directors gave credence to an apparently minority viewpoint and pursued it. This was a delicate time for Christian Science and Stetson appeared to be an "individual"—a dangerous individual whose forceful presence hindered the institutionalization of faith, rendering its doctrine incoherent and compromising a community seeking fellowship rather than charisma.

Indeed, it is appropriate to label Stetson's interpretation of Christian Science "radical" or "apocalyptic," since its root emanates from the finality of its theology. Stetson claimed that a right-thinking Christian Scientist recognized the demonstration over disease and death via healing or spiritual resurrection as an immediate reality and not a future possibility. When Mary Baker Eddy died on 3 December 1910, Stetson, already excommunicated for more than a year, alleged that the physically deceased Eddy had entered a twilight world to battle for spiritual resurrection, much as Jesus did when he appeared out of body after the crucifixion. This appearance was not a "return" in the usual sense since she had never deserted the world spiritually. Instead, like Christ, she had risen to demonstrate victory over death. Eddy's triumph would be evident for all eternity in an outpouring of spiritual Principle and divine Love. Thus, to Stetson, the risen Eddy would happily complete the world's cycle, presiding over the "end of days" initiated by Christ.[59]

The doctrine of theological immediacy went unchallenged by Eddy during her lifetime, despite the voluminous correspondence between founder and disciple, but was unacceptable to the Mother Church directors, especially after the dedication of the New York City church and the *Broadway Magazine* article; both illuminated Stetson's rather than the movement's personality. It is altogether possible that the elevation of traditional Christian Science favorite William McCrackan to the office of lecturer at the First Church of Christ Scientist was a Mother Church rebuke of Stetson, coming as it did just a few months after the dedication of the New York City temple. Eddy may have been consulted about McCrackan or may have taken some responsibility for the overall effort to diminish Stetson but clearly the latter bore her no malice and allocated to her mentor no blame. The king was not at fault, though her preference in disciples may have leaned toward a Mary rather than a Paul; Parliament, (the directors) was in error. "Today it is a question of ecclesiastical control or despotism—official domination . . . as opposed to individual understanding and spiritual sense. . . . They [the Boston directors] have . . . been good business men . . . of a material organization. . . . My defense is . . . divine Love."[60]

Mindful of an earlier (1892–93) failed attempt by a less assured Stetson to assume the editorship of the *Christian Science Journal* in concert with then-editor Joshua Bailey and publisher William G. Nixon, the Mother Church Board of Directors acted. On 25 September 1909 the Board took testimony from twenty-five New York City Christian Science practitioners, most of whom had been trained by Stetson. Six of them claimed that she taught Christian Science erroneously, denied the legitimacy of Christian Science churches in New York City other than her own, tried to exercise a sort of mental control over friend and foe alike and endeavored to "obtrude herself upon the attention of her students in such a manner as to turn their attention away from divine Principle." The contents of the *Report* were forwarded to Stetson and the New York City Christian Science Church Board of Directors, with that body undertaking an immediate inquiry. In the meantime, Stetson's practitioner credentials were revoked, and her advertising card was removed from the *Christian Science Journal*.[61]

With only one dissenter, the New York City Board exonerated Stetson in a *Report* dated 14 October 1909. It gave no credence to the charges, finding them to be the work of a vindictive minority. Therefore, if the Mother Church saw fit to take any negative action, it would have to be at the risk of taking the word of one naysaying New York City trustee opposing seven faithful ones and six anti-Stetson practitioners standing against nineteen loyalists. Nevertheless, such action was taken after Augusta Stetson was interviewed at the Mother Church in mid-November. She deemed it a " 'trial,' " an irregular one, "as I was not confronted by my accusers," was denied the services of a personal stenographer and "no copy of the report of the proceedings has ever been furnished to me." Based on the visible evidence, there is no reason why the Mother Church Board acted to excommunicate Stetson, but that was the result. Equally amazing was Stetson's resolve not to cause trouble. "I shall withdraw from personal participation in my church. . . . I am sending in my resignation as a member of the Board of Trustees. . . . I shall not attend the . . . Annual Meeting. . . . I shall not oppose the orders of the Board of Directors." Determined not to cause a schism, she left quietly and sixteen of the nineteen loyal practitioners were dropped with her from the rolls of the Mother and New York City churches.[62] Though she reviewed the incidents leading to her expulsion in countless letters written between 1909 and 1913, she never implicated Eddy, remained an inspired advocate for "radical" Christian Science and stood firmly as an opponent of the male directorate who, in her opinion, rendered an unsubstantiated verdict.

Augusta Stetson, reared by "Puritanical" parents, was a lot like Mary Baker Eddy, but with greater self-direction and more engrossing intellect. The qualities of self-denial, aloofness and distance are there as is a romantic affinity for the poetry of Whittier, Lowell, Longfellow and Holmes; in a quarter-century at 1 West 96th Street, New York City, she "never attended places of amusement" nor "participated in social functions." If not grimly determined she was at least messianically directed to build on Eddy's "spiritual foundation." By 1910, though, she had become superfluous since a hierarchical leadership enshrining Eddy had supplanted Gilded Age individuality. Ironically, Christian Science was to be a revolt against the cruel individualism of a material age—"I beheld the helplessness of humanity to avert . . . suffering . . . then I cry out . . . all is Mind"[63]—but Eddy became and remained the unassailable figure in Christian Science. This contradiction did not go unnoticed by her alert, aspiring pupils, Stetson among them, who for better or worse were banished into the wilderness.

NOTES

1. Frank Ballard, *Eddyism Miscalled Christian Science: A Delusion and a Snare* (London: Robert Culley, 1909), 181.

2. Martin E. Marty, "Church Looks for Right Path," *Boston Globe*, 15 March 1992, pp. 67–68; Alex S. Jones, "Book on Their Founder Splits Christian Scientists," *New York Times*, 30 September 1991, A1, A10.

3. David A. Rausch and Carl Hermann Voss, *Protestantism—Its Modern Meaning* (Philadelphia: Fortress, 1987), 179.

4. Allen F. Davis, *American Heroine: The Life and Legend of Jane Addams* (New York: Oxford University Press, 1973), 283.

5. Ronald G. Walters, *American Reformers 1815–1860* (New York: Hill & Wang, 1978), 163–66.

6. Julius Silberger, Jr., *Mary Baker Eddy: An Interpretive Biography of the Founder of Christian Science* (Boston: Little, Brown, 1980), 18–19.

7. Oscar Handlin, *Boston's Immigrants* (New York: Atheneum, 1977), 73.

8. Silberger, *Mary Baker Eddy*, 109–11.

9. W. W. Wright to Mary Baker Glover (Eddy), 10 March 1871, Personal Miscellaneous Papers—Mary Baker Eddy, Rare Books and Manuscripts Division, The New York Public Library, Astor, Lenox and Tilden Foundations, New York City.

10. Mary Baker Glover (Eddy) to W. W. Wright, n.d., but ca. 10 March 1871. Ibid. In the same manuscript collection, Eddy uses the word "control" thirty-four years later. See Mary Baker Eddy to Sarah Dean, 22 March 1905.

11. Silberger, *Mary Baker Eddy*, 109–11.

12. Edwin Franden Dakin, *Mrs. Eddy: The Biography of a Virginal Mind* (New York: Charles Scribner's Sons, 1930), 26, 81, 212, 415, 522; Robert Peel, *Mary Baker Eddy: The Years of Discovery* (New York: Holt, Rinehart and Winston, 1966), 257; Georgine Milmine, "Mrs. Eddy and Her First Disciples," *McClure's Magazine* 29 (May 1907): 106–7.

13. Frank Podmore, *From Mesmer to Christian Science*, 2d ed. (New York: University Books, 1963), 269.

14. Stephen Gottschalk, *The Emergence of Christian Science in American Religious Life* (Berkeley: University of California Press, 1975), 145; Briefs for the case of Eddy,

by Next Friends, against Frye, et al. in the Superior Court of the State of New Hampshire, April 1907, 4, 11, Streeter, Eddy Litigation Papers.

15. Silberger, *Mary Baker Eddy*, 213.

16. Podmore, *From Mesmer to Christian Science*, 269.

17. Herbert Albert Laurens Fisher, *Our New Religion* (London: Ernest Benn, 1929), 49; Robert Peel, *Christian Science: Its Encounter with American Culture* (New York: Henry Holt, 1958), 74; Podmore, *From Mesmer to Christian Science*, 269; Silberger, *Mary Baker Eddy*, 131.

18. Sybil Wilbur, *The Life of Mary Baker Eddy* (Boston: Christian Science, 1907), 233; Briefs for the case of Eddy, 1907, 4, 11, Streeter, Eddy Litigation Papers; Silberger, *Mary Baker Eddy*, 131–34; Podmore, *From Mesmer to Christian Science*, 270.

19. Silberger, *Mary Baker Eddy*, 132–35, 138–39, 146, 152, 166–69; Gottschalk, *Emergence of Christian Science*, 126.

20. Brad Holland, "The Price of Faith," *Yankee* 56 (July 1992): 113; Norman Beasley, *The Cross and the Crown* (New York: Duell, Sloan and Pearce, 1953), 97; Podmore, *From Mesmer to Christian Science*, 270; Silberger, *Mary Baker Eddy*, 137–39.

21. Briefs for the case of Eddy, 1907, 16–19, Streeter, Eddy Litigation Papers; Georgine Milmine, "The Massachusetts Metaphysical College and Calvin Frye," *McClure's Magazine* 29 (August 1907), 567–81.

22. Frederik A. Fernald, "Science and Christian Science," *Popular Science Monthly* 34 (April 1889): 808; Gottschalk, *Emergence of Christian Science*, 100; Silberger, *Mary Baker Eddy*, 176.

23. Gottschalk, *Emergence of Christian Science*, 100; Silberger, *Mary Baker Eddy*, 189.

24. Gottschalk, *Emergence of Christian Science*, 101–4.

25. "Christian Science," *New York Times*, 1 November 1887, 3; "An Inspired Woman" (editorial), *New York Daily Tribune*, 12 June 1889, 6; "Christian Science a Public Nuisance," *New York Times*, 30 July 1889, 4.

26. Fernald, "Science and Christian Science," 800; Silberger, *Mary Baker Eddy*, 170–74.

27. Beasley, *Cross and the Crown*, 122–23; Mary Baker Eddy, *Miscellaneous Writings 1883–1896* (Boston: Trustees under the Will of Mary Baker Eddy, 1896), 98–106.

28. Josephine Curtis Woodbury, *War in Heaven* (Boston: Press of Samuel Usher, 1897), 1–70; Frederick W. Peabody, *The Religio-Medical Masquerade* (New York: Fleming H. Revell, 1910), 5–18; "Topics of the Times," *New York Times*, 12 December 1898, 6; Silberger, *Mary Baker Eddy*, 212–13; Mary Baker Eddy, *Miscellaneous Writings 1883–1896* (Boston: Trustees under the Will of Mary Baker Eddy, 1896), 286; Podmore, *From Mesmer to Christian Science*, 295; Georgine Milmine, "Life at Pleasant View and 'War in Heaven,' " *McClure's Magazine* 30 (April 1908): 710.

29. "Brought Seven Libel Suits," *New York Times*, 1 August 1899, 4; Josephine Curtis Woodbury, "Christian Science and the Prophetess," *The Arena* 21 (May 1899): 537; "Christian Science Libel Suit on Trial," *New York Times*, 30 May 1901, 1; "Mrs. Eddy on Trial," *New York Evening Post*, 29 May 1901, 2; "Mrs. Woodbury's Suit Disposed of," *New York Daily Tribune*, 22 April 1902, 1; "Christian Science Case Ends Suddenly," *New York Times*, 6 June 1901, 1.

30. Gottschalk, *Emergence of Christian Science*, 181–89, 192; Silberger, *Mary Baker Eddy*, 208–11.

31. Steno Records, 1907, Folder 1, 100, Streeter, Eddy Litigation Papers.

32. Henry F. May, *Ideas, Faiths and Feelings* (New York: Oxford University Press, 1983), 7–8.

33. "Helen C. Brush Bequest," *New York Daily Tribune*, 14 July 1900, 14; "Fight over Brush Will," *New York Times*, 15 December 1900, 2; "Topics of the Times," *New York Times*, 24 December 1900, 6; "Christian Science an Insane Delusion," *New York Times*, 19 February 1901, 3; "Christian Science Lunacy, He Thinks," *New York Herald*, 19 February 1901, "Calls X-Science Madness," *New York Sun*, 19 February 1901, Newspaper Clippings and Misc., Streeter, Eddy Litigation Papers.

34. "Helen G. Brush's Will Ordered Probated," *New York Times*, 29 August 1901, 3; "Insanity and Religion," *New York Sun*, 21 February 1901, "Says Miss Brush Was Not Insane," *New York Daily Tribune*, 22 February 1901, "Alienist On 'Scientists,' " *New York Evening Post*, 22 February 1901, "Christian Scientists Are Not Insane," *New York Journal*, 28 February 1901, Newspaper Clippings and Misc., Streeter, Eddy Litigation Papers.

35. Streeter Testimony, 23 May 1907, 1, 36; Steno Records, 1907, Folder 1, 101, Streeter, Eddy Litigation Papers; Silberger, *Mary Baker Eddy*, 223–24.

36. Margaret Leech, *In the Days of McKinley* (New York: Harper and Brothers, 1959), 148.

37. Silberger, *Mary Baker Eddy*, 119; Untitled Summary of an Article in the *New York World*, 2 March 1907, 1, Newspaper Clippings and Misc., Streeter, Eddy Litigation Papers.

38. Streeter Testimony, 1907, Streeter, Eddy Litigation Papers.

39. *New York World* abstracts for 1–6, 10–12 March, 22, 28 April, 1907, 1–14, Newspaper Clippings and Misc., Streeter, Eddy Litigation Papers.

40. Silberger, *Mary Baker Eddy*, 135–36.

41. Chandler Testimony, 24 May 1907, 3–4, Streeter, Eddy Litigation Papers; Silberger, *Mary Baker Eddy*, 48.

42. Mary Baker Eddy to George Glover, 12 August 1892, 16 August 1893, 27 April 1898, Steno Records, 1907, Folder 2, 265, 267, 270, Streeter, Eddy Litigation Papers; *New York World* abstracts for 1–6, 10–12 March, 22, 28 April 1907, 6½, Newspaper Clippings and Misc., Streeter, Eddy Litigation Papers; Mary Baker Eddy to George Glover, 26 June 1889; Briefs for the case of Eddy, 1907, 24, Streeter, Eddy Litigation Papers.

43. Mary Baker Eddy to George Glover, 12 March 1903, 25 and 26 December 1906, Steno Records, 1907, Folder 3, 315–16, Streeter, Eddy Litigation Papers; *New York World* abstracts for 1–6, 10–12 March and 22, 28 April 1907, 3, 5, 7, Newspaper Clippings and Misc., Streeter, Eddy Litigation Papers; Mary Baker Eddy to George Glover, 21 August 1900, Steno Records, 1907, Folder 2, 272–73, Streeter, Eddy Litigation Papers.

44. Steno Records, 1907, Folder 3, 315–16, Streeter, Eddy Litigation Papers.

45. Stanley P. Hirshson, *Farewell to the Bloody Shirt* (Bloomington: Indiana University Press, 1966), 12, 121, 140, 154, 182, 208, 237, 249.

46. *New York World* abstracts for 1–6, 10–12, 22, 28 April 1907, 1, Newspaper Clippings and Misc., Streeter, Eddy Litigation Papers; "Sets Them Right," *Concord Evening Monitor*, 5 January 1907, Steno Records, 1907, Folder 3, 318, Streeter, Eddy Litigation Papers.

47. Mary Baker Eddy to George Glover, 11 January 190[7], 12 and 26 January 1907, Steno Records, 1907, Folder 3, 318–19, Streeter, Eddy Litigation Papers.

48. Mary Baker Eddy to George Glover, 19 and 26 January 1907 and 13 February 1907, Steno Records, 1907, Folder 3, 320–23, Streeter, Eddy Litigation Papers.

49. Steno Records, 1907, Folder 3, 330, Streeter, Eddy Litigation Papers; "Ex-Publisher of Eddy Book Gives Hint of a Plot," *New York World*, 12 May 1907, and "Plot to Depose Mrs. Eddy; Put Mrs. Stetson In," *New York World*, 6 May 1907, Newspaper Clippings and Misc., Streeter, Eddy Litigation Papers; Silberger, *Mary Baker Eddy*, 178–79, 191, 205–7, 223.

50. Silberger, *Mary Baker Eddy*, 227, 229.

51. Ibid., 224.

52. "Mrs. Eddy's Next Friends," *New York Evening Post*, 20 May 1907, 12; "Mrs. Eddy's Trustees Defeated," *New York Evening Post*, 5 June 1907, 1.

53. Steno Records, 1907, Folder 1, 96–112, Streeter, Eddy Litigation Papers; Closing Discussion of Counsel and Masters, Steno Records, 1907, Folder 4, 342, 344, 348, Streeter, Eddy Litigation Papers; "Masters Visit Mrs. Eddy," *New York Evening Post*, 14 August 1907, 6; "The Mrs. Eddy Suit Ended," *New York Evening Post*, 21 August 1907, 2.

54. Augusta E. Stetson, *Reminiscences, Sermons and Correspondence Proving Adherence to the Principle of Christian Science as Taught by Mary Baker Eddy* (New York: G. P. Putnam's Sons, 1913), 196.

55. Stetson, *Reminiscences, Sermons and Correspondence*, 5; "Mrs. Stetson and Her Invalid Husband," *New York Times*, 25 February 1901, 12.

56. *Letters of Mary Baker Eddy to Augusta E. Stetson, C.S.D. 1889–1909*, reproduced from the manuscript collection in the Huntington Library, San Marino, Calif. (Cuyahoga Falls, Ohio: Emma, 1990), 84–85, 106–9; Beasley, *Cross and the Crown*, 240; "Mrs. Stetson Resigns," *New York Times*, 28 July 1902, 5; "McCracken Elevated by Mrs. Eddy," *New York Times*, 8 February 1904, 14; Stetson, *Reminiscences, Sermons and Correspondence*, 19, 24–26, 143.

57. Stetson, *Reminiscences, Sermons and Correspondence*, 188–89, 263, 832; *Letters of Mary Baker Eddy to Augusta E. Stetson*, 73, 83, 88–90, 93, 110–11; Silberger, *Mary Baker Eddy*, 202, 235.

58. Stetson, *Reminiscences, Sermons and Correspondence*, 146.

59. Ibid., 205, 342, 359, 363–64, 486, 495, 498, 534, 635, 639, 642, 667, 674, 688, 700.

60. Ibid., 642–43, 645.

61. Ibid., 506–8.

62. Ibid., 230–31, 498–500, 518–35, 1196–97.

63. Ibid., 285, 348–49, 354, 967.

3

Roads Converging and Diverging

The philosophy of Christian Science is both simple and profound. It rejects materialism and reinterprets transcendentalism to mean the perfectibility of humanity through spirit and its divine operation rather than flesh. Nourished by superficial and interior currents that are poetic, psychological, intellectual and religious, Science's truth resonates with the personal experiences of Mary Baker Eddy. She walked well-traveled paths and tore at thickets torn before, sometimes two millennia before. Founders of the faith, its general congregants, casual readers and scholars hold something in common: a tendency to view the Science end product as a self-contained, hermetically sealed entity and not a process. This is a human failing to be sure, born of an intense individual need to be truly innovative. One wishes to present a fully furnished home, a ready-made bicycle path through some primeval forest, an intricately textured sand castle at the seashore and salvation unsullied as a pristine gift, the product of inspiration rather than perspiration. Along the way, an all too human being may consolidate debts, often diminishing them or occasionally forgetting them for the sake of originality. The latter, however, is as much a virtue with a footnote as not, perhaps even more so, since it acknowledges a debt and implies a responsibility to those who minded the store aeons or moments before that all-important, seminal customer stepped across a worn threshold setting off resounding bells.

Transcendentalism is a movement some historians credit Mary Baker Eddy with understanding and experiencing, even incorporating into her Christian Science thought.[1] But it must be a certain sort of transcendentalism since one barely catches an echo of the Cambridge School in her work; its intellectuals were figuratively light years removed from the Massachusetts towns Eddy passed through. So what sort of transcendentalist, if any, moved her? Certainly not the Harvard-educated scholars like Emerson and

Thoreau who wrote essays she never read; or the Unitarian sermonizers like Channing, Parker and Clarke, whose faith seemed a bit cold for a lone woman, despite its exuberant tendency. Pessimistic prophets Hawthorne, Melville and Dickinson were altogether impenetrable for her and perhaps a little frightening as well. In her world, it had to be someone else, someone accessible who might touchingly explain her life and her wandering in ways she could utilize and comprehend; someone or a group of someones with the popular or common touch.

Poets were such people and they could be found in small towns or at the lectern imbuing hard-working, informally educated citizens with a sense of their self-worth. In simple, homely, sentimental, untroubled verse—long on narrative and short on bothersome symbolic depth—James Russell Lowell, Henry Wadsworth Longfellow, Oliver Wendell Holmes and John Greenleaf Whittier could tell ante- and postbellum American generations what to think of themselves in words they could understand and, if they so desired, commit to memory. Without having to ponder too deeply the meaning of existence, the American public liked it. But not merely the American public; American seers too. Mary Baker Eddy wrote poetry and so did Augusta Stetson. They answered each other in verse, often trite and sentimental, but on the lilting Whittier–Longfellow model. For example, Stetson enclosed these lines to Eddy with a live gift—a caged canary:

> If a little bird may say
> What is in his heart today,
> I would say, "A song of glee
> Motherhood of God for thee."
>
> If you ask "Why come you here?"
> I will say "Your home to cheer,
> Life, Love, Truth, the whole day long
> Is the burden of my song."
>
> At the early morning dawn
> I will sing "Our Christ is born."
> And when dawn fades from our sight
> I will sing "Let there be light. . . . "
>
> And as Love appears to me
> I will sing "Truth sets me free!"
> Loud I'll sing "God is the power
> Moving me from hour to hour. . . . "
>
> I will sing a tend'rer song
> And its glad refrain prolong,
> I will trill, Life, Truth, and Love,
> Echoing the choirs above. . . .

And when shadows chase the light
I will sing "There is no night,"
Then will darkness flee away
As I sing "Behold God's day."

If I listen, I shall hear,
"Birdie, you are God's idea,"
Sent to chant your merry lay
Lovingly to cheer my way. . . .

Eddy's reply was well honed since she had expressed herself poetically since girlhood. (Incidentally, she returned the bird.):

I did send your birdie back,
But your song stayed in my heart,
To repeat its strain above,
Wakened by your friendly art.

I have loved and lost—Ah! What—
Many a joy but once a bird
Who did love me—and he died
Of my sorrow sad, unheard.

I have never told my grief,
Yet can never love another,
But your bird-prayer God may grant
Who has given you bird and "Mother."

So sweet nestling sing to her
Whom I love and must not lose,
Tell her I have kept her heart,
Ask her if I may not choose?[2]

The First Church of Christ Scientist, New York City, periodically affirmed its allegiance by letter "to our beloved Leader and Mother, who first taught us to lisp the language of spirit and led us to apprehend the power of infinite love." In expressing the congregation's "unfaltering loyalty," in appreciating Eddy's "wise, dauntless and perfect leadership," the signatories, including First Reader Augusta Stetson, Second Reader Edwin F. Hatfield and eight trustees, assured Eddy that their confidence in her remained unshaken, despite "all that has been said or written by revilers, whisperers or false witnesses, the mouthpieces of anti-Christ." Accompanying this particular missive, dated 28 October 1899, was a Stetson poem:

Oh! hear of the motherhood
  Brooding above,
Soft voicing Thy message
  Through Love's chosen love,
Hear gratitude, voiceless
  And prayers without speech,

> Which soar like the dove
>   Heavens portals to reach.
> Oh! fill us with meekness
>   To sit at her feet,
> Who teaches the pathway
>   To Love's blest retreat,
> Who leads Israel's army
>   In paths Jesus trod,
> The highway of holiness
>   Leading to God.

Eddy's rejoinder, sent from Pleasant View on 2 November 1899, urged a rededication to the divine, spiritual Principle rather than acts—"even the crown of thorns that mocked the bleeding brow of our blessed Lord, was overcrowned with . . . duties"—and offered this poem to "mercifully forgive, wisely ponder and lovingly scan the convulsions of the distempered mortal mind":

> I will listen for Thy voice,
> Lest my footsteps stray
> I will follow and rejoice
> All the rugged way.

Stetson herself pondered the poetic truths of Mary Baker Eddy some years later as she wondered if Christian Scientists were meeting modern religious challenges. Were they recalling the crucifixion of Jesus? Considering the meaning of Good Friday? Meeting the "so-called forces of evil and its claims of life in matter with the spiritual forces of good"? Do they

> [K]iss the cross, and wait to know
> A world more bright?[3]

In sources other than the Gospel, a true indicator of Christian Science may be found in nineteenth-century American verse, especially that of four or five native New Englanders who were, like Mary Baker Eddy, morally opposed to slavery but not necessarily proabolition activists or transcendentalists; interestingly, all were born forty or fifty years before the Civil War, all survived well after its conclusion but none saw the twentieth century. One, John Greenleaf Whittier, had little formal education, learning primarily, as did Eddy, in "Nature's unhoused lyceum";[4] he also resided in the small towns of Eddy's early career, and his work spoke to her struggle. The others were, from a physical standpoint, less accessible since they were Brahmins, editors and contributors to the *Atlantic Monthly* and primarily literary aristocrats whose flirtation with "truth" and "soul"[5] were less esoteric than that of the Cambridge School. As veterans of the lyceum they "might be called perennial and peripatetic schoolmasters of America,"[6]

educating large numbers of people in a popular culture style while maintaining the common touch.

A high point in Eddy's life in postbellum New England was the meeting
she had with Whittier in the summer of 1868, just after she moved in with
Sarah Bagley at Amesbury. Whittier had been a resident of the town since
1840 and remained there until his death in 1892. A great poetic "conscience"[7] rather than an immortal talent or intellectual, he spoke for and
lived among the lower middle and working classes of America. His memories of personal adversity, family poverty, small triumphs and ennobling
past were frozen in his finely etched Currier and Ives-like work, *Snowbound*,
composed in 1866:

> Our uncle, innocent of books
> Was rich in lore of fields and brooks. . . .
> A simple, guileless, childlike man.
> Content to live where life began;
> Strong only on his native grounds,
> The little world of sights and sounds
> Whose girdle was the parish bounds.

To him as well as to her, nature revealed itself geometrically;[8] indeed,
Eddy wrote poetry but Whittier set the standard for people of their class.
In years to come Whittier's lines were employed to describe Eddy's mission
as "God anointed leader of Christian Science . . . groping for the keys of
heavenly harmonies" while leading an "anthem of immortality":

> She is catching gleams of temple spires,
> Hearing notes of angel choirs,
> Where, as yet, unseen of them,
> Comes the New Jerusalem. . . .
>
> In the dual heart of man
> And between the soul and sense
> Reconcile all difference.[9]

Christian Science disciple, trusted lieutenant until 1909 and powerful,
decisive presence Augusta Stetson also esteemed the audience she had with
Whittier, but she entertained a more patrician clientele:

Whittier, Longfellow and Oliver Wendell Holmes I regard among the best American
poets. I have personally met them in their homes and at their firesides. It seems
ungracious of me to favor Whittier,—yet he, of all poets, sweeps his hand across the
heart's harpstrings, and awakens the chords of Soul . . . which flow from a life
consecrated to, and in unison with the source of being, Spirit, God, eternal life, Love
and Truth.[10]

She doesn't list James Russell Lowell, but he is omnipresent as well, quoted a half-dozen times in her *Reminiscences* as an exemplar of truth whose values coincide with those of Christian Scientists.[11] He, like Henry Adams, was a scion of a family rooted deeply in the American Protestant tradition, turned from hoped to ambivalence[12] in his decline, but somehow bore witness to this elusive truth, sought by all humanity in all ages, like the legendary El Dorado. In a May 1911 article for *Columbian Magazine*, Augusta Stetson, though excommunicated, was still called upon to publicize Christian Science to a popular audience. She did so at length, with generous reliance on Pauline spirituality and pre-Church interpretation of Christian immortality, underscored by the voice of truth as elicited in the writing of James Russell Lowell. He seemed to strike just the right note for divine metaphysicians Jesus of Nazareth, Paul of Tarsus and Mary Baker Eddy:

> Once to every man and nation comes the moment to decide,
> In the strife of Truth and Falsehood, for the good or evil side;
> Some great cause, God's new Messiah, offering each the bloom or blight,
> Parts the goats upon the left hand, and the sheep upon the right,
> And the choice goes by forever 'twixt that darkness and that light. . . .
> [H]istory's pages but record
> One death-grapple in the darkness 'twixt old systems and the Word.[13]

Stetson shared Eddy's taste for Whittier and added those of the "Genteel"[14] tradition because their sentiments were consistent with those of Christian Science and its founder. All of them, poet and prophet alike, in their different expressive mediums, recalled a simpler past in America particularly and in Western civilization generally. Quoting tirelessly from Whittier, Lowell and to a lesser extent Holmes in her major Christian Science memoir, Stetson saw the world passing swiftly before her, was deeply skeptical of the industrial-urban future and attempted a final glimpse of supposed perfection before the apocalypse. She, like Eddy, appreciated a comfortable life and eschewed the ideology for an active one. In admiring ethereal concepts of moral heroism, spiritual thought and disembodied truth, Eddy and Stetson revealed a preference for conservatism, prevailing class structure, formalism and the status quo. From a philosophic standpoint, Eddy's calculus was far more dependent on the impressions of religion and poetry than on the precision of mathematics and far more dependent on the culture of her environment than that of the academy, although she never lacked critics or defenders in either locale.

Science was vulnerable to a secular, intellectual critique during the Gilded Age because it was neither secular nor seriously intellectual; eventually, it had little pretense to nor any legitimate claim on human thought. The germ of Eddy's doctrine was contained in the poetry she wrote and heard, the Gospel she wished to rid of judgment, philosophy old and new that had become part of everyday discourse and contents of therapy sessions she had taken to heart but later disavowed. Such sessions stressed interpersonal contact while creative Christian Science opted for impersonal, spiritual New Testament curatives. As the years passed, she claimed less derivation and more innovation: at the end of her life, she was indebted only to divinity and not to humanity. In a material sense, there was nothing to repay and no reason to say "thank you": she believed herself to be liberated from her "debtors" and her past was, at least in her own mind, above reproach and closed to scrutiny. The fact that Eddy was not always candid, often contradicting her previous statements on the origins of Science, merely compounded the confusion and gave the arguments of her detractors a measure of credibility they otherwise would not have possessed.

Daniel Patterson, Eddy's second husband, went off to Washington, D.C. in late 1861, the recipient of a commission from the governor of New Hampshire to smuggle funds to Northern sympathizers in the South. He was captured by Confederate soldiers in the autumn of 1862, escaped from prison and returned home, only to find his marriage and his personal life changed. His wife of nine years, disheartened, alone and chronically unwell, had traveled to Maine to take a cure with a quasi-physician named Phineas Parkhurst Quimby. They had met on a brisk October morning in a year when Eddy was particularly receptive to revelations.[15]

Quimby's importance lies not in his healing methods per se but in his status as transitional figure in the scientific revolution that began three or four centuries before his advent and continues beyond his 1866 death. In brief, the scientific revolution replaced one standard of truth, the Christian faith, with a new standard, science. Reason and its adjuncts—deduction, proof and experimentation—were deemed indispensable for comprehending the universe and natural law. All this implies, of course, that there was no such thing as original sin; on the contrary, it was through reason that humans perceived the patterns of nature and by the proper application of science the possibility of man's harmonious existence with nature and its laws could be realized. The scientific revolution was perhaps the first time a doctrine of progress was espoused for Western civilization.

Promises of this sort would have to be purchased at a high price. Unpredictability and fear of the unknown subsided: a common elite belief of the revolutionary era was that the world was a machine and that its operations could be predictably explained by science. In return a new sort of insecurity was bred among less elite, much less worldly types whose mental state was significant because it was untouched by sophisticated investigatory techniques. Impenetrable and enduring, like an undercurrent of cold clear water, uninhibited by modernity, ceaselessly flowing, the fruit of such thought was unaffected by waves stirring the surface. For that sort of individual, whose opinion dominated the Western mind-set, the earth was deglorified, the universe cold and indifferent and men, including himself, too small to notice. He viewed with dismay the fact that spiritual existence, a necessity for community cohesion, had simply lost its power to influence the physical world.

After scientific, social and political revolutions, wars, diplomacy and the rise of nationalism, Quimby seems rather unimportant, just a folk healer in a backwater of America. But his contribution is greater than that. The trilogy of the scientific revolution—experimental man to biological man to rational/irrational/moral thinking man—was passing from step two to step three when Quimby practiced his unlicensed folk art, soon to be legitimized as psychotherapy, for male and female patients eager to be relieved of physical ailments via counseling. He certainly wasn't "establishment" nor did he represent conventional wisdom of a medical profession struggling for legitimacy. But there was something to it—a folk counterculture of sorts with precedent in the activities of Charles Poyen, who wrote an 1837 work on the concept of animal magnetism in New England and, for those willing to recede a shade further, Franz Anton Mesmer. Founder of the animal magnetism doctrine, later touted by Mary Baker Eddy as an oppositional or counterforce to Christian Science, Mesmer was an Austrian physician and hypnotist who established at Paris in 1782 the Order of Universal Harmony for the Propagation of Mesmerism.

A session with Quimby was a real experience, for one was counseled by every current, medical or otherwise, every philosophy, academic or folkish, which impinged on the man's intellect, with or without his knowledge. Quimby's forté was not terminal or fatal illness but nervous disorder, for which he employed a variety of techniques, all drugless, the most important of which was therapeutic conversation. His medicinal grab-bag included hydrotherapy, hypnotism, occasional reference to Christian spiritual healing and intuition.[16] Though mystical philosophies of both Eastern and Western derivation filtered through the American environment and certainly had their public promoters and places of popularity, Quimby and his "ism" were pragmatic, rock-solid, reliable and workable, as long as the method was not obliged to cover untenable or potentially dangerous situations. This sort of dependability was attractive to Eddy as a student, though the demands of faith and universal application were to take her, for better or worse, far beyond the comfortable, picturesque, undemanding confines of Belfast, Maine.

At the time of their encounter, was Eddy already groping toward a revelatory approach to healing or was her mind activated and subconsciously directed by Quimby? Historians of Christian Science and her biographers hedge because Eddy virtually denied any Quimby influence after the 1875 publication of *Science and Health*; of all the positive and negative developments in Christian Science that Augusta Stetson discusses, none whatever relate to Quimby, and she roams over a period greater than a quarter-century (1884–1913). When constrained to mention Quimby,

Eddy claimed his expertise resided in mind control, that he was a "magnetic" healer while she represented heavenly, impersonal, nonmaterial, immortal Gospel healing. All that can be said for certain is that P. P. Quimby was a leader of a popular mental healing movement in the United States and that he sometimes attempted to identify his theory with theism. "He believed that God must reveal himself to a scientific age through law . . . and if this was so, then the saving knowledge of His holy laws must come as an eternal science."[17] By mixing and mingling different approaches it might be asserted, with some justification, that Quimby was, in his time, an experimenter or pioneer in holistic healing, emblematic of the tortuous path toward enlightenment that mental man had taken but had not completed. His knowledge was available to a wider public than was experimental science and he was well known among women because he offered his services guilt-, surgery- and opiate-free. For the woman in search of stress alleviation, even for the man in search of the same sort of release, it was not merely a breath of fresh air; it was liberating.

Eddy was treated by Quimby from October 1862 until his death in January 1866. Extant letters to 1871 reveal a psychological dependence, as Eddy relied on her doctor in much the same way she would have liked to rely on her father and husbands. She described her condition as chronic gastric and bilious suffering, the result of "spinal inflammations" and evinced complete confidence in his method, whose success had filtered through New England. At the outset, when he didn't respond immediately or personally, she became more insistent and eventually made the trip to Portland in the autumn of 1862. It was obviously worth it: " 'I am . . . a living wonder and a . . . monument to your power. . . . So I have laughed about the wind veering according to P. P. Quimby . . . why even the winds and waves obey him.' " A few months later she continued: " 'Dear Doctor, what could I do without you? . . . I do not want to return to Portland. . . . If I could have my husband . . . at home I would like it there; but! but! but! . . . tis only in you I have any hope.' "[18] And even in the early 1870s, her method had been practiced only once before by a "Dr. Quimby . . . who healed me . . . and made it a research for twenty-five years, starting from the standpoint of magnetism, thence going forward and leaving that behind. I discovered the art in a moment's time, and he acknowledged it to me."[19] Her art, though, was not Quimby's; it was, however, the only way a person of her background could understand him. It was the Red Sea parting; it was intensely devotional; it was her testament.

The assertion that Eddy was groping toward a personal insight prior to her treatment with Quimby is interesting but unproved. Instead of identifying a gradual process and the accumulation of need over the course of years, it is always tempting for writers to offer discovery dates, among them 1853, 1862, 1864 or 1866.[20] Note that at least one of these precedes her treatment with Quimby, placing her creativity within the context of family crises surrounding her son George (no longer living with her), critical relationships with her father and overbearing older sister and her impending second marriage. The latter three dates were equally disturbing for her, as added tension in Eddy's life threatened to overwhelm her. With no palliative for her emotional and physical agony, a portion of which she brought on herself, she may have sought comfort in religious thought rather than church attendance or any other avenue of communal warmth. Abstractions can indeed serve to replace people and have done so for those who either feel or really are isolated.

To continue beyond Quimby, Eddy needed to further concentrate on ideas and principles that rendered her life orderly, disciplined and controlled while distancing her from her all too human afflictions. In idolizing Quimby—he cured her ailments to the extent that she rarely relapsed and never visited a regular doctor for her chronic aches and pains—she learned something that could enhance her religious thought. He had impressed upon her his conclusion that disease was both caused and cured by factors other than drugs or surgery. He believed it was the human mind, but Eddy celebrated Quimby rather than "mind"; part of her attachment to him stemmed, no doubt, from an unsaid conviction that what she witnessed in her own session was not proprietary. On the contrary, it was uncopyrighted. Quimby performed, but it was not Quimby's personal cure; if she thought of him as a mere doctor, it wouldn't be a compliment. Physicians—just like ailments, family members, tragedies and disappointments—came and went; electromagnetic, hypnotic or otherwise organic explanations for healing also came and went. Quimby himself went the way of all flesh. As the agent of spiritual truth rather than its inventor, his achievements lived well beyond his physical presence, which to Eddy was actually unnecessary. Such perfection, relieved of people, and such medicine, relieved of human practice, were the essence of Christian Science and, following Quimby's death, took a number of years to develop. Apparently, as the story goes—and it's been told and retold—Eddy's relationships with people over the next few years did not improve, nor did she become any more optimistic concerning her own personal adjustment. Principles, ineluctable truths and universal Christian "love" moved her much more than service or human contact.

After Quimby died his disciple, Julius Dresser, felt himself inadequate to the task of perpetuating the mental healing philosophy. At this time, Eddy asked Dresser to continue Quimby's work, since her faith in its impersonal, universal workability remained unshaken. Dresser demurred, believing himself inadequate to the task. Sometime between 1866 and 1872, probably closer to the latter date, during the genesis of *The Science of Man*,[21] the component of human healing within the Quimby method was submerged in an idea Eddy knew best and was most at ease with: religion.

The way her inspiration matured during the first decades of industrial consolidation in the United States rendered it an inviting target. To the uninitiated, it appeared to be a religion but claimed to be demonstrable, like a science. Moreover, Eddy shared with Social Darwinist philosopher Herbert Spencer a contempt for mortal man that vitiated her ostensible but not quite transcendental belief in perfection. Her theories on God—his calculus, precision and impersonal demonstration—were, in many ways, as inexorable as natural law. As envisioned by Eddy, the ultimate triumph of the spirit would arrive when material humanity yielded to the love of God, realizing its helplessness and its inadequacy before the divine law.[22] Her belief that evil was unnatural seemed to coincide with the prevailing materialistic ethic, but her consistent rejection of material importance[23] defies categorization of this sort. In the 1870s the contradiction in her thought was already apparent. Her denial of matter, sickness, sin and death was "sensational and sinister" to Herbert Spencer but she also seemed conspicuously uninspired to the more optimistic: "There is no indignation. . . . There is no pity for the sufferings of those around her; the long tragedy of human history leaves her unmoved."[24]

Before the end of the first complete postbellum decade, Eddy became preoccupied with materialism's dark side, establishing her concept of Malicious Animal Magnetism to accuse erstwhile Scientists Kennedy and Spofford, while admitting the existence of evil in the mortal mind for critics[25] who might have thought her unchristian. The artlessness of Christian Science found little currency among American thinkers, although there were persistent pockets of support among those empiricists who believed Eddy offered vital alternatives. Fresh, energetic ideas with a humanistic nucleus inevitably challenged Science and, themselves, underscored the need for varied responses to suit the complexity of the 1880s.

One such movement, New Thought, should be mentioned, if only because former Quimbyites organized it and disaffected Christian Scientists found prominent positions in it. Julius Dresser and a Methodist minister, Walter Felt Evans, developed an optimistic theory—not necessarily religious—harmonizing with the laws of experimental science. Essentially creedless, it, and not Christian Science, was the natural Quimby successor.

Like Quimby, New Thought expressed the idea that mind and matter were separate; although physical disease existed, it stemmed from a basic unsoundness of the mind. New Thought's admission of material reality supported the conclusion that cures were achieved through the use of mental healing in conjunction with formal medical care. Its spokespeople held that absent treatment produced satisfactory results in some situations but, for the most part, an essential physical relationship between doctor and patient was most conducive to the latter's well-being. Finally, they trusted in the power of positive thinking. Concentration on the "higher life" would reduce mental disorders and, therefore, prevent somatic ailments.

Hence, New Thought did not deny the existence of matter and disease; it simply affirmed the power of the mind.[26] Its humanistic moral foundation recalls Pico della Mirandola, the fifteenth-century Florentine thinker who believed every era in history had something positive to offer as did each major philosophy—Christian, Moslem and Jewish—whose common denominator was a universal form of consciousness uniting all men in a single understanding of God. Rather unspecified and unfocused, New Thought never acquired a particularistic core but among its charter members and disseminators were Emma Hopkins, Mary Plunkett and Ursula Gestefeld, former Christian Scientists who sought life-affirming alternatives in other than Christian philosophy; in addition their ability to rise in Science was hampered by the long and demanding shadow cast by the founder.

Dresser and Evans thought they had excellent grounds on which to attack the originality and radicalism of the Eddy doctrine. Speaking at Boston's Church of the Divine Unity on 6 February 1887, Dresser stated that the mental healing component of Christian Science originated from Phineas P. Quimby and that a manuscript stolen from him by Eddy supplied the impetus for her writings. Credence was lent to this argument in 1921 when Dresser's son Horatio published the Quimby manuscripts. Horatio Dresser arrived at the conclusion that Eddy most assuredly "borrowed" from Quimby in formatting her own thought; he also claimed that Quimby's healing employed a modicum of spirituality, since one of its mechanisms was the "divine presence." Every reference to Mary Baker Eddy attempts to confirm her intentional reliance on her former mentor: "The turning point with Mrs. Eddy, as with all who came to Dr. Quimby was . . . the silent, spiritual treatment she received." The manuscript, entitled "Questions and Answers," appearing at the end of each edition of *Science and Health*, was alleged to be the stolen document referred to by Julius Dresser and formerly called "Extracts from P. P. Quimby." The younger Dresser stated that Edward Arens lost his copyright case in 1883 merely because Julius Dresser refused to allow the Quimby manuscripts to be taken to court.[27]

In conclusion, both Horatio Dresser and George Quimby, the mental healer's son, claimed that the system of therapeutics called "Christian Science Healing" was stolen from Quimby. It would be more correct, though, to say that Quimby was a factor in the founding of a religion whose nature, intent and operation had only a peripheral relation to mental healing; actually Horatio Dresser and George Quimby both disclaimed responsibility for the faith allegedly founded on Christian Science healing. In a letter from Belfast, Maine, written in November 1901, George Quimby declared that the "religion she teaches certainly is hers for which I cannot be too thankful, for I should loath to go down to my grave thinking that my father was in any way connected with Christian Science."[28] For her part, there was never a question in Eddy's mind about purloining manuscripts or ideas. In the first place, hers was a religion of spirit and his was human manipulation and there was a world of difference, positive versus negative, between the two. In the second place one could not own God's metaphysics—it was readily available to all—and such knowledge, existing within the public domain, was not stealable. By the close of the 1880s Dresser, Evans and the women composing the Chicago wing of Christian Science thought the Eddy philosophy inexorable, out of touch with contemporary eclecticism. Although New Thought was utopian and did enjoy a following until World War I, when psychotherapy was slowly incorporated into legitimate medical practice, it did not deny a material basis for disease, physical sickness or drug cures. Unlike Christian Science it was unsystematized, diffuse and uncentered, but it lasted thirty years because it heralded new approaches and validated "scientific laws that we see proved every day."[29] Science, of course, made its contribution too, as we shall see, but primarily from the religious standpoint.

Students of Plato, Immanuel Kant, Plotinus, René Descartes, Baruch Spinoza, Johann Gottlieb Fichte, David Hume and Georg Wilhelm Friedrich Hegel might have had something to cheer about and criticize too within Christian Science. One can locate the Western tradition from antiquity through the advent of nineteenth-century German idealist philosophers in Eddy's work.[30] But one hunts in vain for coherent or systematic elaborations; what she offered was entirely in snippets because that was the way Eddy acquired and stored whatever secular knowledge she may have valued. Nevertheless the traces are there[31] and were passed on to leading Christian Scientists. It was not uncommon for Christian Scientists other than Eddy to address students in the following fashion: "Shadows are not substance" or "man is spiritual and not material. . . . matter is . . . a false sense. . . . Truth has shown . . . objects of the . . . material senses to be shadows, while Mind alone [i.e., impersonal, divine mind] is 'substance.' "[32] Objects, truth, substance, shadows, soul and their incorporation into the "Parable of the Cave"[33] influenced Hellenized Judaism and early Christianity. Since Mary Baker Eddy was attuned to Gospel Christianity she was doubtlessly moved by an outline of classical knowledge.

She acquired a nodding acquaintance with these Western concepts and their Christian relevance perhaps from random talk in New Hampshire neighborhoods and Congregational churches but more likely from someone closer at hand, well-respected, accomplished, brilliant in his way and admired by the 1830s Baker household, someone Mary would listen to, enthralled. Although it may be an exaggerated or pretentious claim, Eddy would say upon reflection that her Dartmouth-educated brother Albert, an attorney and political activist in New Hampshire before his death at age thirty-one in 1841, taught her "the classical languages [and] exposed her to classical training."[34] Of course she lost it all upon her acquisition of spiritual verity but not really, since the Western tradition, in certain nonsecular ways, mixed and mingled in Science.

There is a whisper of Kant, and for that matter Plotinus, Fichte, Descartes, Hume and Hegel in the worldview, if one can call it that, of Mary Baker Eddy. None of the names would necessarily prompt a knowing reply or stir a sense of recognition but they were, perhaps, a source of sibling discussion when Albert felt communicative or were admixed in wide-ranging, popular discussion held at assorted breakfast or dinner tables, where Eddy was sometimes welcomed. The commonality in all these is communal disenchantment accompanied by a search for God or ultimate knowledge. Even in the search, there was some sort of law to be grasped, something absolute to hold on to, something elusive yet definable, very much like Christian Science.

Fichte, Kant and Hegel widened the application of Plato and the third-century C.E. Plotinus by rendering their philosophy less antique and much less abstract. Fichte, who became a spokesman for German nationalism during the Napoleonic wars, stressed the importance of the individual inner spirit as creator of its own moral universe. Kant, having been disabused of the philosophes and their reliance on rational, empiric solutions, posited a world of noumena where reality could be known only intuitively, where the sole contact with the real world was a transcendent, true faith. Having lived in a revolutionary environment, Hegel sought to explain causation in terms of motivating ideas that inevitably move the world forward independent of human will. As a matter of fact, human beings had very little to do with the romantic temper of struggle, whose end was foreseen in some all-embracing but not always optimistic law. Reliance on law, in the manner of Descartes who wished to construct a geometrically precise universe, or Spinoza, whose deity was natural, constantly unfolding and not revelational, was, by the nineteenth century, questioned but not quite displaced by philosophers like David Hume who, as a skeptic of rationalism, placed limits on human knowledge rather than the authority of law.

Mary Baker Eddy was not inured to philosophic debate nor was she a philosopher, but, in twentieth-century idiom, you don't have to be a weatherman to know which way the wind is blowing. She felt it and swayed to its Victorian rhythm. In poetic terms, the highly charged, innovative character of Eddy caught the tone of life on a feather, drifting, lonely, trapped and lifting / always seeking / rarely finding / shelter of a harbor. Assuredly, it was this tone of unbending iron law, albeit spiritual, often a melodramatic re-creation of struggle, which informed her personal and public identity; more telling perhaps, especially for a visionary, is that it informed the collective identity of one hundred to two hundred thousand middle-class Americans, sometimes more educated than herself, who shared with her a deep skepticism about human achievement and potential.

Spiritualism, European and American, along with Eastern cosmic philosophies, debuted in the Atlantic world at about the same time as Christian

Science; in the case of theosophy, it was actually coincident. A theosophical society was founded in New York City in 1875, precisely the same year as *Science and Health*'s initial publication. Historian Carlton J. H. Hayes estimates one hundred thousand European theosophists at the 1891 death of its leader, Helena Blavatsky. Just a couple of years later, at the World Parliament of Religions, Christian Science made an impressive showing but was compelled to share the podium with the Swami Vivekananda, "who was swamped with admirers, most of them female," and Annie Besant; the first was an explicator of vedanta and the second was a theosophist.[35] Perhaps it was Mary Baker Eddy's past returning to haunt her since she associated with and attempted to convert those with a spiritualist leaning in the 1860s, before she dealt with mainstream Protestants. More likely, however, this close association was an embarrassment and a source of confusion. Indeed, Christian Science afforded spiritual and/or physical benefit without pain but only through correction of error, practice and demonstration. In its very mundane approach, it proved, in its maturity, to be wedded only to a Western tradition.

In a superficial way, it would appear that Christian Science held something in common with the work of Emanuel Swedenborg and Andrew Jackson Davis. Swedenborg, an eighteenth-century Scandinavian, was a distinguished theologian and mystic whose beliefs were incorporated into a Masonic rite though he never joined the Masons. He was said to have apocalyptic visions of heavenly ascent, conversed with spirits and thought spiritualism and Christianity reinforced each other. Davis, also called the "Poughkeepsie Seer," was not so much a spiritual "rapper" as a cosmic philosopher whose reality was manifested in groups called "Harmonial Brotherhoods." Their mission was to implement his teachings for the purpose of transforming the world. His teachings were not particularly Christian but nonsectarian and universal. He suggested in an overlong tome called *The Principles of Nature, Her Divine Revelations and a Voice to Mankind* how society might be improved. "He endorsed virtually every contemporary reform, including antislavery, temperance and women's rights." His message was really neither mystical nor intuitive; he urged readers to think, to study, to receive wisdom from all sources and to act.[36] More than a handful of reformers would have agreed.

Eddy was not like either of these and any similarity is purely coincidental. Unlike Swedenborg, Eddy would not have entertained Masonry (the order does not recognize the divinity of Jesus); nor did she have ecstatic visions, though she flirted with spiritualism in her postbellum New England environment. In its mature stage, Christian Science doesn't discuss heavenly ascent but spiritual selfhood realizable and attainable in the present. With regard to Davis, involvement in reform was simply not the Eddy style since any sort of materialism detracted from divine Love and Truth, whose major expression was to be found in impersonal Principle rather than social activism. Davis was much too Catholic for her entirely Pauline, John-like re-creation of Gospel Christianity. Far from ecumenical, the Eddy reliance on "Logos" is unmistakably, exactingly Christian.

Meditative, integrative and universalist/brotherhood philosophies of the East competed for American favor along with Christian Science. Yoga aimed at training the consciousness for a state of perfect spiritual insight and tranquility; a system of exercises was practiced to promote control of the body and mind. Buddhism posits that suffering is inseparable from existence but the inward extinction of self and the senses culminates in a state of illumination beyond both suffering and existence. Baha'i, a splinter movement of Islam, was founded by a nineteenth-century Iranian mystic called the *Bab* or the "door" to wisdom. Rather different from the authoritarian Shia faith, the *Bab* taught the principles of sexual equality, ethnic unity, universal rather than a particularistic Moslem God and world harmony. Vedanta is to Hindus what the Koran is to Moslems and the Bible is to Christians. A system of Brahmanic philosophy written in Sanskrit and three thousand or more years old, it is described in the *Vedas*, or sacred writing of the Brahmans. The core belief is in the unity of all real existence, called "soul" or "God," which vanquishes the power of external life or individuality. Some of the *Vedas* or hymns manifest a yearning or groping after the eternal, highlighted by an anxious search for the divine name. Theosophy, whose mystical tenets rest on divine intuition, proposed the regeneration of humanity and its reintegration into that state of primitive innocence preceding Adam's fall and original sin.[37]

Christian Science was none of these. Brotherhood of faith, yearning, suffering, body-soul integration, equality, world harmony and regeneration were foreign to the spirituality of Eddy. She often said that one does not proceed in Christian Science to a point of divinity; if one understands Science, he or she is already at that point. Founded on assurance rather than groping or hoping, suffering was one of those mortal beliefs requiring error "management" rather than endurance; worse than unnecessary, it was incorrect. Finally, Christian Science offered no credence for human absorption into the divine and the loss of individuality. Physical individuality as such was a mortal error that was banished by divine truth; spiritual individuality, the fruit of Jesus' teaching and healing practice, remained distinct, "perfect and eternal," never to disappear. The principle was not grasped by Mary Baker Eddy's critics and, due to the competition for Christian hearts, she felt it incumbent to clarify it in *Science and Health* and two of her other works, *Unity of Good* and *No and Yes*:

This scientific sense of being, forsaking matter for Spirit, by no means suggests man's absorption into Deity and the loss of his identity. . . . Man is not absorbed in Deity; he is forever individual; but what this everlasting individuality is, remains to be seen. That which is born of the flesh is not man's eternal identity. Spiritual and immortal man alone is God's likeness and that which is mortal is not man in a spiritually scientific sense. . . . I do not deny, I maintain the individuality and reality of man; but I do so on divine principle, not based on human conception and birth.

Eddy aspired to the spiritual selfhood of Jesus as explained in John's Gospel. The attainment of such a consciousness, she concluded, would negate fleshly perceptions in favor of God's true likeness: spiritual man and woman, "coexistent and eternal," with the "infinite Father-Mother God."[38]

Some American thinkers roiled Christian Science in an international mix because they were uncomfortable with it as a Western faith; they might have wished, as well, that it could be dismissed as merchandise stolen from P. P. Quimby—as such, it could be bogus or counterfeit but not problematic. In fact, an American critique did develop and featured great enthusiasm but not much insight or originality.

From 1901 to 1910, the last decade of Eddy's life, some Progressives and twilight Social Darwinists combined for a climactic anti-Science salvo. In the Progressive era, the demise of matter was a serious allegation since it meant the rejection of the scientific age and the ability of Americans to fashion their own destiny. John Churchman railed against the notion of nonexistent evil in a society in which corruption was shamelessly flaunted; he called the Science system heresy and its innovator a dilettante and a fanatic.[39] The concept of matter as an illusion seemed closely allied to Social Darwinism's denial of poverty and blithe disregard of immigrant and working classes. The crux of the Progressive intellectual argument was that "matter [in this case, the new scientific discoveries and technological advances of the early twentieth century] was saturated with God; to say that God revealed himself to man in any other way was a monstrous belief. The chief indictment of Progressives against Christian Science was that "it tended to shut off the current of growth and lock the wheels of progress."[40]

However, other Progressive thinkers were more sanguine about Science. To Benjamin O. Flower, editor of the muckraking *Arena*, materialism had paralyzed virtually an entire country. Christian Science was the last expression of moral idealism left. Atheistic idealist Gerhardt Mars identified Eddy with the culmination of the philosophic concept of man's spiritualization. Although he approved of mental healing, he believed it to be most effective when proper medical precautions were taken. In a figurative sense, he interpreted Eddy's faith to be the beginning of man's victory over death; humanity would master its material environment and build a new heaven on earth. Joel Rufus Mosley, a young American thinker, demonstrated the relevance of Christian Science to Platonic thought and the subjective idealism of Berkeley, Kant and Hegel. Thus, the morality, idealism and spiritualization of Christian Science were regarded by some as manifestations of modern idealism rather than an ill-conceived delusion.[41]

Christian Science was buffeted in a philosophic crosscurrent. If Progressives were not completely sold on Eddy's religion, neither were right-wing naturalists. Henry White thought the movement a "medieval revival" while others claimed it was a regressive step on the evolutionary scale, a return to primitive existence.[42] Frank R. Medina presented a comprehensive indictment of Science in which he proved himself an ardent advocate of Spencer:

From the standpoint of evolution . . . Christian Science is a movement backward . . . to primitive man . . . where all phenomena were caused by spirits . . . [and] disease and death [were] produced by supernatural beings. . . . It [Christian Science] is a cult that retards the natural evolution of religious ideas. . . . [I]t is a cult that retards secular ideas as it mixes natural with supernatural which is primitive. Christian Science, by rejecting secularism, is barbarous.

While experience is the foundation of reality, continued the writer, dreams are the foundation of the supernatural. Primitive man could not distinguish his actual beliefs from his unconscious dreams because, to him, both seemed real. As man progressed, his intelligence evolved and his dark, irrational self became less material and more spiritual. Christian Science proposed a return to primitivism by encouraging a revival of humanity's early dream beliefs. Therefore, Eddy and her followers retarded human progress by invoking the supernatural against sin, in defiance of the scientific, rational age: "While the great white sun of science is strong in the outer expanse, the new cult leads the world back into the deserted caves of ignorance and holding up its glimmering lantern cries, 'Behold the light!' "[43]

Those who attacked the originality of Eddy's thought presented bold arguments to justify their position. However, they cast too wide a net in grouping Eastern asceticism, Hinduism and Quimbyism together, intimating that anything and everything was a Christian Science precursor.[44] The riddle of Science origins is explainable in terms of a response to unique personal problems and, less consciously, to societal crises. To a great extent, the Gospel, with its Hellenized, Platonic intent and the verse of popular poets were much closer to Eddy's realm of understanding than transcendentalism, Quimbyism and pragmatism. Hence the first two, to a greater extent than the last three, shaped Eddy's heavenly optimism. Indeed, hers was not exactly the material exuberance fomented in an age of science and urban, managerial reform but neither was it the verdict of Spencer; it is a link between the two.

Eddy adapted a portion of the Quimby writing to fit the religious truth of the Gospel, but she understood and really cared little for the experimental function and curative intent of mental healing. Her true role is reviver of the literal Gospel, not experimenter or nascent analyst. She stumbled onto something but it was incidental to her mission. When she first began to construct her theory, she referred to the Quimby healing practice as the twilight of discovery. The Belfast doctor dealt with the mind as an agency to heal the body. To Eddy, that was impossible, though Quimby was an avenue leading toward ultimate enlightenment. Several recent Christian Science histories, including those of Eddy's supporters, acknowledge Quimby as some sort of vessel through which wisdom flowed and to whom she may owe a debt, though a small one.[45] Eddy's error, then, was not in creatively employing Quimby for a different purpose; it was in opening the floodgates of criticism by unnecessarily denying her debt, especially after the 1880s.

Did Christian Science harmonize in any way with the twentieth century or was it merely a spiritual manifestation of a past time, either antique or Victorian? From the positive standpoint, the Emmanuel movement was regarded as an "Episcopal flirtation with Mrs. Eddy."[46] Inaugurated in 1905 and arising "explicitly in response to Christian Science," the Emmanuel Episcopal Church movement granted to Science a certain innovative credit for attempting to restore to Christianity its "lost therapeutic power," but rejected Eddy's monism. Believing that mental illness could, in some cases, predate physical illness or vice-versa, the Emmanuels united clergy and physicians in an effort to heal the mind and the body. "Troublesome questions still lurked" but medical missions arrived in the slums, divinity students were introduced to religious psychotherapy and, in 1941, when the Emmanuel enterprise ended, new groups in other denominations and faiths were formed for the purpose of promoting clinical training among theologians. "Modern 'pastoral counseling,' "[47] and the need to obtain advanced degrees in this field by ministers, priests and rabbis, date from this period. Emmanuelism, less divine but more material and pragmatic, completed the revolution begun but carried only so far by Christian Science.[48]

Though not a philosopher, muckraking author Georgine Milmine found Mary Baker Eddy's nonmaterial historical perspective narrow and uncompromising: "All the physical sciences are the harmful inventions of mortal mind and the slow . . . painful accumulation of exact knowledge has been but the baser element of human nature. There was never such a discouraging view of human history." Yet in another article, Milmine sneered at Christian Science for appealing to materialism and perpetuating the fiction of a healthy society.[49]

The way to resolve this conflict is simply to say that Science rightfully belonged to several eras, only one of which was contemporary. In the Gilded Age, it offered release to certain disempowered classes, specifically women and entrepreneurial men, whose competitive opportunities were circumscribed by the movement toward consolidation; in the Progressive period, it offered hope but no particular burden of accountability for a large segment of the middle class. Christian Science discarded and added, adapting in its own fashion to the needs of a dynamic society; it stood at the crossroads of American intellectualism. It moved slowly, hesitantly, leaving its mark on a new age, creating no philosophic revolution but, nevertheless, inciting to fresh and evolutionary trends.

NOTES

1. Robert Peel, *Christian Science: Its Encounter with American Culture* (New York: Henry Holt, 1958), xi. A similar theme may be found in I. Woodbridge Riley, "The Personal Sources of Christian Science," *Psychological Review* 10 (November 1903): 606. A few years later, Riley tried to show that Eddy plagiarized from Bronson Alcott and "borrowed" from the writings of the spiritualist Emanuel Swedenborg. See B. R. Wilson, "The Origins of Christian Science: A Survey," *Hibbert Journal* 57 (January 1959): 164.

2. Augusta E. Stetson, *Reminiscences, Sermons and Correspondence Proving Adherence to the Principle of Christian Science as Taught by Mary Baker Eddy* (New York: G. P. Putnam's Sons, 1913), 159–62.

3. Ibid., 166–68, 825.

4. Robert McHenry, ed., *A Documentary History of Conservation in America* (New York: Praeger, 1972), 61.

5. Stetson, *Reminiscences, Sermons and Correspondence*, 46, 205, 354, 640, 880, 992.

6. Alice Felt Tyler, *Freedom's Ferment* (New York: Harper and Row, 1962), 263.

7. Thomas A. Bailey and David M. Kennedy, *The American Pageant*, 9th ed. (Lexington, Mass.: D. C. Heath, 1991), 1:337.

8. McHenry, *Documentary History of Conservation*, 60–61.

9. Stetson, *Reminiscences, Sermons and Correspondence*, 52.

10. Ibid., 967–68.

11. Ibid., 46–47, 354, 640, 880, 992.

12. E. Digby Baltzell, *The Protestant Establishment* (New York: Vintage Books, 1964), 89–90.

13. Stetson, *Reminiscences, Sermons and Correspondence*, 986–1003.

14. Warren I. Susman, *Culture as History* (New York: Pantheon Books, 1984), 72; Henry Bamford Parkes, *The American Experience* (New York: Vintage Books, 1959), 266.

15. Georgine Milmine, "The Encounter with Quimby," *McClure's Magazine* 28 (February 1907): 339–54; Julius Silberger, Jr., *Mary Baker Eddy: An Interpretive Biography of the Founder of Christian Science* (Boston: Little, Brown, 1980), 58.

16. Stephen Gottschalk, *The Emergence of Christian Science in American Religious Life* (Berkeley: University of California Press, 1975), 105–7, 130–31; Silberger, *Mary Baker Eddy*, Chap. 3.

17. Robert Peel, *Christian Science: Its Encounter with American Culture* (New York: Henry Holt, 1958), 114; idem, *Mary Baker Eddy: The Years of Discovery* (New York: Holt, Rinehart and Winston, 1966), 167–68; Mary Baker Eddy, *Miscellaneous Writings 1883–1896* (Boston: Trustees under the Will of Mary Baker Eddy, 1896), 98–106.

18. Silberger, *Mary Baker Eddy*, 61–62, 79, 83–84.

19. Mary Baker Glover (Eddy) to W. W. Wright, n.d., but ca. 10 March 1871, Personal Misc.

20. Georgine Milmine, "The Quimby Controversy," *McClure's Magazine* 28 (March 1907): 508.

21. Horatio Dresser, ed., *The Quimby Manuscripts* (New York: Thomas Y. Crowell 1921), 152–57.

22. Peel, *Christian Science*, xii-xiii, 91, 201–4.

23. Mary Baker Eddy, *Science and Health with Key to the Scriptures*, 11th ed. (Boston: Trustees under the Will of Mary Baker Eddy, 1934), 130, 274; Peel, *Mary Baker Eddy*, 280.

24. Adrian Feverel, "Christian Science: The Cult of the Ridiculous," *Catholic World* 96 (February 1913): 655–60; Benjamin O. Flower, "The Recent, Reckless and Irresponsible Attacks on Christian Science and Its Founder, with a Survey of the Christian Science Movement," *The Arena* 37 (January (1907): 64; Georgine Milmine, "Mrs. Eddy's Book and Doctrine," *McClure's Magazine* 31 (June 1908): 186; Frank Podmore, *From Mesmer to Christian Science*, 2d ed. (New York: University Books, 1963), 291.

25. Georgine Milmine, "The Revival of Witchcraft," *McClure's Magazine* 29 (June 1907): 339.

26. Georgine Milmine, "The Schism of 1888, the Growth of Christian Science and the Apotheosis of Mrs. Eddy," *McClure's Magazine* 30 (February 1908): 390–92; Podmore, *From Mesmer to Christian Science*, 255–59.

27. Julius A. Dresser, *The True History of Mental Healing* (Boston: Alfred Mudge and Son, 1887), 15–17; Dresser, *Quimby Manuscripts*, 12, 15, 154, 389, 433–35.

28. Dresser, *Quimby Manuscripts*, 436–38.

29. Milmine, "Literary Activities," 698–99; Fernald, "Science and Christian Science," 804; Donald Meyer, *The Positive Thinkers: A Study of the American Quest for Health, Wealth and Personal Power from Mary Baker Eddy to Norman Vincent Peale* (New York: Doubleday, 1965), 36–37, 74; Gottschalk, *Emergence of Christian Science*, 99–100, 117–22.

30. H. S. Ficke, "Sources of *Science and Health*," *Bibliotheca Sacra* 85 (October 1928): 417–23; Charles S. Braden, *Christian Science Today* (Dallas: Southern Methodist University Press, 1958), 31.

31. Silberger, *Mary Baker Eddy*, 64; Meyer, *Positive Thinkers*, 73.

32. Stetson, *Reminiscences, Sermons and Correspondence*, 279, 304.

33. Francis MacDonald Cornford, ed. and trans., *The Republic of Plato* (New York: Oxford University Press, 1967), 227–35.

34. Silberger, *Mary Baker Eddy*, 20, 23.

35. Carlton J. H. Hayes, *A Generation of Materialism 1871–1900* (New York: Harper and Row, 1963), 332; Gottschalk, *Emergence of Christian Science*, 150–51; *Letters of Mary Baker Eddy to Augusta E. Stetson, C.S.D. 1889–1909*, reproduced from the manuscript collection in the Huntington Library, San Marino, Calif. (Cuyahoga Falls, Ohio: Emma, 1990), 40.

36. Ronald G. Walters, *American Reformers 1815–1860* (New York: Hill and Wang, 1978), 166–69; Albert G. Mackey, ed., *Encyclopedia of Freemasonry and Kindred Sciences Comprising the Whole Range of the Arts, Sciences and Literature of the Masonic Institutions* (Chicago: Masonic History, 1929), 2:858, 796–997.

37. William Spencer, *The Middle East*, 4th ed. (Guilford, Conn.: Dushkin, 1992), 53; Mackey, *Encyclopedia of Freemasonry*, 1035–36, 1076–77; F. F. Ellinwood, "Theosophy, Esoteric Buddhism and Christian Science," *Homiletic Review* 37 (January

1899): 15–20; Joseph Jastrow, "The Modern Occult," *Popular Science Monthly* 67 (September 1900): 465.

38. Stetson, *Reminiscences, Sermons and Correspondence*, 243, 426, 439, 1104–5, 1109.

39. John W. Churchman, "Christian Science," *Atlantic Monthly* 93 (April 1904): 433–48.

40. John Whitehead, *Illusions of Christian Science* (Boston: Garden, 1907), 214–22; Mary Platt Parmele, *Christian Science: Is It Christian? Is It Scientific?* (New York: J. F. Taylor, 1904), 78–80; B. Calvert, *Science and Health* (n.p., n.d.), 1.

41. Flower, "Recent, Reckless and Irresponsible Attacks," 63; "Christian Science as the Ultimate Philosophy of Life," *Current Literature* 45 (August 1908): 186; Joel Rufus Mosley, "Christian Science Idealism," *Cosmopolitan* 43 (July 1908): 330.

42. Henry White, "Christian Science: Medievalism Redivivus," *The Monist* 17 (April 1907): 161–72; Charles W. J. Tennant, "Christian Science Healing," *Nineteenth Century and After* 98 (October 1925): 563.

43. Frank R. Medina, "Dreams, Beliefs and Facts," *Overland Monthly* 53 (February 1909): 147–52.

44. Clarence Batchelder, "The Grain of Truth in Christian Science Chaff," *Popular Science Monthly* 72 (March 1908): 211.

45. Gottschalk, *Emergence of Christian Science*, 129, 134, 136–37; Peel, *Mary Baker Eddy*, 204–5.

46. "The Larger Aspects of the Emmanuel Movement," *Current Literature* 46 (January 1909): 65–68.

47. Meyer, *Positive Thinkers*, 250–52; Gottschalk, *Emergence of Christian Science*, 214–15.

48. "Christian Science and the Emmanuel Movement," *The National*, 86 (25 June 1908): 572, 575.

49. Milmine, "Mrs. Eddy's Book," 185; Milmine, "Schism of 1888," 400.

4

Swords and Plowshares

"Christianity influences men through the means of men; it has no authority here more than men choose to allow it."[1] An American crowd applauded this sentiment on 4 July 1828, a little more than half a century following the signing of the Declaration of Independence. It was exactly what the audience had come to hear, but it wasn't entirely accurate. Until that time and well afterward, even to the present, Americans have permitted the Protestant form of Christianity a great deal of latitude as an interpreter and symbol of American destiny in both its spiritual and secular form. Citizens of the United States share a belief that the American nation is guaranteed and underwritten by God. They ask their children to recite a daily pledge that subtly equates national aspiration with heavenly objectives. Older and more complex minds are seduced by a currency that attests to the twofold belief that wealth and what it brings must always be good if God has deigned that his name be inscribed—generically—on United States coins. Although all peoples harbor the belief that they are divinely inspired, the degree of their devotion has, from time to time, involuntarily wavered. So has ours, despite the claim to constancy.

Protestantism in its varied forms was transferable and, to some degree, malleable, and both of these accounted for its durability in the New World. But of course it was more than just a religion. Two centuries before the Declaration of Independence, Dutch Calvinists, or followers of the Reformed faith, created the Union of Utrecht that pledged to continue their freedom fight against the Catholic King Philip II of Spain and maintain the Protestant religion. The combination of religious and political agendas was furthered in 1581, just two years after the Utrecht agreement, when the six rebelling northern Dutch provinces announced that they were no longer resisting Philip's counselors: they abjured Philip. As long as the Spanish king respected the rights of his subjects, they were bound to obey, but since he no longer respected these rights, his sovereignty was forfeit. The proper conclusion to draw from these events is that, at a relatively early stage of Protestant development in the Low Countries, an assertion of faith entailed an act of political rebellion. One might even go a step further and suggest that the Protestant religion became synonymous with the polity wherein it resided. Therefore, religion and politics reinforced each other in generating feelings of nationalism in opposition to European absolutists and the Catholic Church. About a century after Dutch Calvinists rendered their emotions tangible, John Locke espoused the same general idea during the Glorious Revolution: that a king must be obeyed as long as he respects popular rights, but if that respect is compromised, the proper course for citizens would be to overthrow him. Thus, the bargain between subjects and sovereign is contractual.

So goes the history of Protestantism, assured, confrontational and often politically subversive, until the nineteenth century. Those who arrived in America during the colonial period commingled social, civic, economic and political obligations until public and private expressions of Protestantism were blurred. For example, it is indisputable that the Massachusetts Bay Colony contributed its share of egalitarian legislation to colonial life, with the Mayflower Compact, higher levels of citizen participation in everyday governmental affairs and the Body of Liberties; but it is also indisputable that this was "Jerusalem on a Hill" and the "Bible Commonwealth," where modes of behavior in the seventeenth and eighteenth centuries, even on the eve of the Revolution, were partly fueled by an antihierarchical, anti-Church militancy.

Religious and secular objectives were mixed in virtually every colony, thus making the Protestant grip on the American mind a tenacious one, even for non-Protestants. The Episcopal form of Church governance, featuring leadership by bishops, retention of traditional Catholic ritual and Protestant doctrine, was regnant in the South but in a much attenuated form. The established Anglican Church of Virginia lacked a real British structure since ecclesiastical courts were absent, there was no Anglican bishop and population was dispersed. Laymen aspired to greater influence in the local church and sometimes controlled the ministry.[2] The Presbyterian, Congregational or Reformed variety of Protestantism derived from the English, Dutch, Scotch and Scotch-Irish demonstrated a marked preference for a Church organization of councils led by Presbyters, either elders or ministers, or a federation of independent churches. New York, Pennsylvania, Maine, New Hampshire, Vermont, Massachusetts, Connecticut and Rhode Island were, to a great extent, influenced by local elites whose experience in government formation was rooted in a European religious past. Some diversity before the American Revolution was presented by the Quakers, whose 1681 Frame of Government was no less an article of their faith than a statement of orderly political processes; Pennsylvania was the only one of the original thirteen colonies featuring a two-chambered legislative body elected by freemen. Interestingly enough, the concept of Church-State separation was not the product of political thought in America but that religious view, growing from Puritanism, which emphasized individual conscience, civil rights, equality of church members, antioligarchical spiritual leadership and the privacy of the conversionary experience. If one wished these benefits, they could be found in Rhode Island as could their seventeenth-century Baptist progenitor, Roger Williams.[3]

The first Great Awakening in North America, part of a general trend sweeping the Atlantic world during the years 1735–50, was the quintessential secular-spiritual mix. Ministers spread the word—George Whitefield in the South, Gilbert Tennent in the Middle Atlantic colonies and Jonathan Edwards in New England. Even young John Wesley, soon-to-be preacher to colliers and quarrymen, crafted an exciting Gospel technique in Georgia, one that would develop a new Protestant denomination and, with his colleagues, inform a rising generation of colonists just an emotion away from Bunker Hill and Yorktown. The new denomination, one of personal experience, moral piety, devotional life and intimate relationship with God, was a form of Pietism called Methodism.[4] But to say you were a Methodist was not sufficient, nor was it sufficient to emphasize a greater democracy in politics (separation of Church and State) or a more humane attitude by the rulers of society toward their fellows (liberty of conscience). In the open air, under leaden skies, in driven snow, by candlelight or morning light, it was a crusade and these were Protestant crusaders. To achieve deliverance, ministers would stress the necessity of conversion, being "born again" in Christ. It was a missionary message with a "new age" cure packaged in assorted wrapping and suitable for export or import. It was delivered uncompromisingly, zealously, passionately, as once Catholics delivered their majoritarian message. It was evangelism and all major Protestant denominations became adept at it. By 1775 the trend toward Church-State separation was enhanced but, at its side, not really out of sight then or ever, was the sacred character with which spellbinding orators endowed the national cause. Thus, for good or for ill, the American persona would be shaped by a civil religion.

The realization of Protestant "nationhood" in the Constitution represented the faith's high tide in American cultural life. In the early days of the Republic, a second Great Awakening swept over the country, which mitigated the Calvinist emphasis on predestination in favor of the idea that America was "chosen by God to perfect the world."[5] Such an interpretation offered Protestantism a highway into the nation's future by guaranteeing that evangelism was not just the sum of America's colonial and Revolutionary experience. Far from ending its participation in 1783 as an active force for change, Protestantism was earmarked for the same role in the coming century. After all, its history had been one of progress, wherein it blessed and accommodated libertarian social and political reality from age to age. There was absolutely every reason to assume that its principle of godly service would enhance the sense of individual freedom that appeared to be the legacy of war and peace. By 1790 church growth was a given, with Methodism leading the way. Sparked, perhaps, by its fresh, individual look, the result of its 1784 breakaway from the Church of England, the newly established Methodist Episcopal Church in America gained 43,000 members.[6] Within a quarter-century, old-time evangelism received a fillip through revivalism, a phenomenon effecting the frontier and the "Ivy League," duly noted by Alexis de Tocqueville during his travels through the United States in 1831 and 1832. Truthfully, revivalism was hard not to notice in either backwoods Kentucky or upstate New York's "burnt-over" district since its originator was the dramatic attorney turned minister Charles Grandison Finney, its message was one of self-improvement through faith and family and its medium was intense, impassioned evangelism driven by public professions of faith. On the road, Tocqueville described the American character through its polarities—restless, optimistic, commercial, idealistic, cooperative, individualistic—and found its strength to be in its vigor rather than its balance. The missionary impulse he found particularly gripping and identified its bond to political democracy in prescient terms: " 'I do not know whether all Americans have a sincere faith in their religion . . . but I am certain that they hold it to be indispensable for the maintenance of republican institutions.' "[7]

From the vantage point of high hopes, Protestantism's descent from glory must appear, like that of the Adams family, precipitous and absolute. Yet it was neither of these: it was gradual and the faith was, in the long run, redeemable. If one was to examine raw membership figures for antebellum evangelical churches no decline would, in fact, be noticeable. Fully two-thirds to three-quarters of America's 14 million denominational Christians in 1850 were Baptist, Methodist, Presbyterian, Congregational or Episcopalian, with 5.5 million Methodists.[8] There were troubling indications, however, that Protestantism as a whole missed or even worse, ignored opportunities to address issues that challenged the faith's central doctrine of human equality before God. Tender or militant oratory notwithstanding, all was not well in the Christian social order. "They," wrote Presbyterian James H. Thornwell, or some combinations of who's or they's, "are atheists, socialists, communists, red republicans, jacobins on the one side, and the friends of order and regulated freedom on the other. . . . The world is the battleground . . . the process of humanity at stake."[9] Dividing the world between "them" and "us" usually reveals less about God's troublemakers than it does about those who perceive a decline in their own authority.

American Protestant churches, those individuals who spoke on their behalf or those apparently secularized American leaders schooled in the Protestant tradition had difficulty commenting on social wrongs or inequities because the nation itself was unimpeachable, at least to the religious establishment, for it was engaged in a holy mission associated somehow with the idea of progress. Protestant denominations felt uncomfortable with a definition of liberty without limits which, in their lexicon, was perilously inclusive, multicultural and multireligious. For that reason, it was a necessary task to send Indians to reservations, thus directing them on an endless path toward the setting sun. By the same token, it was also necessary to turn inward if liberty was not to be understood in its widest sense to mean absolute freedom of conscience or individuality; rather, it would be understood only in its Protestant sense, as a value or system of values with historic meaning dating only from the Reformation. Social and cultural contributions to the nation and the concept of service would then acquire an exclusive or selective meaning. As a matter of course, convents would be leveled in Boston and, if offered the opportunity as Protestants were in the Mexican War, Catholic churches south of the border would be pillaged and Catholic women raped; not only that, those Irish American recruits who attempted to protect lives and property and, incidentally, their own religious culture, would be executed. Senator Stephen Douglas of Illinois was quite confident that he spoke for an American Protestant population generally agreed on blacks when he referred to the Declaration of Independence as " 'the white-man's charter of freedom,' "[10] the inheritance of the Western European Enlightenment, and in no way relevant to "negroes" and "savage indians." By 1855 the Know-Nothing party had excluded Catholics and bartered the Constitution's more expansive intent for a mess of nativist pottage.

Of course, there were certain individuals and groups who were less sure, but they spoke for themselves rather than for institutions or establishments and that is how they are remembered. If one is careful not to judge Abraham Lincoln by twentieth-century standards, his humanity was of a high quality. Unlike most men of his era, he thought beyond mere abolition or even free-soil of which he was an advocate, into the issue of social inequality and its probable future for blacks. Whether there were hostilities or not; whether the Constitution was construed in its narrowest sense as a document for white Protestants of Western European descent—he thought this a ludicrous misreading of the open-ended commitments of the republican patriarchs—he remained unsure of black capabilities and was unwilling to declare potential black freedmen as equal to whites. But he did have a plan that he attempted to implement as president: separation and deportation. Jeffersonian by philosophic inclination with pragmatic inclinations toward colonization, at least he tried. Abolitionists, on the other hand, were gradualists after the example of Theodore Dwight Weld and John Quincy Adams, or immediatists, after the fashion of William Lloyd Garrison or Theodore Parker. They have been called transcendentalists or moral perfectionists— soldiers against the sin of slavery—but they may have been more fatalistic than Lincoln, even with their avowed determination and ostensible optimism. Despite their commitment to black freedom in the abstract, they had no coherent program for blacks in the United States once freedom was achieved. They were "often short-sighted . . . sometimes insensitive" and grimly expedient, especially when none lifted a voice to stay the execution of John Brown, preferring a martyr to a live, if potentially useless, human being.[11]

These were Protestants who thought independently, pursuing a national cause outside established religious institutions, some even outside the arena of conventional social wisdom. But there were also groups who despaired of any solution to the problems created by American capitalism, Southern slavery, massive Catholic immigration and Manifest Destiny. "These pursued religiously inspired reform movements designed to purify the country" and reaffirm the hope that the second Great Awakening was a birth pang for a paradise-like "New Israel"; or they separated, pursuing a Western or revelational inspiration designed to end history or regain Eden.

Temperance movements to rid America of alcohol's sinfulness bloomed; communities like Oneida, Hopedale and Brook Farm were established as alternatives to an increasingly corrupt world. From John Humphrey Noyes' notion of complex marriage (every man married to every woman) to Methodist abolitionist La Roy Sunderland's emphasis on mesmerism and phrenology as cures for sickness,[12] Northern religious leaders waged a battle against the perceived evils of an anti-American, "un-Protestant" nature. Mormons and Shakers opted out of inhospitable climes, and millennial imagery was the innovation of a new Protestant sect, organized by William Miller and inherited by Ellen White, called Seventh Day Adventists. They stressed popular health regimens and mathematical calculations anticipating the fulfillment of Biblical prophecies and the "end of days." Perhaps the most interesting of all was a movement called primitivism, desirous of returning to certain practices of New Testament churches and, in this respect, similar to Christian Science. At first, it "appealed to popular audiences in the western regions of the country" and spawned a successful new Protestant denomination, the Disciples of Christ. The writings of its founder, Alexander Campbell, urged Christians to free themselves of traditions and prejudices by returning to the facts—logical, natural or Biblical—which were fully in accord with stated, specific New Testament practices. Although it retained the Protestant core of viewing America as a Bible civilization, its driving force lay in its challenge to the educated clergy, prestigious churches and existing church authority.

Established Protestant churches and their spokesman parties, like the Whigs who "promoted the Puritan-evangelical" ideas of virtue and hard work and the Democratically oriented Baptists and Presbyterians,[13] could not withstand the onslaught of the free-soilers, abolitionists, separatists and reformers. In 1838 the formerly united Presbyterian church split, apparently over doctrine. "The Presbyterian-led Old School and the Congregationalist-led New School were consumed by the issue of predestination and original sin." The Old School adhered to the traditional view of predestination "while the New School was sure that humanity was free to choose whether or not it would sin." The implications of New School theology for the institution of slavery were ominous. In effect, the New School theology, supported by Charles Grandison Finney and Theodore Dwight Weld, menaced Old School believers who defended the inevitability of the Peculiar Institution. Actually, New School Presbyterians reached a conclusion of the abolitionists, only a little later: that human freedom was ordained by God and consecrated in the Bible. Slavery, on the other hand, as a permanent and irreversible condition, was a sin. Since the Presbyterians could not resolve the issue and the denomination's Southern wing felt that an impasse had been reached, the Church split.

Following the same scenario, Methodist unity came to an end with its 1844 General Conference; it was no coincidence that America's two-party political system began foundering too. The Baptists followed suit in 1845,[14] the same year that Texas was annexed by a joint resolution of Congress. Confronted by the Western frontier and its supposedly endless space, massive population movements, relentless urbanization and intractable slavery, Protestantism surrendered its authoritative position as political and moral focus of authority. It became less of a driving force in Enlightenment discussions and rhetoric and more inexorable in its attempt to impose discipline and order. In a nation with no real elite, no permanent leaders and no venerable institutions, such an effort was bound to fail. A once vibrant evangelical Protestant Church, sundered into sectarian shards and divisive fragments, contemplated the 1850s slide of what clerics might have termed a "missionless" nation that lacked the stamina to check an excessive democratic tide.

The Civil War, an internecine bloodbath that claimed a million casualties in more than ten thousand separate military actions, completed the gradual decline in Protestant authority, a dominating trend for the second half of the nineteenth century. Numbers in mainstream Protestantism are not at issue since membership was rising but competition was persistent, especially from premillennial and Holiness sects, Catholicism of an East European and Mediterranean variety, Russian and Greek Orthodoxy, Islam and Judaism. But the most important factor was established Protestantism's internal weakness, which was highlighted during Reconstruction and the Gilded Age. Undecided and hesitant on the issue of supporting the forces of stability or movement, it supported neither. The individualistic, laissez-faire economic ethic derived from Calvinism, though still bearing the Church imprint of "service," challenged Protestantism to explain and defend its position on unregulated industrialism. Failing to meet the challenge immediately, it withdrew behind closed doors, North and South, to become a self-perpetuating caste system. Even Social Gospel renewal left Protestantism's core unmoved, since its message to action was heeded by women, who were perpetually on the fringe of American public life, and a very limited number of activist ministers.

Some sectors of the Church abjured the acquisitiveness that passed for individualism but some dined at Delmonico's in Manhattan with renowned speaker and international celebrity Herbert Spencer. The guest list for that particular banquet included Henry Ward Beecher, son of the Presbyterian evangelist and abolitionist Lyman, brother to Catherine and Harriet and, toward the end of his own life, "the best-known" and most celebrated preacher in the United States. But he was a puzzle as was Protestantism itself in the 1870s and 1880s. As pastor of the Brooklyn, New York Plymouth Congregational Church, he supported "free soil" prior to 1861 and warmly advocated the antislavery position in Kansas with "Beecher's Bibles," a symbol of armed resistance; after the Civil War, he influenced Americans with editorials in *The Independent* and in his own publication *The Christian Union*, which was renamed the *Outlook* in the 1890s. Though in 1869 he was president of the American Women's Suffrage Association and called for civil service reform, he was a "theistic Darwinist," seeing no contradiction between poverty, social imbalance, natural selection and the realization of a divine, Biblical plan. He was a survivor, after all, as was William Lawrence, Harvard graduate and Episcopal bishop of Massachusetts from 1893 to 1926. Both denied that there was a conflict between wealth and morality.[15] The Protestant ethic survived the epoch of wide-open Jacksonian individualism only to bless entrepreneurialism's less attractive mirror image, consolidation. One did what was necessary to ensure the survival of at least some traditional beliefs within the new order.

So, the religious battle against Christian Science, launched by some clergymen in the 1870s, was fought from a practical standpoint. Weighing and measuring the positives and negatives of Science in a calm, considered fashion, or welcoming candid exchanges, was not what good denominational practice called for on a survival of the fittest landscape, where the recent past showed itself all too vividly and the future was obscure. When, in 1892, the reordered Christian Science Church embarked on a more tightly knit organizational career, it was still winning youthful and elderly converts from the established denominations at an unprecedented rate. Calvin Frye, Eddy's personal secretary, had been a Congregationalist; Ira O. Knapp, whose son Bliss authored a work apotheosizing Eddy and whose estate has recently become the center of a controversial suit pitting the Church Board of Directors against Stanford University and the Los Angeles County Museum of Art, was a Methodist. As a matter of fact, a good percentage of the uncommitted and disillusioned seemed to be composed of Methodists who chose Science if they didn't stay as they were or split into postbellum revivalist sects called Holiness, Pentecostal or Premillennial. Congregationalism, once the religious home of Mary Baker Eddy, secularized its message on the order of Henry Ward Beecher, but lost the trust of those who needed fewer verbal balms and more sympathy, direction and tangible assistance. They, too, chose a Christian Science alternative with regularity. Traditional clergymen, having no centralized authority to lean on were, for decades, thwarted by dissatisfied, neurotic congregants flocking to apparently more tranquil banners, escaping a society that gave them no rest. It is no wonder that hatred and fear of Science, as well as the specter of internal revolt, egged ministers on.[16] The fact that Christian Science "worked" and achieved success heightened their reaction and their desperate helplessness.

Christian Science wasn't even worth throwing stones at in 1866, when it was assailed by the local clergy at Lynn, where Eddy was living. However, her reputation spread rapidly. She was accused of and felt obliged to deny allegations of spiritualism. As one might expect, the Boston pulpit was particularly vitriolic, since it was close by and felt a special discomfort with her "antique" faith which, on the one hand, lacked distinctive ceremonies and rituals, but on the other, struck a discordant, "unenlightened" note, at least according to traditional, and vulnerable, evangelical wisdom. Ministers stated that Eddy was "planning to rewrite the Bible" in the name of "medieval nihilism."[17]

A number of Eddy's indiscretions seemed designed to catch clerical fire. She claimed for her "immaculate idea, represented first by man and last by woman," the power "to baptize by fire." Certainly, the implication and eventually the statement that her belief was divinely inspired would engender no sympathy from the clergy. Her theory of agamogenesis and the acceptance of marriage as a necessary evil, though in itself Paul-like and not unusual in Scriptural and scholarly Christianity, was regarded as an attack on the sanctity of a hallowed religious institution. In 1889 the separatist spirit was climaxed by a resolution of the National Christian Science Association (NCA) exhorting all Christian Scientists who had not already done so, to drop dual membership in Science and their former churches in favor of exclusive adherence to Eddy. Four years later, the Protestant Church was compelled to declaim on two events. First, Christian Scientists were permitted equal participation in the World Parliament of Religions held in conjunction with the Chicago Columbian Exposition; second, Eddy published a book of poems a few months later. The portrait on the flyleaf of a woman, supposedly womanhood joining divine manhood in Christ clasping hands (womanhood bore a striking resemblance to the poetess), gave rise to the clerical attack that Eddy had instructed the artist to use her as a model.[18]

Before specific denominations are dealt with, it is instructive to present the general argument of the Protestant Church:

1. Christian Science was spiritually dead, stark, relentless and compassionless.
2. The belief that sin was an illusion precluded the necessity for divine mercy.
3. Christian Science was unchristian, at least in the contemporary, post-Reformation, post-Enlightenment, proindustrial, pro-Darwinian sense: either it was a form of witchcraft or a throwback to ancient superstition-laden heresies.
4. Science denied Christian religion by undervaluing the Bible's physical representations, challenging the divinity of a personal Jesus and the value of prayer.
5. Its very material basis—large, expensive churches, well-dressed, stylish women, the dispensing of souvenir spoons and healthy, wealthy, aggressive bureaucratic leadership—attested to the fact that Science was oriented toward the pocketbook rather than the spirit.
6. Christian Science, immoral and dangerous to human life, ought to be proscribed by legislative enactment. Finally, the rigidity and lunacy of the leader, critics said, revived the bestiality of the fifteenth-century Catholic inquisitor Torquemada who, "in the name of religion and humanity . . . tortured and put to death thousands of . . . old women, feeble girls and children." One minister wished to close discussion when he branded Science "a disgrace to the intelligence of the age";[19] others were not as kind.

Baptism, an emotional, fervent form of evangelical Protestantism, severed itself from the Anglican Church in the seventeenth century; by inclination, it was individualistic, antihierarchical, loosely federated in terms of church structure, fundamentalist and, according to its own lights, a literal interpreter of Scripture. Therefore, it is safe to say that Baptist criticism of Christian Science was directed at the heart rather than the intellect. One of the first individuals to draw a bead on Mary Baker Eddy was a Boston Baptist minister, Adoniram J. Gordon who, in the 1870s, denounced Christian Science teachings as unscriptural, derivative of theosophy, Buddhism, pantheism and Kabbala, a body of Jewish mystical lore: "It is a sort of witches' caldron with a repulsive, sinless doctrine in which every conceivable . . . Christian heresy is found seething and simmering." Above all, he must be credited with consistency. One of the most vituperative attacks leveled against Christian Science was made in Boston's Fremont Temple on 26 February 1885 by the Reverend Joseph Cook, reading and interpreting a letter of Adoniram Gordon. Three weeks hence, on 19 March, Eddy was permitted a ten-minute rebuttal but the audience barely listened. A minister who followed the events denigrated the "Boston craze," hoping it would be relegated to limbo upon Eddy's demise.[20]

By far, the most critical clergy were evangelicals, who drew meaningful equations between themselves and liberty's historic American meaning. One very active Baptist respondent was Isaac M. Haldeman, whose tracts were occasionally published by a well-known evangelical press, Fleming H. Revell. His *Analysis of Christian Science*, a 1909 pamphlet, is an itemized list of the Baptist stand. According to it, Science (1) denied the existence of matter; (2) denied sin; (3) denied disease and sickness; (4) denied death; (5)

denied the creation of man from dust (since immateriality was paramount to Christian Scientists, there could be no physical creation); (6) denied God's personality (to the Scientist, God was principle); (7) denied the death of Christ; (8) denied the personality of the devil since evil is unreal to the Scientist; (9) denied the doctrine of justification by faith (if there was no sin, there was no need to repent); (10) denied the resurrection and the second coming; (11) denied the last judgment (if there was no sin to the Scientist, there could be no judgment); (12) denied the utility of prayer; (13) denied the sanctity of marriage; (14) denied the divinity of Jesus and the Bible as the infallible word of God; (15) denied cures through the application of medicine or drugs and claimed to heal the sick by what was, in reality, hypnotism. Haldeman called Christian Science one of the "many Antichrists already in the world; the darkling shadow of that final Antichrist." He claimed that Christian Science was intellectually and morally bankrupt, the paralyzer of human sympathy, a great success at fooling people, a perversion of the divine order and last, but certainly not least, a deadly peril.[21]

Fundamentalists like Haldeman detested Eddy because they had created an anthropomorphic God, replete with devil and hellfire; to them, true Calvinism was being undermined by a female apostate. By the end of 1885 there was scarcely a pulpit in Boston that was not fulminating against Christian Science theology. The Lutheran minister K. K. Reed agreed with the fundamentalist preacher and missionary William E. Blackstone that Mary Baker Eddy was the incarnated Antichrist. The Reverend Amzi Clarence Dixon stressed the immorality of Eddy and the pagan quackery of her cult. In another essay, the minister denied the Christianity of Science and scored its demented doctrine on disease and the illusion of existence. To him, Eddy was nothing more than an avaricious, lustful, money-hungry "woman pope."[22]

The *New York Times* fed the clergy raw meat. In 1901 an inflammatory piece was written about the death of a Baptist who had resigned from his church in 1897 to become a Scientist. The man died of a treatable ailment because he allowed no doctors to attend him; instead, he relied exclusively upon the ministrations of Christian Science practitioners. Once again was heard the lament that it was far better to walk "rejoicing through the fiery affliction through which all must pass" than to become a heretic. The fatal fallacies of denying a personal, living God, the reality of matter and disease and death[23] were indiscriminately paraded for another impetuous perusal.

The ultimate transgression to the Baptist was the Science denial of a personal God and the material component of the Calvinist ethic. Dr. Frank Rogers Morse of the New York City's Sixth Avenue Calvary Baptist Church was not at all illuminating when he lashed out at the "cunningly written and terribly misleading" Science; A. Lincoln Moore of the Riverside Baptist Church, also located in New York City, thought the Christian Science doctrine of sin "a most welcome announcement to the modern" evildoer.[24] It is very clear from this sampling of sermons that more than a few Baptist leaders were scared. For those who censured Science because of its apparently perverse nature, it must have seemed as if three centuries of Protestant, republican stewardship in America had dissolved into a single generation of panic.

The Methodists lacked originality—much of what they said aped the Baptists—but not ferocity, primarily because their defection rate into Christian Science was high. The Reverend Samuel Fallows, Methodist bishop of Chicago, doubted Eddy's claims to have cured patients mentally. Continuing in a Baptist vein, he assailed the Science tenets of an impersonal God, illusory matter and nonorganic illness. He concluded that the Eddy system was, like P. P. Quimby's, telepathic, with mind rather than religion the controlling factor. *Zion's Herald*, a Boston Methodist newspaper, carried an open letter to the editor from local theologian Luther T. Townsend claiming that Eddy was a fraud; Iowa minister S. C. Brown "exposed" Eddyism as a "subtle delusion" that taught "white is black." Writing for the *Methodist Review* in 1898, M. W. Gifford was typically abrasive and predictably uncreative. In a "ho-hum" sort of diatribe, Christian Science went beyond "un-" into antichristian and was linked to pantheism and superstition.[25] Unhappily, this kind of ploy was becoming commonplace.

Early in the twentieth century heated discussions, sometimes motivated by conversions, stirred the air in Methodist churches. In 1901 the Reverend S. E. Simonson adopted the Christian Science faith and in response, the Reverend Willis P. O'Dell of New York City's Calvary Methodist Episcopal Church delivered an uncompromising sermon whose message was direct and unmistakable. Indeed, Science was a moral evil cultivating egoism on the part of its followers and it was also insidious and heretical, but its crowning blasphemy was that "it is hostile to the Evangelical faith held by the great body of Christendom."[26]

The Reverend James Monroe Buckley, another "guardian of orthodoxy," was a leading Christian Science critic and editor of the "influential" New York *Christian Advocate*, a Methodist publication. He attempted a fair and even-handed approach to Science in a July 1887 article for *Century*, a periodical with a significantly urbane but limited readership. It worked for a while because he distanced himself from Science as a Christian religion; rather than a faith, it was a form of mental healing that would never displace "either the skilled surgeon or the educated physician." But it didn't work permanently. In the long run Buckley owned up to "Eddyism" as a "false religion," like Mormonism. Commenting on the "absurd paradox of Christian Science" for *North American Review*, once edited by disillusioned reformer Henry Adams and, in 1901, a journal of patrician sensibility with a stance favorable to the Gospel of Wealth, economic imperialism and the White Man's Burden, Buckley made a final, unconvincing stand: "Christian

Science is pleasant while health lasts. . . . When the sickness is unto death the dream becomes a nightmare," but one of pagan rather than Methodist proportions. The Methodist minister who compared Eddy to a "fungus growth" was less diplomatic but more honest, as was Charles Edward Locke, a Los Angeles pastor who wrote *Eddyism, Is It Christian? Is It Scientific? How Long Will It Last?* His replies weren't optimistic. "It's doomed" he cried, but one could expect little else from writing that drew on Baptist Isaac M. Haldeman for inspiration.[27]

Doom was a chief motivator of the Presbyterians, too. A number of them saw Christian Science, allied with Brahmanism, Buddhism and the Kabbala, as a religion from hell. It was examined in a number of journals and in a number of places, anywhere from *Homiletic Review* to Sing Sing (now Ossining), New York, and its prognosis was not very encouraging. It was "unscientific" because its principle rendered "all knowledge of chemistry, anatomy, geology" and "astronomy . . . obsolete and worthless"; it was misleading with regard to bodily healing—Christian Science could neither treat nor cure; it was unchristian since its sources were pagan; it was immoral because ethical distinctions were obliterated by practitioners; it was unscriptural and unwholesome, since it was stolen from P. P. Quimby. The chorus, however, was always the same: it was an aberration because it was not evangelical. At Witherspoon Hall in Philadelphia, Reverend B. Campbell Morgan of the Northfield Presbyterian Conference scored the evangelical faiths for not reaffirming old beliefs in an age of materialism.[28]

The secretary of the Presbyterian Board of Foreign Missions proclaimed Science to be primarily Eastern with some Christian trappings. He detailed the similarities of Eddy's doctrine and theosophy: (1) both claimed that the spirit was supreme and the body unreal; (2) both claimed occult powers over others at a distance, for example, absent treatment and Malicious Animal Magnetism (MAM) in Christian Science; (3) both rejected the existence of a personal God; (4) both systems were pantheistic and monistic—*The Monist*, a journal of opinion published a generally favorable review of Science from free-thinker Robert Ingersoll, whose father was a Presbyterian minister; (5) both dispensed with prayer; (6) both were derivatives of Indian philosophies, like Yoga, Baha'i and Vedanta; and (7) both abhorred the Christian Church.[29]

Though steeped in trivialities, the arguments of George Francis Greene touched on some of Mary Baker Eddy's essential inconsistencies. He stated that the religious truths of Science included some fantasies such as the evil eye, witchcraft, voodoo and MAM. To the extent that Eddy influenced the movement and its system of therapeutics, this was quite a proper criticism and relevant to the substantial medical danger inherent in Science healing. He also mentioned the failure of Science to enter the area of Christian missionaryism in China or India and, closer to home, in the London or New York City slums. In Greene's opinion, idealism notwithstanding, the "gospel" of Christian Science, if it had one at all, bore no similarity to Christ's. The Presbyterian *New York Observer* referred to Science as "a craze of speculators and clairvoyants."[30]

Christian Science offered a vigorous response when offered the space to do so. On 8 February 1900, *The Evangelist* published an article by the Reverend Chauncey W. Goodrich, pastor of the St. Cloud Presbyterian Church in Orange, New Jersey. Less combative than most, he actually had an appreciation for some of Science's salubrious effects. First, he observed among Scientists "a certain quietness and serenity of spirit, not common to members of other churches"; second, they possessed an "exceptionally vivid consciousness of the Divine," perhaps demonstrating that they touched a "great truth" uniting all those who love Christ. Goodrich erred, though, in assuming that this fundamental human truth resided in "human mind power" when, in fact, divine mind made it all possible.

Augusta Stetson answered, as she was wont to do, in a complete and detailed letter to the editor. According to the Christian Science interpretation of the Gospel, Jesus' self-revelation was entirely spiritual, and perfection in healing was to do as the Father had done—healing the sick, raising the dead and casting out devils—through the implementation of God's spiritual Principle. By attending and perfecting such spiritual practice, Science realized Christianity in its purest, crystalline form: that of awakening humanity from the carnal, material, bodily "Adam-dream" to divine Christian reality. And Mary Baker Eddy's role was central, the same as the patriarch Abraham's. Like the great iconoclast of the Old Testament, she crushed before her every idol blocking spiritual completion. In closing, Stetson listed the Christian truths and adhered to them all—the one God, the one Christ, the destruction of sin, the efficacy of atonement, the centrality of crucifixion and resurrection, and the healing ministry to the sick—but her interpretation empowered no earthly, human or material force.[31]

Christian Science in England, led by Eddy protegé Mrs. Field-King, rocked British evangelism. Most disconcerting was that her teaching created a vogue, acceptable to "the educated . . . cultured and . . . thoughtful." When lords and ladies, dukes and duchesses and sundry nobility deserted Anglicanism for the new wave, hypotheses began to flow. English theologians concentrated on Science's rejection of the cross, public prayer and Anglican communion; British animosity was stimulated by a desire to defend the scientific age and the discoveries of Bacon, Newton, Galileo, Faraday and Huxley. Christian Science, clerics intoned, was unscientific: its healing was a form of mental suggestion and its objective the acquisition of wealth and power. On the religious questions, Science was predictably pantheistic; medically, it was suicidal and delusive. Yet the feeling that Science attracted people because a deficiency existed within the traditional Church was disquieting. The British journalist and clergyman Herbert Horwill pointed the direction in which twentieth-century theology would have to move if it wished to compete with unusual or modernist doctrines. He said that Christian Science was not only gaining converts because of its mental healing ability but also because of its simple theology and practical church organization. He focused on the absence of liturgy, the plain, uncomplicated service, the lack of a distinguishable hierarchy and the centralization of authority as factors in the movement's spiritual and material success.[32]

The American Episcopal Church, the Congregationalists and the Unitarians, representing a higher degree of sophistication and a more rational approach to Protestantism, offered a controlled but not always laudatory appraisal of Christian Science. Only in these groups, whose theology was "open-ended"[33] in comparison to evangelicals, did Mary Baker Eddy find a measure of support or, at least, a "wait and see" attitude. Interestingly, a most popular Eddy biography among contemporary Christian Scientists— it is available for sale at Christian Science reading rooms and is marketed as part of a service by the Christian Science Publishing Society—is one written more than sixty years ago by Lyman P. Powell, an Episcopalian minister.

It is quite possible that Episcopalians were willing to entertain Science as essentially Christian and worthwhile because counseling, by way of the Emmanuels' pastoral sensitivity and an integrated healing approach, featuring psychology and medicine, was of interest to them. To be sure, Episcopalians, much like the other denominations, harbored "true believers" who marched to the beat of that "old-time religion"; Southern Episcopalians may have felt at ease with comfortable, familiar reference points as did Andrew F. Underhill, whose *Valid Objections to So-Called Christian Science* was printed in New York. But among Eddy's supporters were weighty individuals. One of these was Phillips Brooks, rector of Boston's Trinity Episcopal Church, a favorite speaker among Philadelphia's Victorian gentry and, in the Gilded Age, a man, it is said, who still could influence those outside the faith in the community at large. He took note of "the wise and learned . . . methods of reaching physical" health through the exploration of changing "mental states," but cautioned against its overzealous application. The Reverend Richard Heber Newton, "an Episcopal clergyman prominently identified with liberal theological and social views," was unwilling to dismiss Christian Science therapeutics out of hand. "While rejecting the Scientists' denial of the material body and their repudiation of the physician," he was cognizant of their success with various types of mental disorders and believed that they pointed toward the metaphysical healing method of the Gospels as employed by Jesus. Meeting at Providence, Rhode Island, in 1900, the Episcopal Church Congress debated the topic of Christian Science. During the exchanges, a number of delegates argued convincingly in Science's behalf—that the movement represented a doctrinal return to the religious teachings of Christ and was justified in adapting those teachings to modern society.[34]

Encouraging Christian Science in Unitarian circles were a pair of friendly voices, those of Andrew Preston Peabody and Cyrus A. Bartol, "a latter-day descendent of Ralph Waldo Emerson. . . . While rejecting its pantheistic aspects," Bartol praised Science as more than a passing craze, deserving of wider "attention than it has received." But kudos from waning transcendentalism carried a little less influence than *Outlook*, the opinion periodical edited in turn by Congregationalists Henry Ward Beecher and Lyman Abbott. Known for its presentation of "a religious version of Darwinism that found favor with many Protestants," *Outlook* affirmed a threefold truth in Christian Science: first, that man is not a machine but a living spirit; second, that spiritual truth is not immediately discoverable by scientific processes "but . . . known by spiritual vision; third, that Christianity has the power to heal." Arriving at these truths, however, took a dozen years and *Outlook*, symbolic of Protestants generally, remained ill at ease. "In a word," stated an *Outlook* writer in 1894, "let him recognize frankly and maintain stoutly all that is good and true and beautiful in Christian Science, dissociated from its unthinkable philosophy and practical extravagance." These extravagances, according to *Outlook*, included its medical practice that endangered children, its quality as opiate rather than cure for social ills and its erratic leader. The faith would survive, predicted the magazine, as a "religion of comfort rather than service" but with limited growth potential.[35]

Washington Gladden, the Columbus, Ohio, Social Gospeler and Congregationalist minister, spent a lifetime working for individual reclamation and urging government intervention on behalf of the poor. His program for American improvement included a defense of labor's right to strike, "the institution of maximum hour laws . . . factory inspection and . . . regulation of . . . monopolies." As such, he rejected the concept of sin's illusory quality and found the denial of sickness and poverty to be wicked and unrealistic; he believed flesh to be the servant of spirit rather than a purposeless illusion. But this most involved of Protestants favored the essential revolt of Christian Science against materialism and stated authoritatively that "this truth will last long after the garnishings of Mrs. Eddy's . . . cult have disappeared."[36]

Of the nearly 2 million Jewish immigrants entering the United States between 1881 and 1914, only a small number were attracted to Christian Science and, of those, a handful actually converted. Orthodox, atheist, radical, anarchist, revolutionary or intellectual, Eastern European Jews had a visceral attachment—whether secular, nationalist or religious—to their shared past. As immigrant newspapers like Abe Cahan's *Forward* indicated, new arrivals were hoping to be Americanized, not Christianized, and that, of course, was the great conundrum of American culture: How does one accomplish the first without "being" the second? Russian and Polish Jews didn't philosophize about it; much like athletes in *Nike* commercials they just "did it." A large percentage were urban, having come from places like Kiev and Odessa, and entered the clothing industries, needle-trades and businesses dealing in mass-produced, ready-to-wear garments; those with agricultural or pioneer/Zionist inclination, or both, moved west and founded colonies in Louisiana, Oregon, South Dakota, Colorado, New Jersey, Kansas, Virginia, Wisconsin, Michigan, Maryland, California, Illinois, Alabama, Pennsylvania and Texas. Social organizations were invariably founded, from fraternal to cultural to benevolent.

As Jews became acclimated, it was common for them to participate in those areas of human endeavor from which they had been harried, dispossessed and excluded, like the arts, politics, finance and reform. Nurtured in the ghetto, the Pale of Settlement and the village, this culture would communicate human and humane messages to Americans; nevertheless, it remained sensitive to those Christian ideals claiming universality but practicing it imperfectly. It would be difficult though, if not impossible, to "love" Christian Science's impersonal, spiritual Principle founded on the Gospel, which reveals in a favorable light the trials of universal Israel, whose leader was called an "Israelitish Mother" and whose antagonists were, according to Scripture, particularistic, carnally minded troublemaking Jews and sly, smiling and materialistic Pharisees, all living grandly in "gorgeously" ornate synagogues. In *Science and Health* and in *Miscellaneous Writings*, Mary Baker Eddy offered a widely accepted Christian understanding of Jewish history. In the former text, "Jesus acted boldly . . . against . . . Pharisaical deeds and practices and . . . refuted all opponents"; in the latter, Jesus "was ready to stem the tide of Judaism . . . to . . . lay himself as a lamb upon the altar of materialism."[37]

Western European Jews arriving between the years 1815 and 1881 and composing what is called the second Jewish migration to America were fewer in numbers—only 230,000 by an 1878 American Jewish Committee census—were not nearly as sensitive and embarked upon their own journey toward self-realization. Products of the Enlightenment, secularization and Napoleonic freedom doctrines, they witnessed the ghetto collapse and opportunity rise between 1789 and 1815. Accommodation was the key tactic in Germany, France and England and, if carried through, would hopefully climax in ending historic Jewish isolation.

The strategy worked rather smoothly in Great Britain, only intermittently in France and not at all in Germany, where nationalism and state building eventually drove some of the more liberally minded, with the brightest egalitarian dreams, out of the country. Once in America, these Reform Jewish thinkers became even more creative in a country with no apparent boundaries—at least no one talked as if there were—and infinite possibilities. Arriving in 1854, Rabbi Isaac Mayer Wise became Reform

Judaism's chief spokesman and innovator, settling in Cincinnati and founding, in 1875, Hebrew Union College, a seminary training and ordaining rabbis in the Reform theology. An 1885 statement of Reform objectives called the Pittsburgh Platform became the movement's raison d'etre for half a century. It stated that the unique religious heritage of Judaism had preserved the people for five thousand years. After the destruction of the Second Temple, the Jews ceased to exist as a national entity, became dispersed and were henceforth charged with a universal mission: to witness "God among the Christian nations, illuminating a path reaching up from the darkness to redemption. Their duty was to promulgate moral and ethical concepts as a preliminary to realizing a world brotherhood of man. Nationalism, locked in a shadowy, dead past" was, like distinctive ceremony and ritual, "an enigma to them." Apparently, such a mission was safe enough for other ethnic groups, but deadly for the Jew; behind it lurked the charges of "separatism, particularism and ghettoism." Intermarriage, Sunday sabbath and Felix Adler's ethical culture as assimilationist prototypes were tacitly acknowledged as strategies by which Jews might attain parity in Christian society.[38] Within this context, it is easy to understand the attraction Christian Science might have for Reform Jews.

Science did exert an influence sufficient for their consideration at the 1912 Central Conference of American Rabbis. Meeting at Baltimore in April, Reform spokesmen offered telling observations about their own movement as well as Eddy's. Religion, generally, seemed a bit too mechanistic and Christian Science, like Reform Judaism, offered little in the way of emotion or mysticism. For those Jews who wished to convert to Christian Science, a rationalization would be that, superficially, the two were roughly equivalent, with the latter advantaged since it offered a more direct path into the American mainstream. Rabbi Maurice Lefkovitz refuted any notion of equivalency in the strongest possible terms. Unlike certain Christians, who claimed an Asian or Indian provenance for Science, Lefkovitz "clearly grasped the point" that it was entirely Christian in derivation and point of view. "The man who subscribes to the creed of Christian Science affirms his belief in this unique unmatched, and unmatchable position of Christ Jesus!" The body of Reformed rabbis grasped the Lefkovitz argument that "twofold membership in synagogue and church was incompatible with Judaism" and a resolution to that effect clarified the issue.[39]

In religion, however, as with most issues of humanity and community, what is needed is closure—some psychic need for ending or shifting debate—rather than votable resolutions. Christian Science remained on Judaism's periphery for at least another decade and its presence encouraged Rabbi Morris Lichtenstein to counter it with an innovation called Jewish Science. In Jewish Science, all necessary Biblical sources for healing were located in the Old Testament, specifically the Prophets, and if Jews sought a cure for modern maladies, they could well be directed there.[40]

Soon, though, a confluence of positive and negative occurrences, among them the multicultural, pluralistic philosophies of Randolph Bourne, Horace Kallen and Louis Brandeis, rising Continental and American antisemitism, immigration quotas and fascism's imminence spurred warm, intimate responses to divinity and the advent of the "I-Thou" personal dialogue with God. The Europeans Franz Rosenzweig and Martin Buber, followed by the American Abraham Joshua Heschel, were to be strong Jewish voices ringing the curtain down on a mechanistic age which, a few years after Mary Baker Eddy's death, was fast running its course.

Christian Science rippled across a formidable Catholic lake and left a memory of its passing but only that. There were the usual bizarre or sensational stories—three Catholic sisters driven insane at a faith cure prayer meeting and a Catholic refusing medical assistance dying of typhoid—and some conversions[41] but insignificant in comparison to the thoroughgoing Americanization process of the American Catholic Church and its constituents in the last quarter of the nineteenth century. That was the "real" story and, indeed, all else was beside the point. In 1906 11 million Americans (out of 77 million) were Catholic. Fully aware of this, ethnic policymakers within the Church hierarchy established an educational priority and placed on the agenda some controversial items, like labor unionism and social justice, though a debate ensued as to their ultimate realization within the framework of Papal pronouncements and established Church doctrine. More often than not the advocates of Americanization, among the most celebrated being James Cardinal Gibbons, archbishop of Baltimore, and the colorful Republican John Ireland, archbishop of St. Paul, Minnesota, voiced sentiments congenial to Protestantism—"for" patriotism, "for" democracy, "for" imperialism, "for" Church-State separation—and thus shaped a useful community of interest that would likely serve to breech historic barriers dividing Protestants and Catholics. Nativist Protestant groups blamed Catholics for hard times—the American Protective Association crested in 1894, enjoyed a rush of popularity in the Midwest, far West and East[42] following the panic and depression of 1893—but it hardly ruffled the Church hierarchy. Not always in agreement with its membership, it nevertheless charted a safe and sane course for the faith's perpetuation in Christian America.

If Catholic commentators and opinion makers employed anti-Christian Science invective as an Americanizing tool—and they probably did—it was only after the death of Pope Leo XIII and the 1903 accession to the pontificate of Pius X, a man of humble origin and an avowed anti-Modernist.[43] Virtually all the essays and articles condemning Christian Science were published after 1903,[44] and continued thereafter for a decade. It is conceivable that they served a multiple purpose: for one thing, hopping on the anti-Science bandwagon certainly appeared to be culturally correct, the "Protestant" thing to do; for a second, it would distract American, anti-Catholic crusaders;

for a third, conservative clerics disliked and found distasteful a primitive, pre-Thomist, pre-Augustinian, pre-Constantinian heresy whose byword was a faith cure anathema. To be absolutely fair, Eddy found "pagan" Catholicism detestable, with salvation dependent and impressed upon the carnal, intrinsically evil "body of the Church." Nevertheless she swallowed hard, saving her choicest epithets for Christian Science group discussion; in public, she limited offensive remarks and called upon diplomatic reserves if the occasion demanded.[45] Catholics didn't need the call to restraint: they were one-seventh of the entire American population and, if any deference was owed, it would only be to Protestants.

Not many Catholics thought Science to be a clear and present danger to worldwide Catholicism[46] but most writers used well-worn Protestant arguments adjusted to apparent Church exigencies. Louis Lambert, a priest from Waterloo, New York, and editor of *The Freeman's Journal*, agreed with the Reverend Walter Drum and T. J. Campbell that *Science and Health* was "a perfect ragbag of shreds and remnants, of fancies, platitudes, half-truths, gross errors and extravagantly pietistic statements to which her followers have attached every conceivable form of Cabalistic [*sic*] signification. . . . She is Manichean . . . and a pantheist." Lambert debated the issue in print with William D. McCrackan, an important figure close to Eddy in the Christian Science movement and a lecturer at the New York City church. Since it rejected materiality and the tangibility of bodily disease, Science was the "antithesis of Christianity" and, by inference, death to the right-thinking Catholic. The fact that these unfriendly confrontations were motivated by anti-Modernism's rise is clear. Christian Science, Campbell intoned, "fits in with the growing belief that criminals are victims of physical conditions." Virgilius H. Krull took *A Common Sense View of Christian Science* when he listed its prime religious heresies—its denial of the trinity, Jesus' divinity, Mary's mothering a divine son (Christian Science holds that Mary conceived the *idea* of God), creation, original sin, hell and bodily resurrection—concluding that Eddy's belief was "a part of Modernism which Pope Pius X has condemned."[47]

It must have been disheartening for more progressive Catholics to see *Catholic World* enter the fray on the "wrong" side. Founded by a Paulist, Isaac Hecker, "an early herald of the liberal spirit," *Catholic World* was to act as a "harbinger of truth to Protestant America," breaking down "barriers of mistrust"[48] while vindicating Catholicism's role in the progress of civilization. In this instance, the magazine compromised the high hopes of its founder.

Having searched in vain for a Christian Science meaning in his January 1905 essay for the *American Catholic Quarterly Review*, Walter Drum could not locate the faith at all within Christian tradition the next month. It was, as many Christians had so far concluded, divorced from Christianity, lacking the meekness, poverty and charity of Jesus; in her attempt to twist the Old Testament, alter Christ's divinity and recast the doctrines of grace, sin and poverty, he found Eddy to be a schemer and a pirate.[49] Catholics, though, were less concerned with "exposing" her than with Science's aversion to traditional Church practices. Doing away with penance and sacraments was expected, but marriage? That was the question posed by Adrian Feverel, a Drum disciple no doubt, in a series of four punitive articles published in *Catholic World* during the final months of 1912 and the first of 1913. To Feverel, Christian Science was immoral in denying human free will, its capacity to sin and its institution of marriage. After all, which Christian ever regarded marriage as an encumbrance to the attainment of true spirituality? Was Christian Science "unchristian" as well, "unscientific," "ridiculous"? It was, according to Feverel, all of these: it had no soul, used no medicine and negated the material universe. Christian Science was all an illusion and a hoax, with the "every man his own doctor" philosophy dangerously apropos to "Modernism."[50]

In 1905 an interesting experiment in forbearance and maturity, if not in actual conciliation, occurred at four Protestant churches in New York City: St. Paul's Methodist Episcopal, Park Presbyterian, Fourth Presbyterian and Riverside Baptist. Their unified approach to Christian Science was this: it could not be deemed "unchristian" because, in intent, it was probably more Christian "than any other religion practiced today"; it made life clean and worthwhile. The only means of defeating it lay in educating people in mental healing while offering them at least a rudimentary understanding of disease. To Eddy's credit was the creed of hard work, mission and spartan repudiation of luxury she instilled in her congregants. Attacks on Christian Science founded on the assertions that it was unscriptural and unhygienic contradicted reality and would not help in loosening Eddy's grip upon the public. A lesson learned from Christian Science was that institutionalized theology must rationalize, not mechanize, its appeal and adapt[51] to a changing milieu. Henry Ward Beecher who, incidentally, was an admirer of Eddy's work, shared with her the belief that the Age of Science might receive light from and bring insight to the Age of Faith. Eddy once circled a paragraph from one of Beecher's sermons that contained the phrase: " 'It is the business of preachers to readapt truth, from age to age, to man's ever-increasing wants.' "[52]

Protestant orthodoxy in America received invaluable aid from Christian Science. The five-word catechism it learned from Eddy was that you can't go home again. Faith cannot reflect dogma if it hopes to remain vital in a vital society; it cannot always teach old lessons to a new generation. In 1914 a Protestant theologian, J. Winthrop Hegeman, wrote that when he first studied Christian Science he was repelled; upon closer inspection, however, he realized that it was reviving the ancient teachings of Jesus which, if incorporated into the regular Church, "would constitute a world-regenerating power."[53] It is a step on the road to progress when organized religion realizes the morality of learning from its failures.

NOTES

1. William B. O. Peabody, *An Address Delivered at Springfield before the Hampden Colonization Society, July 4, 1828* (Springfield: S. Bowles, 1828), 4.

2. Michael Kraus, *The United States to 1865* (Ann Arbor: The University of Michigan Press, 1959), 75–76.

3. George M. Marsden, *Religion and American Culture* (New York: Harcourt Brace Jovanovich, 1990), 19–20.

4. Dorothy Marshall, *Eighteenth-Century England* (New York: David McKay, 1966), 245–46, 248, 250.

5. William G. McLoughlin, *Revivals, Awakenings and Reforms* (Chicago: University of Chicago Press, 1978), 105.

6. Douglas Mellard, "The Religious Dispute over Slavery" (Unpublished Bachelors Essay, College of Charleston, 1992), 10.

7. Marsden, *Religion and American Culture*, 48–53.

8. Ibid., 87.

9. F. D. Jones and W. H. Mills, *History of the Presbyterian Church in South Carolina* (Columbia, S.C.: R. L. Bryan, 1926), 62.

10. James M. McPherson, *Abraham Lincoln and the Second American Revolution* (New York: Oxford University Press, 1990), 52–53.

11. Kenneth M. Stampp, *America in 1857: A Nation on the Brink* (New York: Oxford University Press, 1990), 133; Richard N. Current, *The Lincoln Nobody Knows* (New York: Hill and Wang, 1969), 232–33; Gerald Sorin, *Abolitionism: A New Perspective* (New York: Praeger, 1972), 167–68; Stephen B. Oates, *With Malice toward None* (New York: New American Library, 1978), 76–77, 317; Stuart E. Knee, "John Brown and the Abolitionist Ministry," *Negro History Bulletin* 45 (April–June 1982): 36–37, 42.

12. Mellard, "Religious Dispute over Slavery," 21.

13. Marsden, *Religion and American Culture*, 58–59, 88–89.

14. Mellard, "Religious Dispute over Slavery," 36, 38–39, 44, 48.

15. Paul E. Boller, Jr., *American Thought in Transition: The Impact of Evolutionary Naturalism 1865–1900* (Chicago: Rand McNally, 1970), 31–33, 37, 47–48, 118, 122; Lois W. Banner, *Elizabeth Cady Stanton* (Boston: Little, Brown, 1980), 95, 117; Margaret Beecher White, "Beecher and Christian Science," *Cosmopolitan* 45 (August 1908): 320–22.

16. Clifford A. Woodward, "Recent Growth of Christian Science in New England," *New England Magazine* 51 (April 1914), 56–66; Raymond J. Cunningham, "The Impact of Christian Science on American Churches 1880–1910," *American Historical Review* 72 (April 1967): 894; Lawrence J. Goodrich, "Judge Sends Knapp Trust Dispute to Trial," *Christian Science Monitor* (21 September 1992): 8; T. G. Moulton, *An Exposure of Christian Science* (London: James Nisbet, 1906), 117–23; "Dr. Cookman's Theorists," *New York Times*, 31 May 1889, 5; Stephen Gottschalk, *The Emergence of Christian Science in American Religious Life* (Berkeley: University of California Press, 1975), xvii; Marsden, *Religion and American Culture*, 153–58.

17. Mary Baker Eddy, *Science and Health with Key to the Scriptures*, 11th ed. (Boston: Trustees under the Will of Mary Baker Eddy, 1934), 70–100; Georgine Milmine, "Six Years of Wandering," *McClure's Magazine* 18 (April 1907): 614, 619; Robert Peel, *Christian Science: Its Encounter with American Culture* (New York: Henry Holt, 1958), 105; Norman Beasley, *The Cross and the Crown* (New York: Duell, Sloan and Pearce, 1953), 39, 108–9, 113.

18. Frank Ballard, *Eddyism Miscalled Christian Science: A Delusion and a Snare* (London: Robert Culley, 1909), 184; Mary Baker Eddy, *Miscellaneous Writings 1883–1896* (Boston: Trustees under the Will of Mary Baker Eddy, 1896), 311; "Topics of the Times," *New York Times*, 3 September 1899, 16; Cunningham, "Impact of Christian Science," 892–93; Beasley, *Cross and the Crown*, 242.

19. H. M. Dexter, "Common Sense as to Christian Science," *Chautauquan* 10 (March 1890): 721; Frank Podmore, *From Mesmer to Christian Science*, 2d ed. (New York: University Books, 1963), 283, 292; B. Calvert, *Science and Health* (n.p., n.d.), 7; A. F. Frost, "Christian Science," *New Church Review* 3 (January 1896), 32; Georgine Milmine, "The Revival of Witchcraft," *McClure's Magazine* 29 (June 1907): 348, and "Literary Activities," *McClure's Magazine* 29 (October 1907): 698; Cunningham, "Impact of Christian Science," 899–900; C. H. Pritchard, "Mens Sana in Corpore Sano," *Nineteenth Century and After* 98 (October 1925): 565–80; J. A. Schaad, *Only a Mask: A Comparison of the Teachings of Christ and of Christian Science* (Kansas City, Mo.: M. C. Long, 1910), 1–56; A. W. Patten, *Facts and Fallacies of Christian Science* (Chicago: n.p., 188_), 10; Albert G. Lawson, *A Short Method with Christian Science* (Philadelphia: American Baptist Association, 1902), 50; W. S. Auchincloss, *The Mask of Eddyism* (New York: n.p., 1907), 1–5, 8; Clifford P. Smith, *Historical Sketches* (Boston: Christian Science, 1941), 205–8; Frederick W. Peabody, *A Complete Expose of Eddyism or Christian Science and the Plain Truth in Plain Terms Regarding Mary Baker Glover Eddy* (n.p., 1901), 28–45; "Christian Science Belief," *New York Times*, 22 May 1899, 5; T. G. Moulton, *An Exposure of Christian Science* (London: James Nisbet, 1906), 113.

20. Adoniram J. Gordon, *Christian Science Not Scriptural* (Boston: n.p., 187_), 5–6; Beasley, *Cross and the Crown*, 107–9; Cunningham, "Impact of Christian Science," 888, 890; Gottschalk, *Emergence of Christian Science*, xv–xxix.

21. Isaac Massey Haldeman, *Christian Science Unveiled in Its Own Words* (New York: n.p., 192_), 1–48; idem, *An Analysis of Christian Science: Based on Its Own Statements* (Philadelphia: School of the Bible, 1909), 1–37; idem, *Christian Science in the Light of Holy Scripture* (New York: Fleming H. Revell, 1909), 8–33; idem, *Mental Assassination or Christian Science* (New York: n.p., 192_), 1–25.

22. Amzi Clarence Dixon, *The Christian Science Delusion* (London: Marshall Brothers, 1918), 37–57; idem, *Is Christian Science a Humbug?* (Boston: James H. Earle, 1901), 1; "Condemns Christian Science," *New York Times*, 10 June 1901, 1; Cunningham, "Impact of Christian Science," 899; Robert Peel, *Mary Baker Eddy: The Years of Discovery* (New York: Holt, Rinehart and Winston, 1966), 251.

23. "A Christian Scientist Dead," *New York Times*, 21 October 1901, 2; A. H. Barrington, *Anti-Christian Cults* (Milwaukee: Young Churchman, 1898), 166; Ezra Morgan Wood, *Schools for Spirits* (Pittsburgh: Joseph Horner, 1903), 33.

24. "Dr. Morse's Sermon," *New York Daily Tribune*, 3 June 1901, 5; "Mrs. Eddy's Book Assailed," *New York Times*, 20 August 1900, 1; A. Lincoln Moore, *Christian Science: Its Manifold Attractions* (Harrisburg, Pa.: Star Independent, 1906), 7.

25. S. C. Bronson, *Delusions* (Burlington, Iowa: Acres, Blackman, 1895), 71–86, 104; M. W. Gifford, "Christian Science Against Itself," *Methodist Review* 80 (March 1898): 281–91; "What's to Be the Future of Christian Science," *Current Literature* 41 (August 1906): 202; Beasley, *Cross and the Crown*, 107, 111.

26. Reverend Willis P. O'Dell, *A Sermon on the Theology of Christian Science, Delivered at the Calvary Methodist Episcopal Church* (New York: n.p., 1904), 8; "The New York East Conference Excited," *New York Times*, 11 April 1901, 8; "Topics of the Times," *New York Times*, 15 May 1901, 8; "Methodist Conference Opposes Christian Science," *New York Daily Tribune*, 30 September 1900, 3.

27. James Monroe Buckley, *Science and Kindred Phenomena* (New York: Century, 1892), 290; idem, "The Absurd Paradox of Christian Science," *North American Review* 163 (July 1901): 34; "Speaks of False Religions," *New York Times*, 17 June 1901, 1; James Monroe Buckley, *Christian Science and Other Superstitions* (New York: Century, 1899), 102; Cunningham, "Impact of Christian Science," 891; Gottschalk, *Emergence of Christian Science*, 73, 112, 202; Boller, *American Thought in Transition*, 55, 219, 239; Henry Adams, *The Education of Henry Adams* (Boston: Houghton Mifflin, 1961), 234; "Dowie and Mrs. Eddy as Fungus Growths," *New York Times*, 10 June 1901, 1; Charles Edward Locke, *Eddyism: Is It Christian? Is It Scientific? How Long Will It Last?* (Los Angeles: Grafton, 1911), preface.

28. "Attacks Christian Science," *New York Times*, 5 January 1904, 1; A. Nelson Hollifield, *Christian Science or Mind Cure: A Sermon Delivered at Third Presbyterian Church, Newark, New Jersey* (Newark: Advertiser, 1889), 21; Reverend J. R. Walker, *Eddyism* (Nashville: Cumberland, 1899), 9–10, 13, 61–62; "No Faith in Christian Science," *New York Times*, 15 March 1892, 9; Reverend George Francis Greene, *Christian Science and the Gospel of Jesus Christ* (Cranford, N.J.: Chronicle, 1902), 11; "Christian Science Denounced," *New York Times*, 10 June 1901, 1.

29. F. F. Ellinwood, "Theosophy, Esoteric Buddhism and Christian Science," *Homiletic Review* 37 (January 1899): 18–19; E. T. Brewster, "The Evolution of Christian Science," *The Monist* 17 (April 1907): 186–99.

30. Greene, *Christian Science and the Gospel*, 11–13, 19; *Current Literature* 41 (August 1906), 202.

31. Augusta E. Stetson, *Reminiscences, Sermons and Correspondence Proving Adherence to the Principle of Christian Science as Taught by Mary Baker Eddy* (New York: G. P. Putnam's Sons, 1913), 842–47.

32. "The Origin of Christian Science," *Blackwood's Edinburgh Magazine* 165 (May 1899): 852; "Christian Quackery," *Blackwood's Edinburgh Magazine* 165 (April 1899): 659–68; *Editorial Comments on the Life and Work of Mary Baker Eddy* (Boston: Christian Science, 1911), 29; Moulton, *Exposure of Christian Science*, 2; Charles F. Winbigler, *Christian Science and Kindred Superstitions* (London: Abbey Press, 1900), 21, 38, 145, 158, 163; Dean Hart, *A Way That Seemeth Right: An Examination of Christian Science* (New York: James Pott, 1897), 6–22; Ann Harwood, *An English View of Christian Science: An Exposure* (New York: Fleming H. Revell, 1899), 2–27, 43–94, 102–17; "An English Explanation of the Growth of Christian Science," *Current Literature* 43 (December 1907): 65; Frank Ballard, "The Menace of Eddyism," *London Quarterly Review* 146 (July 1921): 58–71.

33. Cunningham, "Impact of Christian Science," 887.

34. Andrew F. Underhill, *Some Valid Objections to So-Called Christian Science* (Yonkers, N.Y.: Arlington Chemical, 1901), 1–46; Cunningham, "Impact of Chris-

tian Science," 887–8, 897, 902–3; "Episcopalians and Christian Science," *Brooklyn Daily Eagle* (14 November 1900): 4; Baltzell, *Protestant Establishment*, 113, 181.

35. Cunningham, "Impact of Christian Science," 887; Boller, *American Thought in Transition*, 33, 37; "Truth and Error in Christian Science," *Outlook* 83 (23 June 1906): 405; "Inoculating for Error," *Outlook* 49, (24 March 1894): 527; "Metaphysical Healing" (editorial), *Outlook* 42 (15 July 1899): 607; "Concerning Christian Science" (editorial), *Outlook* 68 (6 July 1901): 526; "Modern Witchcraft," *Outlook* 93 (23 October 1909): 363; "Mrs. Eddy," *Outlook* 96 (17 December 1910): 844.

36. Washington Gladden, "Truths and Untruths of Christian Science," *The Independent* 55 (19 March 1903): 777; Boller, *American Thought in Transition*, 120–22; David W. Noble, *The Progressive Mind 1890–1917* (Chicago: Rand McNally, 1970), 75.

37. Stetson, *Reminiscences, Sermons and Correspondence*, 120, 126, 134, 141, 435, 664, 979, 1101, 1139, 1152.

38. Isaac W. Bernheim, *The Reform Church of American Israelites* (n.p., 1921), 4–7, 10, and, *An Open Letter to Rabbi Stephen S. Wise* (Louisville, 1922), 1, 6–10; "Bernheim Article Provokes Much Discussion," *The Jewish Review and Observer* 47 (21 October 1922): 1; Kerry M. Olitzky, "The Sunday-Sabbath Movement in American Reform Judaism: Strategy or Evolution?" *American Jewish Archives* 34 (April 1982): 75–88; Benny Kraut, "Not So Strange Bedfellows: Felix Adler and Ahad Ha'am," *American Jewish Archives* 37 (November 1985): 305–8; Stuart E. Knee, *The Concept of Zionist Dissent in the American Mind 1917–1941* (New York: Robert Spencer, 1979), 43–44.

39. "Judaism Against Christian Science," *Literary Digest* 44, (4 May 1912): 940; Cunningham, "Impact of Christian Science," 896; Gottschalk, *Emergence of Christian Science*, 84.

40. Donald Meyer, *The Positive Thinkers: A Study of the American Quest for Health, Wealth and Personal Power from Mary Baker Eddy to Norman Vincent Peale* (New York: Doubleday, 1965), 326–27.

41. "Three Sisters Driven Insane," *New York Times*, 4 March 1890, 3; "Christian Catholic Dead," *New York Times*, 1 September 1899, 1; Cunningham, "Impact of Christian Science," 895.

42. Kerby A. Miller, *Emigrants and Exiles* (New York: Oxford University Press, 1985), 528–32; Robert D. Cross, *The Emergence of Liberal Catholicism in America* (Chicago: Quadrangle Books, 1968), Chap. 7, 52–53, 89–94, 101–4; John F. Wilson, ed., *Church and State in American History* (Englewood Cliffs, N.J.: D. C. Heath, 1965), 140–41; Marsden, *Religion and American Culture*, 105, 136–38; John Higham, Strangers in the Land (New York: Atheneum, 1970), 80–87; Gottschalk, *Emergence of Christian Science*, 3.

43. H. Stuart Hughes, *The Obstructed Path* (New York: Harper and Row, 1968), 71, 116–17, 248.

44. One wasn't. See Charles Caverno, "Why I Am Not a Christian Scientist," *Bibliotheca Sacra* 59 (October 1902): 682–95.

45. Gottschalk, *Emergence of Christian Science*, 196.

46. Robert Hugh Benson, "Christian Science," *Dublin Review*, 143 (July 1908): 61–62, 71.

47. Virgilius Herman Krull, *A Common Sense View of Christian Science* (Collegeville, Ind.: St. Joseph's Printing Office, 1908), 7; T. J. Campbell, "The Delusion

of Christian Science," *Catholic Mind* 24 *(22 December 1906): 49, 495, 502; "The Roman Catholic Response to Christian Science," Current Literature* 46 (April 1909): 408–10; Walter Drum, "The Meaning of Christian Science," *American Catholic Quarterly Review* 30 (January 1905): 133.

48. Cross, *Emergence of Liberal Catholicism*, 42.

49. Walter Drum, "Is Christian Science Christian," *Catholic World* 80 (February, 1905): 638, 642–43, 646, 648, 651.

50. Adrian Feveral, "Christian Science: The Cult of the Immoral," *Catholic World* 96 (November 1912): 185, 190; "Christian Science: The Cult of the Unchristian," *Catholic World* 96 (December 1912): 362; "Christian Science: The Cult of the Unscientific," *Catholic World* 96 (January 1913), 466, 469, and "Christian Science: The Cult of the Ridiculous," *Catholic World* 96 (February 1913): 655–60.

51. "Crusading Against Christian Science" (editorial), *New York Evening Post* 21 June 1905(1), 6; James M. Gray, *The Antidote to Christian Science* (New York: Fleming H. Revell, 1907), 97, 105, 108, 119.

52. Peel, *Mary Baker Eddy*, 278.

53. J. Winthrop Hegeman, *Must Protestantism Adopt Christian Science?* (New York: Harper and Row, 1914), vii-ix, 31–32.

5

Live and Let Live

According to the 1989 edition of the *Medicare Handbook*, a publication of the United States Department of Health and Human Services, Medicare hospital insurance can defray the cost of inpatient hospital and skilled nursing services received at participating Christian Science sanatoria, provided they are listed and certified by the Boston Mother Church.[1] Recognized as an alternative form of treatment, with licensed practitioners and fully protected under the Constitution's First Amendment, it is no longer as controversial as it once was, although it still provides sleepless moments and plenty of courtroom action for those who are convinced that what takes place during a healing is medical, though drugless, as well as spiritual. Stephen Gottschalk is not confused with the provenance, progress and utility of spiritual healing, but he is nevertheless instructive as to where the ambiguity may lie. In his *Emergence of Christian Science in American Religious Life*, he states the function of the Christian Science Church to be the reinstatement of primitive Christianity's "lost element of healing"! As a religious figure, Mary Baker Eddy would, therefore, minimize liturgy and maximize healing works, requiring the faithful to perform rather than pray. About one hundred pages later, while Gottschalk distinguishes between Quimby's mental cure and Science, he says the latter is a "religious teaching and only incidentally a healing method."[2] What he means is that Science is not medical in an organic or psychoanalytic sense: it heals, as did Jesus, through the conduit of divine knowledge. Unchallengeable, unassailable, eternal and truthful, it is covered by United States law that exempts those endeavors identified as entirely religious from medical or political constraints.

Physicians have never felt entirely at ease with this definition and the concomitant exemption but no more so than at the height of their collective vulnerability, during America's Victorian age. Modern medicine had yet to make its appearance in 1866, the year of Mary Baker Eddy's mishap on the ice but also a year in which an estimated fifty thousand Americans died of cholera; five years later, the last great cholera epidemic seized the nation.[3] Typhoid, diphtheria and smallpox threatened to reach or actually reached epidemic proportions in 1895 Indianapolis; 1903 Allegheny, Pennsylvania; and 1904 Stamford, Connecticut; individual cases were reported on an everyday basis. Tumors, hemorrhages, cancers, appendicitis, diabetes, pneumonia, tonsillitis, spasms and influenza, a panoply of contagions and malignancies, spotlighted the medical establishment, or what passed for it, in what could rightfully be characterized as its century of inadequacy.

By the 1890s doctors liked to be thought of as performing more professionally but they were still a heartbeat, or perhaps more succinctly a flatline, away. Since the opening of America's first medical school in 1765, a decade before the Revolution, theoretical approaches to curing advanced haltingly, primarily because native orientations in this discipline were predictably, as they were in several others, directed toward pecuniary advancement and cultural validation. The development of anaesthesia by Morton is always mentioned as an exception, but in this case the exception proves the rule as proprietary hospitals and profit-making staffs appeared to have availed themselves of the new procedure to induce dreams of self-congratulation rather than realize scientific aspiration.

If a serious student sought a teaching university, a clinic, a laboratory, a worthy scholarly journal or a discussion of cutting edge research in, shall we say, bacteriology, he or she would find it in Germany, France or, perhaps, England where lived the "giants"—Lister, Koch and Pasteur. For a short time anyway, one could escape the American doldrums of low standards, inadequate training, limited ability, apprenticeships, erratic licensing and "do it yourself" patent medicines, whose value in 1910 was $141,942,000.[4] The American Medical Association (AMA), founded in 1846, failed to elevate standards appreciably or inspire young American physicians with a feeling of self-worth. Public health was simply not a compelling nineteenth-century issue and Freud was Americanized only after 1909. Before that time, psychiatry, psychology and psychoanalysis appeared in the American lexicon as synonymous with faith healing, wholly misunderstood, poorly investigated and seemingly irrelevant to the bedrock volunteerism of the American character. This was the "medical trust," so named by Mary Baker Eddy in 1899, whose abuses and inadequacies were evident in its drumbeat aggression upon Christian Science. "Be as you are wise as serpents in publishing an attack on the MD's but defend our cause squarely and convincingly . . . let [them] commit suicide."[5] It so happened they wouldn't commit suicide and neither would she but the two seemingly incompatible, polar positions, one somatic and one spiritual, would have to evolve more flexibility in order to accommodate elastic twentieth-century medicine. In short, there would really have to be a "healing."

It was not apparent that such a healing or its possibility existed in 1887. State laws were generally as vague on medical practice as on monopoly and, in the absence of definitive federal interest or interpretation, what was or was not acceptable treatment varied from state to state; what's more, drugless medicine was not considered an acceptable alternative to conventional treatment. In the absence of consistent regulation and standardization, and, until the 1893 founding of Johns Hopkins Medical School with its viable philosophic foundation,[6] it was every man—or woman—for himself. There was little Christian Science had to fear except acquiring a bad reputation and that from allopathists or homeopathists who already owned one. Any claims Eddy made as Christian healer—"I healed consumption in its last stages that the M.D.'s by verdict . . . declared incurable; I healed malignant tuberculous, diphtheria and curious bones that could be dented by the finger, saving them when the surgeon [was] . . . ready for their amputation; I . . . healed at one visit a cancer"[7]—were no more outlandish than the charges that her faith caused epidemics; in truth, no more outlandish than the relentless environment in which she lived and worked. Both she and it would reach a plateau of adjustment that would occur in due time and with the acquisition of some wisdom, though problems and dramatic courtroom cases remain even in the contemporary era.

Little was known in the 1870s of the supposed healing qualities of Christian Science outside Mary Baker Eddy's immediate neighborhood. However, her excursions into the realm of spontaneous healing led local doctors to accuse her of practicing medicine without a license. The tension between faith cure and drug cure mounted. Two problems emerged: first, the morality and safety of the faith cure; second, the threat to individual liberty if faith healing were outlawed.[8]

No answer was evident in either this or the ensuing two decades, but plenty of opportunities were found for self-expression, recrimination and shifting responsibility. Since he was unable to discuss the efficacy of spiritual or mental approaches to the treatment of mental illness, Dr. S. V. Clevenger thought it safe to offer a $1 million bounty to anyone who could offer a successful "metaphysical cure for cancer, a real migraine, an actual lung consumption . . . or the amputation of a leg." Writing for the *New York Medical Times* a year later, in 1888, Dr. David Allyn Gorton could hardly grasp the idea that thinking and doing the "right" things, even if they didn't always appear correct or even rational, could allay illness; Dr. Albert H. Burr of the New York City's College of Physicians and Surgeons could indeed grasp the idea if Eddy could make her treatment depend on psychic rather than divine law, though drugless therapy in any way, shape or form, he feared, would be trouble, a potential hornets' nest of "willful murder" charges. Leave it alone, concluded Dr. Henry Reed Hopkins; "as a medical system, Eddyism claims to make obsolete the sciences of anatomy, pharmacy, therapeutics, obstetrics and hygiene."[9]

The thoughts of these physicians are in several ways analogous to the more familiar ideas of Gilded Age industrialists, who sought to regulate their competition rather than themselves. For both, self-restraint was unthinkable but, ironically, each sought protection from grassroots or middle-class movements they couldn't control. In the case of railroads, for example, state regulation didn't work. Courts accepted such rulings in the absence of federal initiative during the Jacksonian period but post-1850 competition between companies led to wasteful duplication of lines, destructive competition among towns, villages and cities for spurs and construction before there was an actual need. By the 1870s citizens affected by all this became disillusioned with railroads, despite their great technological and economic potential. Farmers resented discriminatory rates, railroad building resulted in depression if it occurred too rapidly and was overcapitalized, and fraud, as in the case of the Erie Railroad with accompanying machinations of Jim Fiske, Daniel Drew and Cornelius Vanderbilt, was commonplace. A modern corporate executive summed it up "feelingly: 'I would be very glad if we knew exactly where we stand, if we could be free from danger, trouble and criticism.' "[10]

State laws proved to be inadequate for the steamroller economy but, in the absence of federal commitment, it was from that sector that laws were enacted. A combination of merchants and farmers in Iowa, the Grangers, formed associations militating against "long haul-short haul" discrimination. Granger laws stated that when a business was in the public interest, it was subject to regulation; furthermore, the right to regulate belonged to the states until the federal government stepped in. The Grangers made railroad rates subject to state legislatures in important cases, one of which was *San Mateo v. Southern Pacific* (1882).[11] In 1886 the decision was reversed in *Santa Clara County v. Southern Pacific* in which the railroad was equated with a person, whose property would be jeopardized by the fixing of low rates by state legislatures.[12] Apparently, a complete review of state laws and state regulations was necessitated by the 1886 Wabash decision, which declared them all unconstitutional.

The era of federal regulation began in 1887, the same year that Dr. S. V. Clevenger's diatribe against Christian Science appeared in the *Open Court*. Under the Interstate Commerce Act, whose regulatory agency was the Interstate Commerce Commission, all railroad charges had to be "reasonable and just"; there were to be no illegal rates and discrimination between people and places was outlawed; finally, no railroad company could exact higher rates for the short than for the long haul if the railroad traveled over the same track in the same direction. Smart attorneys found obvious loopholes and, by 1900 a series of court decisions, among them the 1897 Maximum Freight Rates Case and the 1898 Alabama Midlands Act, rendered the Interstate Commerce Act harmless. In business pursuits other than railroading, Supreme Court interpretations of individuality, as in *U.S.*

v. E. C. Knight (1895),[13] *U.S. v. Addyston Pipe and Steel* (1899)[14] and *Standard Oil Co. v. United States* (1911)[15] eviscerated the 1890 Sherman Anti-Trust Act. In industry as in medicine, there emerged a need to introduce positive self-images based upon responsible behavior. A flurry of crises was bringing the Gilded Age rollercoaster to a screeching halt.

But who really wanted to pay the price for maturity in the medical field? It was as difficult to locate visionary doctors as it was visionary capitalists. If there were emerging professionals who cultivated the long view, they were temporarily overcome by the financial panic obscuring the vision of 1890s profit makers—and again let us emphasize the fact that Mary Baker Eddy was no more extreme than her critics.

According to the press, Christian Science treatment didn't work as a ripple of failure became a steady stream in the last dozen years of the nineteenth century. Dentists liked the Science view of deceptive pain and utilized it to achieve their own ends; beginning on 6 November 1884, they advertised regularly in the *Christian Science Journal*. Unfortunately, pandemics, tumors and a variety of potentially life-threatening disorders proved somewhat more intractable to practitioner treatment. "Christian Science Victims" read exciting editorials from the *New York Daily Tribune*, and even more exciting were victim descriptions in the *Brooklyn Daily Eagle*, two of which were a mother and baby, the family of an H. W. Fitch, president of the Washington National Bank. Distraught over the death of his wife and child, he invoked the aid of a Christian Scientist to resurrect them.[16] Front-page or near front-page headlines were made in Jamestown, Albany, Buffalo, Utica, Mt. Vernon and Brooklyn, New York, as Christian Scientists were ridiculed for their callousness and held responsible by relatives and the state for deaths by cancer, dropsy, tuberculosis, appendicitis, pneumonia, typhoid, diabetes, spasms and starvation. Normally the charge was negligence—not calling a physician—indictments by grand juries occurred regularly[17] and issues related to freedom of choice, individual liberty and religious protection under the Constitution were thrashed out by lay jurors often ill-equipped for debate.

And these were by no means the most electrifying of cases. Santiago Porcella charged Mrs. Joseph B. See, leader of a Christian Science church in Cranford, New Jersey, with his wife's murder. In Marion, Indiana, George and Sarah Archer, assisted by William Johnson, treated Mrs. Johnson, who died of a hemorrhage; all three, by the coroner's recommendation, were to be held for murder. Treatment that was "base, diabolical and voodoo"-like was also at the bottom of an Indianapolis diphtheria epidemic, which seemed to have fallen into the grip of Science "perverts," "imbeciles" and "criminals," all of whom practiced a "form of idiocy" degenerating "into a homicidal mania." For society's protection, concluded the *New York Times*, they should be jailed since their accusers, now mute, "lie in rows in every graveyard."[18]

Something to capture the public imagination, if indeed it required further capturing, occurred in late October 1898 when Harold Frederic, London correspondent for the *New York Times* and American literary realist, died after being attended by Christian Scientists. Frederic was not merely a reporter and his case merited wide and sometimes sensational coverage because he was a celebrity. Knowledgeable on the Mohawk region of upstate New York, he produced a best-selling novel about that area in 1896, just published in England, entitled *The Damnation of Theron Ware*. It was an exposé of American faith generally and American Methodism particularly, recounted through the travail of a young fin de siècle minister who seeks prizes greater than his provincial Protestant environment can offer; instead of attaining them, he plunges into a spiritual abyss, suffering a tragic "loss of innocence and moral vision." It was all about America, its religious dilemma and its future possibilities: as such, it was both popular and profound, all the rage in 1896.[19] The *Times* was shrill, coarse and medieval as it rose to the defense of both public figure and employee.

The story, indeed, had sensational possibilities if managed in the appropriate fashion—and the *Times*, to be sure, had excellent management potential. Two London Scientists, Athalie Mills and Kate Lyons, attended Harold Frederic, who died during the course of their treatment. They were taken into custody and questioned in England but they were tried in the columns of the *New York Times*. As unlicensed medical practitioners, or so they were made out to be, they were "criminals" meriting conviction: decisive, punitive action overseas would demonstrate the course America should taken in its own cases of "faith cure murder." Some invective was even worse, having overtones of Kiev, Odessa and Bialystok, where religious minorities were mistreated and pogroms had become a household word: the "hand" appeared before a man whose "wonderful" faculties were "clouded" by illness. "Outstretched . . . rapacious," it reached "for the sick man's gold." The *Times* and other newspapers wanted more than jail but they got less. On 5 December 1898 the charges were dropped, with Lyons and Mills being discharged.[20]

Children were also targets. A mother was denied custody of her child by the New York State Supreme Court because she was a Christian Scientist who treated another of her children unsuccessfully; in Kansas City and points east, Christian Scientists and contagion made an explosive brew. It wasn't "medicine," but it was vilified by the medical world for being "unmedical," meaning unsanitary, unhygienic, unclean and "mischievous."[21]

Science can indeed be criticized for its activities at this time, but not in those terms. It was not unsanitary, unhygienic, unclean or mischievous. In a way, its anti-Protestant orientation caused a medical aversion to it as well as the religious one, already detailed. Although it operated Sunday schools, Christian Science was not a Sunday school faith; although Scientists offered a "truth cure" for bodily ills, bodily ills were as illusory as bodily pleasure. Maybe Santa Claus was there but impersonal Principle was all that mattered; perhaps parents were there, but warmth and wonder were all "by the way"; after all, it was time to put away childish things, since this was not at heart or in spirit a children's faith. It was a rule, proclaimed by Eddy, who had her difficulties with children, both natural and adopted; it was perpetuated in New York City for a quarter-century by Augusta Stetson on whose ocean of *Reminiscences* children were but a tiny speck.[22] Even today, as Christian Science accustoms itself to the concept of children's rights and parents must defend themselves for religious treatment deemed permissible under state law, a recent and sympathetic writer notes: "I saw no children. I found this in every church I visited: small numbers, few children."[23] No children, few children or unmentioned children rendered the faith susceptible to allegations of child insensitivity, however unwarranted. At this juncture states, often at the urging of somatically oriented physicians or associations, took the lead in defending and circumscribing Christian Science practice just as they had done, with mixed results, for railroad and industrial magnates.

Some states, whose inclinations were directed at limiting the practice of Christian Science, defined it as less of a faith and more of a medical practice or healing business. By some circuitous logic, the *New York Times* concluded that proscribing Christian Science would in no way interfere with religious liberty. That newspaper was closer to the truth—or its own truth—a few months later when it classified the Christian Scientist as a criminal if he or she practiced medicine and was unqualified to do so.[24] The ambiguity of the situation facing state courts was plain: if Christian Science was a religious healing system with no claim upon medicine regularly defined, one could not prosecute a Scientist, for to do so would infringe on his or her First Amendment liberties; to try an individual on the basis of his or her theology would likewise inhibit freedom of choice. However, if Science was a system of therapeutics that could be legally defined as medicine a practitioner could be charged with its unlicensed practice; should his or her patient become gravely ill or die, a Scientist could be held and tried on any number of serious criminal charges.

New York and Illinois, both active Christian Science centers, leaned toward the medical definition of Science, probably because each state had vociferous and influential medical societies which, as the occasion arose, acted as lobbies. In 1893, nearly at the height of Chicago's involvement in Christian Science via the leadership of Mary Plunkett, Emma Hopkins and Ursula Gestefeld, the state of Illinois passed an "antidiploma" law that prohibited societies organized for medical purposes under chapter 115 of the public statute from conferring degrees or issuing diplomas unless authorized to do so. In order to curb Christian Science, the Chicago Board of Health opted for legislation that would prevent the practice of medicine by any but licensed practitioners.[25] Three thousand Christian Scientists in New York City rejecting medical treatment and spoken for by John Lathrop, a competitor of Augusta Stetson, aroused the ire of medicolegal society president S.B.W. McCord and Board of Health director Michael C. Murphy. Within a few months, Murphy gained the support of the Kings County Medical Society, but not that of Governor Theodore Roosevelt, in his efforts to eradicate faith healing. Roosevelt was invited but chose not to attend an anti-Christian Science rally sponsored by the Medical and Legal Relief Society and held at the Waldorf Astoria. At this gathering, the prospect of presenting a bill to the state legislature banning faith healing as a treatment for organically ill patients was discussed.[26]

Remunerated Christian Science healing was already a misdemeanor in Albany and the charge of manslaughter was soon to ignite passions in Rome, New York, and New York City. In the former instance, there was more at stake than a controversial treatment: Mrs. Moses A. Davis, the decedent, bequeathed half her estate to Christian Science. In the latter affair, John C. Lathrop's failure to cure by spiritual Principle resulted in his indictment by a Westchester grand jury. A seven-year-old girl had succumbed to diphtheria and the New York Times marched at the head of a parade opposing a "brutal slaughter which only costs one dollar per treatment." Westchester County coroner Banning was supported by the medical community in a successful effort to convince the grand jury that a manslaughter charge correctly interpreted the evidence. According to official Christian Science records, the defendant was not abandoned by Augusta Stetson and the First Church of Christ, Scientist, both of whom supported his not guilty plea with spiritual and monetary resources.[27]

Doing an injustice to the medical profession was a theme that played well in New York and Illinois; it was also rather durable in Pennsylvania, Indiana, the far West and South. Between 1897 and 1903 Judges Arnold and Pennypacker periodically refused to grant a charter to a Christian Science church in Philadelphia because the movement was everything but a religion; it was, they ruled, a business, a faith healing movement and an organization practicing unlicensed medicine. It seems they were unsure as to what Christian Science really was. What they were convinced of, or were convinced by medical societies to believe, was that they wished to uphold an act of 1877 that prohibited the practice of medicine unless proof of competency could be shown in the form of a medical diploma.[28] Attorney General Taylor of Indiana shared the same opinion, grouped Christian Scientists with all manner of faith healers and warned that they break the law, as do osteopaths, if they prescribe unlicensed medical cures. Conversely, Attorney General Boyle of Kansas would not prosecute Scientists. The attitude of the New York Times was succinctly put: "All the homicidal cranks in the country ought to instantly betake themselves to Kansas."[29]

As the old century limped away, doctors and the media demonstrated little inclination for either reason or widened perspective. Dr. John Ferguson differentiated between faith healing (immediate cure through God's personal intervention), mind cure (human mind is directed at a single object cure) and Christian Science (which, he concluded, was "mind over matter"). Of the three, Ferguson thought the least of Christian Science with its absurd "sickness is an illusion theory." Its logical conclusion would always be a "disregard for hygiene and a reckless unobservance for health precautions . . . even soap and water." William Purrington, a lecturer at the Bellevue Medical College, labeled the Eddy system of healing "a travesty and a burlesque," the religion an ignorant, irreverent, vain, vulgar incoherent fraud and its founder a sorceress-magician preying on helpless children."[30] Unfortunately, prejudice became a by-product of the legislative process which, by 1901, included stringent anti-Science laws in Montana, Kentucky, Tennessee, West Virginia, Oklahoma and Georgia. The New Jersey Grand Council of the Royal Arcanium denied insurance to Christian Science "fanatics" residing in the state; next door, a Buffalo mutual benefit society, the Supreme Lodge of the Knights of Honor, restricted membership to non-Christian Scientists. Meanwhile, parents in Hopewell, Pennsylvania, removed their children from the local school and established their own rather than allow a teacher with Christian Science principles to "inculcate" young minds with heresy.[31]

Five states chose to assert libertarian principles on the issue of Christian Science. Besides Kansas, Colorado, under Governors Thomas and Peabody, vetoed legislation against Christian Science on four separate occasions between 1899 and 1905. The rationale for nonpassage was not love for Science but distrust of enhanced "police power" free of constitutional restraint; encroaching on the prerogatives of citizens "with experimental laws" was "no less dangerous because it was well-meant." In yet a third western state, Ohio, a Cincinnati judge fined two Christian Science practitioners for ministering without a license, thereby contributing to the death of Thomas McDowell from typhoid fever. On the very next day, the judge reversed his decision, ruling Science a religion, its services religious and hence not germane to those sections of the state registration law dealing with medicine. The verdict was therefore invalidated and the State Board of Health deeply disappointed.[32] If these were Christian Science victories, they were dubious ones: it was just a matter of time before the motivation for prosecution would be less legally and more morally based.

In *State v. Walter Mylod* (1898), Rhode Island ruled Christian Science a religion rather than a system of therapeutics, thus protecting the defendant from prosecution.[33] But it was in Massachusetts, home of the Mother Church, that one of the most interesting conflicts occurred. In that state, a statute outlawing unqualified medical practice failed to pass, primarily because Christian Science was included in the testimony of and had found a defender in philosopher-physician William James. His statement to the state legislature—actually a defense of faith healing as a nonmedical practice—did not limn Science properly, at least to followers of Eddy, but achieved the desired objective. The *New York Times* was unhappy and suggested that Harvard University might consider taking action against its wayward professors, who dared to defend the "creed of the Scientists . . . self-styled spiritualists" and suspiciously anti-American: "Is Professor James . . . to retain his place in one of America's greatest institutions of learning and, by preaching wild and perilous follies . . . bring . . . reproach upon our civilization?"[34]

Over the course of two Republican, Progressive administrations the relationship between Christian Science and professional medicine improved incrementally. There was softening and adaptation on both sides, but in no way does this mean a collapse or surrender of position. For her part, Mary Baker Eddy continued her assault upon "materia medica" which, to her, was an art rather than exact science; conversely, Christian Science mind healing, founded on the "spiritual attainment of 'Christ Mind,' " was in fact, an always demonstrable science. Augusta Stetson continued in exactly the same path, at least rhetorically,[35] until she ran afoul of the Mother Church Board of Directors who were willing to approach, if not always interact with, a revitalized and quickened medical establishment.

For their part, physicians acquired a better self-image between 1901 and 1912 and therefore were a little more at ease with Science. Since President Theodore Roosevelt's field of expertise was political and urban oversight, he probably hoped that the trickle-down theory, now a political staple, would nourish ethnicity and culture, thus spurring social consciousness and activism. As an imperfect reformer, who may have succeeded in preserving the status quo, at least he provided an arena for social engineering in which various professions, including medicine, felt comfortable. In 1901 the Rockefeller Institute for research in the biological sciences was founded and, five years later, permanently endowed; in the same year, the American Medical Association was reorganized into a twentieth-century professional society with a national membership—8,400 in 1900, 70,000 in 1920—scientific standards, strict evaluation procedures and a commitment to improve the quality of medical services and physicians. State and local governments showed an interest in the Association and its objectives, especially after its successful insurgency on a federal level. Joining hands with Senators Heyburn of Idaho, McCumber of North Dakota, chief chemist of the United State Department of Agriculture Harvey W. Wiley and *Ladies Home Journal* editor Edward Bok were muckraking authors Samuel Hopkins Adams and Upton Sinclair; all sought and won congressional approval for the Pure Food and Drug Act.

Along with the Pure Food and Drug Act, the 1902 founding of the United States Public Health Service represented the limit of federal involvement. But they were a start and a further incentive to the medical community to continue in the direction of rationalizing its discipline. Employed by the Carnegie Foundation for the Advancement of Teaching, researcher Abraham Flexner produced a famous report entitled *Medical Education in the United States and Canada* that exposed the deep, historic decadence in the American medical profession and recommended solutions. As a result, the number of fraudulent medical schools declined, as did the number of doctors produced, health care as a whole improved and basic medical research, conducted in laboratories, yielded finds in hormones, vitamins and x-ray therapy.[36] By 1912 public health, including nursing, became respectable parts of medical practice.

Nevertheless, there existed in medicine an aura of incompletion between 1900 and 1914, very similar to the racist veil drawn over ethnics and black Americans. What should have been an era of realization fell short because the Progressives, in essence, were satisfied with a shortfall. It has been pointed out, with much justification, that the period 1890–1920 was a nadir for race relations in the United States, with the last of the southern states disenfranchising blacks, segregation a given and violence gnawing and habitual. For ethnics other than blacks, quota laws, discrimination and outright exclusion made cultural and political achievement all the more remarkable.

Physicians might have thought about this, but not very long or hard since their work was physiological and their data quantifiable. Those who might have evaluated such struggle in terms of class consciousness, interior drives, youthful motivations and unresolved conflict were not yet popular and most were not yet at work in the United States. The majority were in Europe, perhaps Germany or Austria, studying with or at least gravitating to the office or home of Sigmund Freud. Any Americans who studied the mind were not given to Freudian pessimism; they rejected it in fact, in favor of a more exuberant environmentalism and a more optimistic nineteenth-century holdover called positivism. After all, insecurities bred by nationalism, competition and militarism had not yet made the trip across the Atlantic, although breezes were abroad and storm clouds were already racing across the sun.

Psychiatrists and psychologists operating in the United States in the first decade of the twentieth century tended to ignore Freud altogether or to evaluate his work as contemptible. As his popularity grew, they proffered him reluctant notice by dumping his work in the nonobservable, unquantifiable category of faith healing, osteopathy, yoga and Christian Science. James J. Putnam of the Harvard University Medical School warned neurologists at their 1910 conference to "take a stand against Transcendentalism and supernaturalism," and crush out "Christian Science, Freudism and all that bosh, rot and nonsense." Apparently, the doctor could not appreciate anything he could not see.

Until Freud's 1909 visit to Clark University in Worcester, Massachusetts, this is the way psychologists and psychiatrists in the United States continued to feel, even if they were a little uneasy. The American hero—and he would remain so for a generation beyond World War I—was the behaviorist John Watson, who was committed to engineering personalities which, to him, were entirely mechanical and material. In his 1914 work, *Behavior: An Introduction to Comparative Psychology*, he encouraged psychologists to mold human characters at will. Though certainly not as radical, the convictions of experimental psychologists G. Stanley Hall, president of Clark University, and Edwin Bisell Holt, who taught psychology at Harvard and Princeton Universities, tilted toward a system "dominated by Watson's psychology and the ethics" of the renowned educator John Dewey. In brief, all believed that unhealthy psychic energy, unpredictable behavior, seemingly subliminal, antisocial, hostile and destructive drives could be sublimated in what might be called a "Protestant" way, through the attainment of self-knowledge, the acquisition of restraint, the striving for social and ethical responsibility and the achievement of some sort of moral or transcendent perfectionism. Essentially what they did was to discard Freud's tragic, sometimes too tragic, vision of reality, and replace it with Polyanna, wherein an idealized, unreachable happiness became consistent with friendly cooperation, productiveness and Protestant morality.[37] If this was not the true Freud, and it certainly was not, neither was it the true Christian Science, which also bore no resemblance to typical Protestant adjustment. But there would be concessions from all sides, as the unitary Protestant approach was superseded over the course of years. Real accommodations, however slight, were forthcoming from Eddy and were then continued by the Mother Church Board of Directors. Major Scientists like Augusta Stetson were left behind, not so much because they were wrong or misguided but because they were purists for whom truce was betrayal. Eventually such a truce brought a period of adjustment, Science faded from the headlines, Mary Baker Eddy won some posthumous accolades from doubters, and the faith won kudos from those who favored a more holistic orientation to therapeutics. Although some of her early pronouncements were surprising, the heart of Christian Science remained intact and, in the opinion of its followers, inviolable.

As an archfoe of Christian Science, the *New York Times* continued its barrage during the final months of William McKinley's presidency and into the Theodore Roosevelt years. Four weeks after New Year's Day 1901, a Bronx woman, Grace Hopper, died of blood poisoning after a Christian Scientist administered a heavy dose of prayer and baked apples. The regular physician and two nurses walked off the case when the Science metaphysician arrived, only to return at the pleading of the patient's husband. The incident was brought before the County Medical Society for investigation.[38]

Another headline-grabbing story occurred four months later and involved the practice of drugless obstetrics, a Christian Science staple since the early 1880s and favored by Eddy in both her published works and private correspondence. To her hesitant adopted son Dr. Ebenezer J. Foster Eddy, who was under attack by the Board of Directors of the Mother Church in the 1890s, she wrote: "teaching obstetrics will open your way to . . . heal the sick, and organize a church of your own." It didn't and it also became page one news for the *New York Times* five years after Eddy's admonition to her adopted son when a Chicago woman was "killed by Christian Science." With her Christian Science sister-in-law in attendance and a second practitioner as well, a Mrs. Vance died of a hemorrhage following the birth of her child;[39] over a year later a Boston Scientist, Putnam J. Ramsdell, died of smallpox after refusing to be vaccinated. Indeed, the cases kept up a steady, unsettling rhythm. After "spurning physicians," a sixty-five-year-old woman succumbed to Bright's disease. Four months later, heaped on dozens of stories already like it, a Mt. Vernon, New York Scientist with tuberculosis refused traditional medical care and died, despite the pleadings of his wife. Diphtheria and smallpox epidemics in Stamford, Connecticut, and Allegheny, Pennsylvania, respectively, were traced back to teenagers and "schoolboys" who had been treated by Christian Scientists. The *New York Times* carried many stories of afflicted or afflicting Scientists, provocatively written to arouse public indignation.[40]

Legal action continued apace, although Christian Scientists won their fair share of decisions. Scientists were threatened by litigation in Jacksonville, Florida, following a death certificate report of two physicians charging attending Scientists with homicide. On several occasions in New York City, grand juries sought but could not obtain indictments against Scientists. In 1901 Luther Pierson was alleged to have permitted the death by pneumonia of his five-year-old daughter, but two years later the appellate court reversed the lower court decision because of Science's borderline legality. No less than the son of Queen Victoria's personal physician wrote a stirring appeal, published in *Current Literature*, advocating freedom of choice for adult Christian Scientists but making it mandatory for their children to receive medical care.[41] If Science was a religion, the Constitution's First Amendment would preclude such action.

And, indeed, doctors hoped this was a religion—just as ministers hoped it was a medical practice—because they ardently wished to distance themselves from any intangible, unmeasurable "cures." Meeting in midtown Manhattan at the turn of the century the Society of Medical Jurisprudence savaged mind healing as a whole but reserved some choice epithets for Christian Science. The general feeling was that Science was fraudulent, unlicensed medicine that did an "injustice to the medical profession"; but the audience was corrected by Charles M. Demond, who denounced Science not as quack medicine but as a "religion gone mad." Given the status of the medical art in 1901, this was probably the safer course. James Taylor Lewis, counsel for the New York State Medical Association, found himself in complete agreement with Demond, was duly horrified and vindicated the medical position in a letter to the editor of the *New York Times*.[42]

There were a number of doctors and writers on medical topics who employed the scattergun approach on the hot potato when confronted with Christian Science. They couldn't follow a line of thought on Science—say its unhygienic or unmedicinal qualities—to a rational conclusion. Usually it started out well, but by page seven or eight, spontaneous degeneration occurred. Those who thought it a health hazard affirmed it a philosophic hazard too, or hypnotic, delusive, even demonic; and they couldn't resist all the other issues that were not only beside the point—like Eddy's wealth, dissent within Science and Church censorship—but upon which they were unqualified to comment.

A pair of articles, one in the *Montreal Medical Journal* for August 1904 and the other in *The World To-Day*, a Hearst publication, for April 1905 are notable for two things: first, how far afield a doctor could go; and second, how much physicians could echo ministers. In the first of these, Dr. George Gould kept focused for one sentence—"Every modern discovery in biology, sociology and medicine is ignored" by Christian Science—only to derail in the second, losing his audience and his sanity, appearing in the guise of an old-time abolitionist hanging John Brown rather than a twentieth-century physician: "It [Christian Science] is the spook of the Middle Ages, ludicrously gibbering in a new epoch of science . . . and reason. It is . . . the old barbarism freed by democracy." Psychologist James Rowland Angell offered the pre-Freudian, functionalist viewpoint on the Eddy movement: demand that it respect basic laws of hygiene and pray that it falls to pieces; the battle against Christian Science would not be won by "outsiders," like himself. "Such attacks are . . . likely . . . to give" the decadent Christian Scientists "martyrdom."

The real problem for Christian Science could be summarized for physicians in the same fashion it was summarized for clerics. One author, opposed to *Science and Health* and Eddyism as a "crutch for the mentally indolent, a censer for the spiritually dead," claimed the movement offered unrivaled benefits: it shook Old Church theology from its lethargy and "it has broken the fangs of the medical monster." He advised doctors to give "the devil" its due by examining Christian Science capacities in alleviating mental and nervous disorders. A second writer, Gordon Clark, commented in his tract *The Church of St. Bunco* that blatant disregard for hygiene measures—cleanliness, quarantine and vaccination—was unacceptable. Neither religion nor medicine, Christian Science masqueraded as both; it was a dangerous form of insanity and a rigid belief totally at odds with American Protestantism.[43]

Courts, however, were more circumspect than doctors or journalists and, continuing the pre-1901 trend of religious liberty, cut through polemics when called upon to do so. Judge Reed of Ohio declared the Ohio State medical registration and examination law unconstitutional because it limited the practice of drugless medicine to osteopaths. The judge claimed that it ought to be amended to allow Christian Scientists to register as nondrug practitioners and to practice after passing an examination. Christian Science healing was legalized in Ohio with major qualifications. The Ohio Supreme Court maintained that the practice of unlicensed medicine was still illegal; however, as a pure religious belief, Science could not be circumscribed. In addition, Scientists could charge a fee only on the condition that they presented proper medical certification. To stop paying unqualified healers for services rendered was a valid exercise of state police power and was therefore constitutional.[44]

In the Progressive era, governors and state courts generally upheld the rights of Christian Scientists to practice and choose drugless treatment. Nebraska's governor vetoed a legislative bill opposing Christian Science on the grounds that it would have hurt osteopaths as well. From a purely legal standpoint, according to Judge Clifford P. Smith, the primary objective in considering Christian Science cases was "to maintain the right of every American citizen to choose the method or system he will employ to preserve his health . . . and to have the aid if he so desires of a practitioner of that system." And that is precisely what occurred in two 1905 landmark cases. In the first of these, the New Hampshire Supreme Court in *Spead v. Tomlinson* ruled in favor of the defendant Irving C. Tomlinson, former Universalist minister and then reader at the Christian Science Church at Concord, New Hampshire, upholding his right to practice healing in the state.[45] This ruling also overturned a previous decision of the lower court. In the second, *State v. Briggs*, Chief Justice Clark of the North Carolina Supreme Court upheld the view that all the state could do was regulate the use of dangerous drugs;[46] it could not proscribe the practice of drugless medicine since medicine itself was an "experimental rather than an exact science."[47]

The cumulative effect of epidemics, indictments, nativism and state court decisions was draining and debilitating. In the face of prejudice and insecurity, dogmatism doesn't help and Christian Scientists insisted on divine Principle's infinite ability to destroy "malignant cancer, consumption, tumors, locomotor-ataxia, blindness, deafness, drunkenness and immorality . . . to make men and women 'well,' morally and physically by the touch of divine love." Starting in 1901, 3,331 healers in the United States retreated[48] but did not quite submit. They were compelled, in certain ways, to "meet the law of the land" as it was then understood but the future would vindicate at least some of their practices.

Obviously something happened. It wasn't earth-shaking, but it was enough to quell the most bitter anti-Eddy tide and, most important, ease Christian Science into the twentieth century while, in essence, retaining the core of Gospel healing. Science in practice remains on a perilous tightrope and reverberates dangerously even in contemporary American life. Are there mutually exclusive systems of healing and, if so, should there be precautions against their implementation? Are such systems dangerous to nonusers living side-by-side with practitioners and, if so, how does a free society save the one without trampling the rights of the other? Where does liberty of religious practice end? Is there a boundary beyond which one cannot go? Must each case be decided individually?

In 1901, in response to negative publicity generally and infant mortality particularly, Mary Baker Eddy, nearly eighty years old, rescinded the Christian Science ban on vaccination; interestingly, we would be correct today if we defended an individual's right "not to be vaccinated against a contagious disease." The following year, the teaching and practice of obstetrics was given up, although in contemporary society, natural childbirth in a controlled environment, with physicians in attendance, is entirely acceptable. At about the same time, Scientists forswore a variety of surgical practices; today regular physicians are permitted to perform upon Scientists "mechanical procedures" not requiring drugs, such as filling cavities or setting broken bones. Vision adjustment through the fitting of eyeglasses is also considered consistent with Christian Science. However, whether Scientists are, as has been claimed, "free moral agents" not to be shunned by the church of their choice if they pursue traditional medical care is a matter of debate.[49]

William McCrackan, soon to be Augusta Stetson's replacement at New York City's First Church of Christ, Scientist, and, in 1902, head of the Christian Science Publishing Committee, vigorously defended Scientist John C. Lathrop, whose failure to heal seven-year-old Esther Quimby resulted in her death by diphtheria. Different forms of treatment, he stated, were permissible and legal if the parents so wished them; a Christian Science practitioner, just like a doctor, could not be held responsible for a patient's death. Two and a half weeks later, in the wake of these front-page headlines, manslaughter indictments and imminent trials, McCrackan, speaking on behalf of the Mother Church and Mary Baker Eddy, changed fronts. He ordered practitioners to cease treating infectious disease until laymen became better acquainted with Christian Science.[50]

In another apparent reversal, Eddy took hypodermic injections of morphine in 1903 to relieve the intense pain she suffered from kidney stones. Obviously it was not a step taken lightly at her Pleasant View home, since it would be "potentially embarrassing" should the procedure become public knowledge. It did not, at least immediately, since key members of her household constituted themselves as a "Board of Missionaries" whose function it was to "take instruction in the proper administration of hypodermic injections" so that Eddy might be cared for in the privacy of her own home.[51] At previous times in her life and at this point, too, she acted as only a nineteenth-century mortal would; the call to consistency was not nearly as driving as the twin voices of prophecy and divinity.

By the time of Mary Baker Eddy's death and shortly thereafter, the Christian Science Board of Directors, empowered to lead, inched ever so slowly toward some sort of medical compromise but in so doing, left important disciples—one might even say "purists" or "true believers"—behind. The issue was the proposed establishment of a Federal Health Bureau, which would standardize a number of health and disease-prevention practices. Founded in opposition to such a health bureau was the National League for Medical Freedom (NLMF) which was dedicated to the maintenance of citizen rights "against unjust, oppressive, paternal and un-American laws . . . related to the subject of health." Its president was Benjamin O. Flower, former editor of the *Arena*, a pro-Christian Science periodical.[52] On its advisory board were osteopaths, antivaccinationists, antivivisectionists, retail druggists, authors, corporate officials, ex-governors and ex-senators. A declaration of principles for the organization, adopted at its Chicago conference 21 November 1911, contained propositions opposing healing practice "monopolies" granted to any healing system, the attempt to remove the element of "choice" from those who used it to employ disparate modes of healing, the establishment of a "state" medicine, compulsory medical treatment, the infringement of federal "bureaucratic power" upon states' rights, discrimination in favor of any "healing" school, the use of public funds, public schools or other public institutions for the dissemination of literature favoring a particular healing system and the prosecution of a campaign denying the right of the sick to choose the sort of health care system they wished.[53]

Flower was quoted as saying that the NLMF contained "thousands of earnest, conscientious, scholarly and successful physicians. . . . These men will know that the healing art is an *art* rather than an exact science." The organization contained Christian Scientists, too, and was commended for its work by the Mother Church Board of Directors, from whom it solicited donations and "with which it acts in cooperation." This was not the first time the Board had acted in concert with a material organization since the death of Mary Baker Eddy. By effective lobbying, it convinced President Taft to amend "his general executive order relative to Panama, by virtue of which . . . Christian Scientists may continue" their healing practice in the Canal Zone. What the founder's personal reaction to these events might have been is unknown, since they occurred after her death, but one conclusion is sure: they anticipated an improved relationship with the public or, at least, some of the public. Not everyone was pleased, though, especially a once influential "true believer" who had viewed the Board's activities with a jaundiced eye several years before her own excommunication.

Augusta Stetson was an expert at interpreting the works of Mary Baker Eddy and nowhere could she find a passage giving license to Christian Scientists to join or fund material organizations. But she did find numerous passages to the contrary and she was still sufficiently influential to have her views printed in major magazines. "I understand that some members of the material organization of the Mother Church have given their weight to that League's [NLMF] efforts—they have united with material law . . . in direct disobedience to both the letter and the spirit . . . of *Science and Health* . . . and the other inspired writings." Like a reading of the Decalogue, Stetson cited chapter and verse:

Miscellaneous Writings, pages 79–80: Beware of joining any medical league which in any way obligates you to assist . . . vendors of patent pills, mesmerists, occultists, sellers of impure literature. . . . By rendering such a service, you lose much more than can be gained by mere unity on the single issue of opposition to unjust medical laws.

Miscellaneous Writings, page 81: To prevent all unpleasant and unchristian action . . . let each society of practitioners, the matter physicians and the metaphysicians agree to disagree and then patiently wait for God to decide . . . which is the true system of medicine.

Science and Health, p. 445: You render the divine law obscure and void when you weigh the human in the scale with the divine, or limit in any direction the omnipotence of God.

Science and Health, p. 444: If ecclesiastical sects or medical schools turn a deaf ear to the teachings of Christian Science, then part from these opponents as did Abraham when he parted from Lot. . . . mortals . . . are false . . . brethren.[54]

Stetson's feelings and actions with regard to the medical community and those who took issue with it were rather like George Washington's in his 1796 farewell address: friendships with all, alliances with none. Or, in the parlance of Christian Science, no compromise with boards, leagues, physicians, humanity or demonstrable, spiritual, truthful Christian Science law. Too idealistic and, perhaps, too willing to wish away or ignore the human frailties and distinctive personality of Mary Baker Eddy, Stetson could neither lead nor follow; and she certainly was not of a mind to treat with the "medicine men." Therefore, her alternative, as shaped by the 1909 decision of the Mother Church directorship, was to leave. Even if Science was to change little, it encouraged physicians to take another look.

What facilitated a modicum of Christian Science acceptance in the long run was not its intrinsic ability to respond. Universal healing faiths positing the illusory qualities of sickness, disease and death and derived from antique Gospel incidents do not respond much, nor are they supposed to. That is why they are protected by the religious clauses of the Constitution's First Amendment, though they practice a curative discipline with patients that potentially puts them all—patients and practitioners alike—at risk. In the first instance, the risk is mortal; in the second, it is usually legal. Some facts, however, support a *material* organizational shift, albeit slight, toward a truce, at least for the time being. The founder herself, her spokesmen and the Mother Church Board did place certain strictures on uninhibited Science healing practice between 1901 and 1903; after Mary Baker Eddy's death the Board, having scotched the Stetson insurgency, inclined further into the realm of participatory democracy with its Canal Zone minivictory, its alliance with the NLMF and its continued commitment to public visibility, balanced judgments, topical affairs and readability in the *Christian Science Monitor*. If nothing else, the Progressive period taught the Mother Church that there might be some benefit in curbing the faith's alien, un-American potential though detente, to use a term apropos to Theodore Roosevelt, might not be possible.

For its part American society did alter its response in the direction of tolerance to but not outright license for Christian Science. Freudianism finally arrived in the United States and became the rage of the 1920s, after a decade or so of transition and remolding in the collective works of Hall, Putnam and Holt. Descendant schools of psychotherapy, modeled on the ideas and investigations of Harry Stack Sullivan, Erich Fromm and Karen Horney "were eagerly developed in the American environment" and adapted to meet American needs. Social interactionists on the Dewey model, such as Charles H. Cooley and George H. Mead, put further stress on the "openness of . . . personality," its malleability and its "responsiveness to influences in the social environment, rather than the decisive formation of a fixed character" during childhood development. In the field of experimental medicine, the somatists gave way to comprehensive teaching and research institutions, staffed by researchers, clinicians and directors like Dr. William H. Welch of Johns Hopkins.[55] Germ theorists in the Pasteur mode, bacteriologists, virologists and their antibiotic discoveries—from crude Salvarsan to Penicillin—began to make inroads during the age of Roosevelt. In short, things unseen, whether personality disorders, microbes or "Scientific" Christianity no longer seem as formidable, impenetrable or resistant to analysis. At least one Christian Science detractor noted this, however grudgingly. In 1909 Frank Ballard saw an unbridgeable gulf separating Christian Science from modernity. A dozen years later, in another critical piece, he observed that "Mrs. Eddy's mental cure" anticipated psychotherapy as it was then being practiced in the 1920s.[56] The twain might never meet; the war of the Gospel healing Christian Scientists versus the physicians would continue ceaselessly, but it was a reprieve.

NOTES

1. *Medicare Handbook* (Baltimore: U.S. Department of Health and Human Services, 1989), 10.

2. Stephen Gottschalk, *The Emergence of Christian Science in American Religious Life* (Berkeley: University of California Press, 1975), 23, 130.

3. Charles M. Dollar et al., *America: Changing Times*, 2d ed. (New York: John Wiley and Sons, 1982), 316.

4. *Messages and Papers of the Presidents*, 20 vols. (New York: Bureau of National Literature, 1914), 19: encyclopedic index.

5. Mary Baker Eddy to Col. Sabin, 6 March 1899, Steno Records, 1907, Folder 2, 260, Streeter, Eddy Litigation Papers.

6. Donald Fleming, *William H. Welch and the Rise of Modern Medicine* (Boston: Little, Brown, 1954), 82, 106–7, 113.

7. Chandler Testimony, 24 May 1907, 28, Streeter, Eddy Litigation Papers.

8. "A Check to Christian Scientists," *New York Times*, 22 May 1890, 1; Norman Beasley, *The Cross and the Crown* (New York: Duell, Sloan and Pearce, 1953), 59.

9. S. V. Clevenger, "Christian Science," *Open Court* 1 (21 July 1887): 322; David Allyn Gorton, "The Conflict Between Mysticism and Rational Philosophy," *New York Medical Times* (December 1888): 21–28; "Personal" (editorial), *New York Times*, 14 March 1898, 6; Henry Reed Hopkins, *The Progress of Eddyism* (*American Medical Quarterly* Reprint, January 1900), 5.

10. "Is John Sherman's Antitrust Obsolete?" *Business Week*, 23 March 1974, 47.

11. San Mateo v. Southern Pacific, 13 F. 145 (1882).

12. Santa Clara County v. Southern Pacific, 118 U.S. 394 (1886).

13. United States v. E. C. Knight Co., 156 U.S. 1 (1895).

14. Addyston Pipe and Steel Co. v. United States, 175 U.S. 211 (1889).

15. Standard Oil v. United States, 221 U.S. 1 (1911).

16. Herbert Albert Laurens Fisher, *Our New Religion* (London: Ernest Benn, 1929), 65; "Christian Science Victims" (editorial), *New York Daily Tribune*, 25 September 1889, 6; "Christian Science Victims" (editorial), *New York Daily Tribune*, 5 February 1893, 18; "A Vagary of Christian Science," *Brooklyn Daily Eagle*, 12 March 1892, 1.

17. "Christian Science Extraordinary" (editorial), *Brooklyn Daily Eagle*, 8 August 1892, 4; "Victim of Christian Science," *New York Times*, 10 May 1890, 1; "A Check to Christian Scientists," *New York Times*, 22 May 1890, 1; "More Medicine and Less Faith," *New York Times*, 3 September 1890, 2; "Christian Scientists Indicted," *New York Times*, 23 January 1894, 3; "Topics of the Times" (editorial), *New York Times*, 20 October 1898, 6; "Faith Healers Arrested," *New York Times*, 9 May 1899, 7; "Diphtheria Cases," *New York Daily Tribune*, 2 June 1899, 4; "Cure Treatment Fails," *New York Times*, 22 June 1899, 3; "Dr. Called Too Late," *New York Times*, 8 March 1900, 7; "Woman Refuses Aid and Dies," *New York Times*, 6 November 1900, 7; "Killed by Christian Science," *New York Times*, 30 May 1901, 1; "Christian Science Arrests," *New York Times*, 25 May 1899, 1.

18. "Death Due to Faith Cure," *New York Times*, 24 June 1899, 2; "Christian Science as Crime," *New York Times*, 1 June 1898, 7; "Editorial," *New York Times*, 3 February 1898, 6; "Editorial," *New York Times*, 2 October 1895, 4; "Topics of the Times," *New York Times*, 8 November 1900, 6.

19. Gottschalk, *Emergence of Christian Science*, 6–7; Lloyd Morris, *Postscript to Yesterday: America, The Last Fifty Years* (New York: Random House, 1947), xxiii.

20. "Topics of the Times," *New York Times*, 28 October 1898, 6; "Faith Cure Murders" (editorial), *New York Times*, 11 November 1898, 6; "Attended by Christian Scientists," *Brooklyn Daily Eagle*, 20 November 1898, 1; "Christian Science" (editorial), *Brooklyn Daily Eagle*, 5 December 1898, 3; "Harold Frederic," *Brooklyn Daily Eagle*, 19 October 1898, 6; "Faith Curists Released," *New York Daily Tribune*, 6 December 1898, 1.

21. "A Blow at Christian Science," *New York Times*, 5 October 1890, 4; "Christian Scientist Fined," *New York Times*, 22 January 1898, 11; "Faith Cure Fails Again," *New York Times*, 26 February 1900, 1; "Christian Scientist Arrested," *New York Daily Tribune*, 8 November 1897, 7; John Knott, "Christian Science," *Westminster Review*, 167 (February 1907): 169.

22. Augusta E. Stetson, *Reminiscences, Sermons and Correspondence Proving Adherence to the Principle of Christian Science as Taught by Mary Baker Eddy* (New York: G. P. Putnam's Sons, 1913), 405–13, 1044.

23. Brad Holland, "The Price of Faith," *Yankee* 56 (July 1992): 119, 123.

24. "Topics of the Times," *New York Times*, 26 March 1898, 6; "Topics of the Times," *New York Times*, 31 October 1898, 6; "Christian Science Churches as Irreligious Corporations" (editorial), *Brooklyn Daily Eagle*, 24 August 1901, 4.

25. William A. Purrington, "The Case Against Christian Science," *North American Review* 169 (August 1899): 199, idem, *Christian Science: An Exposition* (New York: E. B. Treat, 1900), 7–26; "To Curb Christian Science," *New York Times*, 29 July 1899, 7.

26. "The Christian Scientists," *New York Times*, 13 November 1898, 12; "To Abolish Faith Healers," *New York Times*, 12 May 1899, 12; "Against Christian Science," *New York Times*, 9 July 1899, 1; "To Check Faith Curists," *New York Times*, 14 July 1899, 1.

27. "Christian Scientists Win," *New York Times*, 17 March 1898, 3; "Christian Scientists Win," *New York Times*, 23 November 1901, 3; "Mrs. Moses A. Davis's Bequest," *New York Daily Tribune*, 24 July 1900, 6; "Christian Scientist Held for Manslaughter," *New York Times*, 24 October 1902, 1; "Christian Scientists Must Stand Trial," *New York Times*, 31 October 1902, 1; "Quimby Child's Death," *New York Daily Tribune*, 22 October 1902, 6; "Coroner Begins Inquiry," *New York Daily Tribune*, 23 October 1902, 7; "Coroner's Jury Verdict," *New York Daily Tribune*, 24 October 1902, 4; "Christian Science as Manslaughter" (editorial), *Brooklyn Daily Eagle*, 2 November 1902, 7; Stetson, *Reminiscences, Sermons and Correspondence*, 525.

28. "Philadelphians Refused a Charter," *New York Daily Tribune*, 17 September 1902, 27; "Court Says Christian Science Is a Pernicious Fallacy," *New York Times*, 5 October 1902, 32; Ezra Morgan Wood, *Schools for Spirits* (Pittsburgh: Joseph Horner, 1903), 62.

29. "Rights of Faith Curists," *New York Times*, 5 August 1899, 3; "Personal" (editorial), *New York Times*, 24 March 1898, 6.

30. John Ferguson, "Faith Healing, Mind Curing, Christian Science," *Canadian Magazine* 6 (December 1895), 183, 185–86; "War on Faith Healing," *New York Times*, 2 April 1900, 5; Purrington, "Case Against Christian Science," 192, 197, 199–200, 204, 206; "Christian Science and Liberty," *Spectator* 81, (12 November 1898): 681; "Inverted Witchcraft" (editorial), *Spectator* 86, (25 May 1901): 761.

31. "Christian Scientists Banned in Oklahoma," *Brooklyn Daily Eagle*, 8 March 1899, 5; "Georgia Refuses Charter," *New York Daily Tribune*, 21 April 1901, 4; "Metaphysical Healing" (editorial), *Outlook* 62 (15 July 1899): 606, "Topics of the Times" (editorial), *New York Times*, 9 May 1901, 8; "Topics of the Times" (editorial), *New York Times*, 20 June 1900, 6; "Topics of the Times" (editorial), *New York Times*, 29 July 1899, p. 6.

32. Clifford P. Smith, *Christian Science and Legislation* (Boston: Christian Science, 1905), 16, 22–23, 35; "Topics of the Times" (editorial), *New York Times*, 24 December 1898, 6; "Topics of the Times" (editorial), *New York Times*, 31 December 1898, 6; "Ohio Court Decision in Favor," *New York Daily Tribune*, 18 November 1903, 5.

33. State v. Walter Mylod, 20 R.I. 632 (1898).

34. Carol Norton, *Legal Aspects of Christian Science* (Boston: Christian Science, 1899), 5–14; "Metaphysical Healing" (editorial), *Outlook* (15 July 1899), 62, 606; "Faith Cure and Medicine" (editorial), *New York Times*, 10 March 1898, 6; "Personal" (editorial), *New York Times*, 12 March 1898, 6; "Punish the Impostors," *New York Times*, 25 November 1898, 4.

35. Stetson, *Reminiscences, Sermons and Correspondence*, 23, 68–69, 94, 115, 917, 964, 1133, 1143.

36. George E. Mowry, *The Era of Theodore Roosevelt and the Birth of Modern America 1900–1912* (New York: Harper and Row, 1958), 207; Fleming, *William H. Welch*, 143, 152–55, 173–74; Dumas Malone and Basil Rauch, *The New Nation 1865–1917* (New York: Appleton-Century Crofts, 1960), 295.

37. F. H. Matthews, "The Americanization of Sigmund Freud: Adaptations of Psychoanalysis before 1917," *Journal of American Studies* (April 1967): 39–62. Included in *Builders of American Institutions*, 2d ed., ed. by Frank Freidel et al. (Chicago: Rand McNally, 1972), 2: 160–62, 166, 173–76.

38. "Christian Science Startles Physicians, *New York Times*, 28 January 1901, 1.

39. Mary Baker Eddy to "Benny" (Ebenezer J. Foster Eddy), 29 October 1896, Steno Records, 1907, Folder 2, 253, Streeter, Eddy Litigation Papers; "Killed by Christian Science," *New York Times*, 30 May 1901, 1.

40. "Dies of Disease He Defied," *New York Times*, 26 July 1902, 5; "Dies Spurning Physicians," *New York Times*, 3 March 1903, 7; "Christian Science Fails to Cure," *New York Times*, 6 November 1903, 1; "Christian Science Did It," *New York Times*, 19 August 1903, 1; "Topics of the Times," *New York Times*, 9 November 1904, 8; "Christian Scientist's Death," *New York Times*, 21 July 1903, 11; "Rochester Woman Dies Refusing Aid," *New York Daily Tribune*, 1 August 1906, 4.

41. "Doctors Attack 'Healers,' " *New York Times*, 11 June 1901, 1; "Court of Appeals Decision on Pierson Case," *New York Daily Tribune*, 14 October 1903, 14; "Pierson Conviction Reversed," *New York Daily Tribune*, 27 March 1903, 1; "New Trial for Christian Scientist," *New York Times*, 10 May 1903, p. 16; "Stemming the Christian Science Tide," *Current Literature* 47 (July 1909): 71–73.

42. "Mind Healing Attacked," *New York Times*, 15 April 1902, 2; "Danger of Public Health" (Letter to the Editor), *New York Times*, 12 November 1904, 8.

43. George M. Gould, "Some Intellectual Weeds of American Growth," *Montreal Medical Journal* (August 1904): 2–4; James Rowland Angell, "Christian Science from a Psychologist's Viewpoint," *World To-Day* 8 (April 1905): 406; B. Calvert,

Science and Health (n.p., n.d.), 7, 10–11, 13, 22; Gordon Clark, *The Church of St. Bunco* (New York: Abbey Press, 1901), 25.

44. "Favors Christian Science," *New York Times*, 19 April 1904, 1; "Ohio Court Decision in Favor," *New York Daily Tribune*, 18 November 1903, 5; "Against Christian Science," *New York Times*, 3 March 1905, 1.

45. Spead v. Tomlinson, 59 A. 376 (N.H. 1904).

46. State v. Briggs, 41 S.E. 676 (N.C. 1902).

47. Smith, *Christian Science and Legislation*, 12, 15–16, 23, 26–28, 36; "New Hampshire Court Decision," *New York Daily Tribune*, 7 October 1903, 2.

48. Chandler Testimony, 1907, 28, Streeter, Eddy Litigation Papers.

49. Burt Neuborne, "In Praise of Inconsistency: The Religious Clauses of the Constitution," *Congress Monthly* 59 (November–December 1992): 3; "Literature," review of Georgine Milmine, *The Life of Mary Baker Eddy* and Francis Edward Marsten, *The Mask of Christian Science* in *The Nation*, 15 (10 February 1910), 138–39; Holland, "Price of Faith," 112, 114.

50. "Ready to Aid Healer," *New York Times*, 25 October 1902, 6; "Christian Scientists' Change of Front," *New York Times*, 14 November 1902, 2.

51. Julius Silberger, Jr., *Mary Baker Eddy: An Interpretive Biography of the Founder of Christian Science* (Boston: Little, Brown, 1980), 215.

52. See, for example, Katharine Coolidge, "Modern Expressions of the Oldest Philosophy," *The Arena* 7 (April 1893): 554–67.

53. Stetson, *Reminiscences, Sermons and Correspondence*, 1156–57.

54. Ibid., 961–66, 1133, 1137–39, 1155, 1158–59.

55. Matthews, "Americanization of Sigmund Freud," 177–78; Fleming, *William H. Welch*, 202.

56. Frank Ballard, "The Menace of Eddyism," *London Quarterly Review* 136 (July 1921): 62.

6

Monopoly and Muckraking

Beneath the cold eye of a microscope, an object under observation is magnified hundreds or thousands of times. Often, most of the mass is ignored, no matter how large, as the fine adjustments are manipulated and the lens is focused on a single particle of interest. Muckrakers, journalists so named by President Theodore Roosevelt at a 17 March 1906 meeting of the Gridiron Club and renamed with negative connotation a month later at a public ceremony laying the cornerstone of a congressional office building,[1] operated in much the same fashion during their 1902–6 heyday and their 1907–12 decline, but the objects subjected to their unblinking gaze were human and the heat generated by their journalistic light as it descended upon the intended prey was nearly unbearable.

Following Mary Baker Eddy's 1881 departure from the small town to the big city, the rise of Christian Science was meteoric, spectacular and successful. Even her most implacable opponents suggested that Eddy possessed a great deal of business acumen, perhaps born of a need or compulsion to survive alone in a dog-eat-dog world. Much like Rockefeller or Carnegie, it seemed, she consolidated her organization and concentrated decision-making power in her own hands; she was the picture of a daring entrepreneur and was labeled a "robber baron" by social and political commentators. Her religion offered the businessman precisely what he needed: "Overworked . . . overwrought and overworried, his practical training affords him no philosophy. His one need is serenity and . . . mental rest. He needs a mental anchorage that sustains . . . but across the anchor must be written 'absolute certainty.' There must be no questionings. . . . Christian Science affords its believers just that."[2] Characteristically, a muckraker on the offensive would spin that piece, taken from the Spokane, Washington *Inland Herald*, until it achieved a negative rotation. The *Atlantic Monthly*, a genteel journal on the wane and not known for muckraking, had this to say about the public's desire and taste for Christian Science a month after Theodore Roosevelt took the oath of office as the nation's twenty-sixth president: "the public wants . . . to obtain . . . cloying sweetness . . . optimism . . . and peppermint sayings. . . . [It] pays a high price to Mrs. Eddy for the privilege of being deluded into believing that all is sweetness and light in an era of stress and materialism."[3] And this was 1901, just before the rush to reform. With the ascendancy of Progressivism, there occurred a reorientation of the anti-Christian Science argument into a more hostile framework. Journalism, catering to a mass market, employing modern technology, boosting sales via enormously well-packaged, literate exposés on a variety of topics—political, ethnic, industrial and religious—offered the enterprising writer an opportunity to investigate, embroider and sensationalize. The technique, introduced by Populist muckraking antecedent Edward Bellamy in his proregulatory *Looking Backward* (1887) and honed in *Wealth v. Commonwealth* (1894) by Standard Oil critic Henry Demarest Lloyd was perfected after 1900 by the volatile muckrakers.

Having graduated from the Gay Nineties, which was really a time of conflict for all those below the management level in American life, the public was assaulted by strikes, like that of 1902 in the anthracite coal fields, murder, as in the 1906–7 accusation leveled against miner/unionist "Big Bill" Haywood by the state of Idaho and highway robbery, like that indulged in by the Northern Securities Company and the beef trust. The "chosen" would answer—those whose weapons were realistic novels, satire and periodicals other than the worn-out *Century*, *Harper's* and *Scribners*; those whom Theodore Roosevelt claimed could not see the crown for the thorns or the mirror through the mire; those for whom the muckraker of John Bunyan's 1687 *Pilgrim's Progress* bore a special meaning. There was, nevertheless, an affinity that Roosevelt shared with the writers: youth, except in the case of Mark Twain, a certain tendency toward moralizing, preachiness and a pugnacious, confrontational character. Where they diverged was in perspective; while the muckrakers stated the American dilemma, Roosevelt emphasized a direct solution.

The muckraker "family" was large and varied. There were some tireless investigators and journals, while others in both categories exposed only intermittently. A favorite topic of the *Ladies Home Journal* was patent medicine as was medical quackery with *Collier's*, whose ace reporter in this area was Samuel Hopkins Adams. *Everybody's*, with a circulation of 735,000 exceeded only by *McClure's* and *Collier's*,[4] favored Thomas Lawson's insider exposé of stock market speculation in his serially run "Frenzied Finance," while *World's Work* was known for its authoritative articles on Chicago's stockyards and *Women's Home Companion* concentrated on child labor. In 1906 popular author David Graham Phillips blew the lid off legislative skullduggery in his "Treason of the Senate," which increased the circulation of *Cosmopolitan* by 50 percent.[5] Equally adept at outselling the literary periodicals of the pre-Progressive years were *Human Life, Hampton's, Success, Pearson's* and *Hearst's Magazine*. Either you had to go with the crowd or you gave way.

Assigning a single agenda to muckrakers doesn't do them or their commitments justice. "Cleanup" is a rather vague term with many nuances and meanings. It could be individual, communal, moral, political, social, technological or any combination of them. For example it might be convenient to group David Graham Phillips, Upton Sinclair and Charles Edward Russell as Socialists, though they wrote on a diversity of topics, including New York City's Trinity Church as slumlord, the case for government ownership of railroads, machinations on Capitol Hill and the meatpacking industry. The post-1907 editor of *McClure's*, Burton J. Hendrick, declaimed on insurance fraud while George Kibbe Turner's beat was municipal corruption at Tammany Hall, intemperance, prostitution and concentrations of wealth. Research or editing for many of the *McClure's* pieces was done by either Mark Sullivan or Willa Cather, the latter in the early stages of a distinguished literary career that would include a Pulitzer Prize in 1922 and such classic works of fiction as *O Pioneers!, My Antonia* and *Death Comes to the Archbishop*.

In essence, the *McClure's* group sounded and acted very much like their boss, Samuel Sidney McClure, an Irish immigrant and a believer in the American ethic of Horatio Alger success. He had been educated at Knox College in Galesburg, Illinois, where he became inured to the heady mixture of Republicanism, revivalism and idealism that seemed to trail farm boys and village youth who chose to make their fortune back east. As a result of his own initiative, fundraising and recruitment abilities and organizational talents, *McClure's Magazine* was founded in 1893. It was challenged by a host of publications, including newspapers, but it remained the nonpareil of muckraking until the owner lost control in 1911.

Reform, to McClure, meant the New Nationalism, Theodore Roosevelt's program of democratized Hamiltonian ideology, suitable for industrialized America and fully articulated in Herbert Croly's 1909 Progressive summation, *The Promise of American Life*. Croly stated that corporatism was permanent, as was big labor and technology. Realistically, the United States could not—and should not—return to Jeffersonianism; the twentieth-century triumvirate was here to stay and the national agenda was to learn to live with it. As for the fate of efficient government, it rested, or should rest, in the hands of enlightened leaders, presumably powerful officials operating in a powerful state free from selfish interests. All *McClure's* challenged was capitalism's lawlessness, not the free enterprise system as a whole. It was, thus, in tune with Roosevelt and bore the stamp of social Christianity. An early McClure acquisition was former Knox College president and intellectual Presbyterian—John Huston Finley. With an already enviable career and more to come as president of City College of New York, commissioner of education for the State of New York, associate editor of the *New York Times* and commissioner for the American Red Cross in Palestine following World War I, he was always a man with a "Christian" message. "America," he said in 1919, "you must send not only the Red Cross to this front. You must send . . . Christ. . . . [Y]ou must have a part in the redemption of the Holy Land." McClure himself felt that "the one great rallying point is the Golden Rule; and the never failing guide is the life and teachings of Jesus Christ."[6]

Such was the shared philosophy at *McClure's* and its burden of redemptive, sociological Christianity weighed heavily on an earlier group, arguably more talented than those already mentioned. With the exception of Ida Tarbell, who was six to eight years older than the rest and born in Pennsylvania, all were born after the Civil War in the Midwest or far West—Kansas, Illinois, California, Wisconsin; their mentalities were not given to the psychological and physical borders of the East. Two of them had a tenuous connection with Knox College—William Allen White's mother was educated there and the father of Lincoln Steffens was located in that region until the Civil War; Tarbell attended Allegheny College in Meadville, Pennsylvania, an equally "congenial environment" for "abolitionist, temperance and suffragist sentiments."

Educated at Michigan State, Ray Stannard Baker had an American dream but it withered rapidly. His father was a "bankrupt . . . merchant and manufacturer" who had gone west in search of acreage to farm, fresh opportunity or sheer survival. Lincoln Steffens' and Ida's Tarbell's fathers did the same. Speaking for them all might have been the younger Baker, who wrote of his father's search " 'in America, or indeed . . . the world . . . for free land, free forests, free rivers . . . we were living on the last frontier.' " Whether he found it wasn't as vital as the quest; and, in the case of Tarbell, the father's adventure ended in his return to Pennsylvania, his emergence as an independent oil entrepreneur and his victimization by a greater entrepreneur, John D. Rockefeller.[7] From the creative tension of their parents' lives there emerged in the children a common religious and political bond forged in adulthood at *McClure's* and culminating in *The Shame of the Cities*, "The History of the Standard Oil Company" and *Following the Color Line*. Though the last was produced out of *McClure's* direct influence, all of these classics said as much about the spiritual proclivities of the authors as they did about social injustice.

"A Jesus complex" was what non-McClurist muckraker Upton Sinclair was said to possess; a little strong, perhaps, but only a little, when applied to the *McClure's* staff of 1902–6. "Many of the muckrakers had been exposed in childhood to . . . gospel Christianity" which, in turn, suffused their mature writings. Ray Stannard Baker was reared on "the stern old Presbyterian Bible" and he tried to sway President Roosevelt to the belief that the color line in the South, much like the plight of the coal miners, "demanded the 'teaching of . . . Jesus Christ—which works in the individual man,' " who must, of necessity, "replace his selfishness with a social conscious-ness." Ida Tarbell was born in a log cabin in Pennsylvania, resided in somewhat more sophisticated Paris, researched and wrote on Napoleon, Lincoln and Rockefeller with admirable clarity but the experience bubbling to memory's surface was the mourner's bench of her girlhood church, kneeling there, knowing she was a sinner. Why did she judge John D. Rockefeller? He is a Christian, she once said, and the "Golden Rule" gives me the right.

The "Golden Rule." As doer and dreamer, over a long career as journal-ist, lecturer, political philosopher, elder statesman to expatriates and editor of *McClure's Magazine* in his mid- and late thirties, Lincoln Steffens was, at heart, a utopian. His exacting, heavily documented, sociological case stud-ies of urban corruption in 1904 St. Louis, Minneapolis, Pittsburgh, Phila-delphia and Chicago won him popular recognition as did his later unorthodox views on revolution and communism. He persuaded millions of readers to reexamine the nature of American truth, and he sometimes played the anticlerical, but he returned again and again to his core, like going home to the California of his imagination. Perhaps it never was, but he thought it was, and that made it so. Steffens, as a reformer, was an evangelist, an advocate of Christian solutions to social problems, a burning conscience as was his grandfather, "a rigid Catholic in his youth," but a convert "to the Methodist church militant." Like Diogenes in search of an honest man, Steffens searched for a real " 'Christian in politics.' " Reform Darwinists all, the muckrakers sought the desideratum of social Christians, a more respectable level of the status quo.[8] That desire rendered them shakers, not movers, having more in common with the management-ori-ented Theodore Roosevelt than even they realized. Had they reflected upon it a while, they might have even softened on Christian Science, whose evolutionary rather than revolutionary principles gave scientists, psy-chologists, ministers and philosophers some "new age" sustenance. But the business of *McClure's* wasn't compromise nor was it Mary Baker Eddy's. So, it was natural that she'd be taken to task by this ardently militant and neoconservative group.

When Eddy retired voluntarily in 1889, the future of her movement was jeopardized. Obviously, the loose, informal structure of her organization, fine for rural New England, would require revamping in metropolitan Boston. Crises that would have started tongues wagging in Lynn became major disasters forty miles away; matters once settled in a relatively private fashion, albeit bitterly, were now debated at breakfast tables across the nation. The 1892 "return" of Eddy at age seventy-one indicated, at first, that she had solved the problem. Only when she appeared remote, absolute[9] and male-dominated was her actual intent, or lack of such, suspect. No matter what the cost, it appeared that consolidation would instill sanity and respectability to her offspring.

Provisions were undertaken for the building of a Mother Church in Boston to be named *The* Church of Christ, Scientist, and presided over, at least nominally, by Eddy. Twelve loyal adherents composed the Board of Trustees whose duty it was to pass on all membership. In the ensuing fifteen years, the Scientists founded branch churches in many major cities, totaling nearly seven hundred by June 1906, the date of the Mother Church's extension and ceremonial rededication.[10] A number of these churches were not modest edifices but large, impressive, stone-solid monuments. The treasury was filled because Eddy and staff gave nothing away; she sold her Bibles, books and trinkets to those who had already invested time and money in her religion; in 1910 her personal fortune was estimated—perhaps overestimated—at $7 million.[11]

Her personal and organizational inconsistencies were apparent. Christian Science was a protest against materialism; yet the foundation on which it rested contradicted its premise. Going a step further, the movement's success was based upon its ability to promote, sell, persuade and recruit a group in America who looked for relief but were not impoverished. This is not a crime, not even a misdemeanor. Nor is it a fault for a faith to concern itself with fiscal affairs because money is essential to its survival, solvency and growth; the smaller the group, the greater the demand. Unfortunately, when Science flourished at the turn of the century, the media offered its journalists no Emmys for objectivity or awards for comparative research into similar institutions. "Debunking was the order of the day"; sometimes means and ends were either tangled or ill-defined by muckrakers and independent reformers. Science affirmed that social change and reform were not enough; spiritual change, an involuntary "logos," must complement them. As social Christians, the muckrakers did not analyze the differences in emphasis[12] and cared even less; they were young, energetic individuals, who tended to see the opposition, if that's what it was, as "the other"—false rather than flawed. In Boston, Eddy became the object, not of sober examination, but urban cleanup.

Due to the small town nature of Christian Science, Mary Baker Eddy's trained healers escaped a great deal of devastating publicity prior to 1889. Following the reorganization three years later, the faith, at its new location, was inundated with unwanted notoriety. No longer amused, reporters covered Eddy's lectures with mounting interest. It seemed as if Christian Science were concealed behind a wall of mumblings and ineffectual gibbering. Even if she was incautious, and Eddy often was in the Massachusetts villages, it was possible to maintain low visibility, but her rural "fortune" deserted her in Boston. The Woodbury humiliation, misapplication of treatment resulting in death,[13] assorted indictments against practitioners, unfavorable court decisions and tensions of long standing between the old guard (Augusta Stetson) and the new (the Mother Church Board of Directors) created a flammable pile and, at *McClure's*, 1906 was a flammable year.

Some of the bad news in American society had dissipated by summer, with the passage of the Meat Inspection, Pure Food and Drug and Hepburn Acts. This was good for Americans but probably the opposite for *McClure's* muckrakers and, by inference, Mary Baker Eddy. Outside of David Graham Phillips' "Treason of the Senate" for *Cosmopolitan*, there was simply less to write about. The pro-Square Deal staffers at *McClure's* respected the president's technique. After all, they were a lot like him: none were revolutionaries, merely service-oriented Protestants[14] with a hint of condescension, a whisper of status anxiety, properly directed militance within a capitalist framework and, possibly, a waning raison d'etre. They were restless and within a year the team of Steffens, Tarbell, White, Baker and satirist-cartoonist Finley Peter Dunne bid *McClure's* farewell to launch their own *American Magazine*. The research undertaken by others for a potentially good Eddy exposé would be the next administration's responsibility. It would have to smooth the kinks and the quirks but no one famous jockeyed for the story.

Caught in an administrative transition, the Mary Baker Eddy saga was not all it could have been. Superficially, it was a compelling replacement for improperly labeled drugs, rapacious magnates, exploited miners and corrupt mayors: it had a unique feel, replete with social, economic, medical and religiously un-Protestant ramifications. At the time they took it on, in the summer of 1906, all they knew at *McClure's* about Eddy was what they read in the papers and the curious fact that an octogenarian failed to appear at the rededication of a Church she had founded. There was a lot of work to be done by December, when an editorial heralding the series anticipated the unmasking of a "slightly deranged woman of mystery . . . a pernicious peddler of lies and the queen of a well-fed, profitable business enterprise called Christian Science."[15] It is difficult to say what the editorship really felt. Both shifts, outgoing and incoming, and owner Samuel McClure said little according to *McClure's Magazine* biographer Harold Wilson. He devotes virtually no space to this story or its creator, a New York housewife,[16] obscure before its writing and equally so thereafter, by the name of Georgine Milmine. Her chief assets may have been her abilities in gathering gossip and absorbing criticism; she was thoroughly edited by Mark Sullivan and novelist-in-training Willa Cather.

A neat mingling of events made the Milmine series hot. In the early months of its run, Joseph Pulitzer's *World* collaborated with Eddy's two sons in fomenting the "Next Friends Suit," which didn't play out until September; Mark Twain could hardly contain himself either and material he had published in 1899 and 1903 was reissued in 1907 by Harper and Brothers. Indeed, this was not a kind and gentle world but there was something unsavory and unseemly in these disclosures. Targeting an old woman, near the end of her life, must have violated some code of Victorian fair play, which seemed to be going the way of Victorianism generally.

Perhaps that is the reason this tale, too good to miss in terms of circulation, was gladly passed to Milmine by star-studded journalists.

Milmine's byline appeared on what really amounted to a book—more than two hundred pages—in fourteen installments between January 1907 and June 1908. The facts of Eddy's life are there as are depositions from a host of relatives, quasi-friends, acquaintances, doctors, mental healers, spiritualists and entrepreneurs who walked a mile or more with her in the previous four decades. What should have emerged—it might be asking too much for 1907—is a gender portrait of a Victorian life, its discontents, inspirational moments and individual eccentricities. Whether it adds up is anybody's guess but it doesn't mean the attempt should be abandoned; if, indeed, that's what it means, actor Charles Laughton should have walked off the *I, Claudius* set in 1937 instead of muttering, as he stalked around the stage, "I can't find the man." He realized that there exists a vital, perhaps indispensable connection among art, biography and personal history. In justice to her subject, Milmine should have struggled to "find the woman." What she found were readers.

Milmine's treatment of Mary Baker Eddy's youth, maturity and career was in the best *McClure's* tradition: unrelentingly hostile. Since the question of Eddy's sanity was raised during the "Next Friends" affair, Milmine's relating themes of Eddy's alleged history of mental imbalance, spiritualist and Malicious Animal Magnetism (MAM) preoccupations, and "masterful" personality were in vogue. *The New York World* and *McClure's* condemned Mary Baker Eddy before a gavel commanded silence in a court of law, while the celebrated alienist Alan McLane Hamilton reiterated his 1900 sentiments, expressed during the Helen Brush litigation—that Christian Science was an insane delusion and its founder a hopeless lunatic. Dorian Gray came out only slightly worse with Oscar Wilde. As a caricature, Eddy became the evil genius, twisted with raging passion and consumed by a lust for power; amply endowed with shrewd, peasant cunning, she charmed her followers and erected marble churches.[17]

Somehow, it never occurred to Milmine and staff that the facts don't always speak for themselves, especially when one deposes all sorts of people, some of whom are requested to recall and remain objective about associations and events from a deep, but not quite dead, past. Acquaintances with grudges were welcomed, one of whom was Hannah Sanborn, "a source of . . . sensational charges" against Eddy, who recalled how the latter once, seventy years before, stole her beau. A "muddled" statement of a Mrs. Richard Haseltine, included by Milmine, misrepresented Eddy's claim of spiritual control by Jesus Christ to mean that she was a medium; on several occasions, Eddy's early associations with spiritualists was taken to be "full-fledged" belief. Usually, Milmine knew when she employed sources with a bias, but abjured a "balance."

In her seventies, Mrs. M. C. Whittier, Eddy's second cousin, fourteen years of age at the time of Abigail Baker's death, testified that young Mary's troubles stemmed from " 'hysteria mingled with bad temper' "; she volunteered that older Mary traduced sensible people into malign beliefs; had she lived in 1692 Salem "I'm sure her life" would have been " 'taken upon the gallows.' " George Quimby, Phineas's son and no admirer of Mary Baker Eddy, questioned Milmine's fact-gathering technique in the composition of a passage involving his late father's work. On 13 March 1906 he wrote her concerning "Questions and Answers," a manuscript Eddy carried in the late 1860s but did not display; "she allowed a few of her early students to read it but did not teach from it." Apparently all, or significant portions of it, were derived from Phineas P. Quimby. An elderly Horace Wentworth, deposed by Milmine, claimed Eddy relied upon it as a method of instruction. " 'Why don't you find out certainly whether Mrs. Eddy did teach from that article? . . . I've only the Stoughton man's word for it.' " But Milmine knew what she was doing; she later wrote that her sources and witnesses were not unimpeachable.[18]

Milmine was not always wrong, especially in describing the controversy surrounding the pre-1881 career of Mary Baker Eddy, but she is untrustworthy because her information is skewed and she casts a jaundiced eye at her subject, vouchsafing her few, if any, human qualities. Eddy is, by turns, guilty of vanity, ignorance, theft, vengefulness, compulsions, witchcraft, mesmerism and the evil eye. One forgets after a while—and Milmine certainly would applaud this—that hindsight creates its own motives and opportunities.

Foresight might, too, but it's neither as predictable nor accurate. Georgine Milmine lacked the foresight to change her strident tone and insistent judgment in the final installments of her series run. In just a few short months, she and *McClure's*-type journalism lost their base. Following the recession of 1907, U.S. Steel executives H. C. Frick and E. H. Gary bought Tennessee Iron and Steel, thus stabilizing the American economy by creating a bigger and more efficient combine. Presiding over and encouraging the formation of efficient consolidation in the national interest was Theodore Roosevelt, beloved at *McClure's*, but making good on his 1904 declaration to decline any future nomination. With his departure, the urge to muckrake just wouldn't be the same. "Mrs. Eddy's Book and Doctrine," a ten-page indictment of Christian Science and Christian Scientists, was anticlimactic when it closed out the series in June 1908. In the same month and year, Roosevelt was playing tennis when his hand-picked successor, William Howard Taft, Secretary of War and stolid legalist, was nominated on the first ballot by the Republican party. He was lauded by the outgoing president as a man equally in touch with all his constituents "upright, disinterested, sympathetic, hard-working, honest, dutiful, fearless" and pragmatic; a "big boy" with glowing face who could not, on 19 June

1908—might never be able to—find the words to express his pleasure. He was "proud and happy"[19] as was his mentor, Theodore Roosevelt, who within a month sent the Great White Fleet out of San Francisco to impress the diplomats of East and West, but particularly the Japanese. The Eddy piece was thankfully concluded but it aged immeasurably in 1908; in tone and presentation, much like *McClure's* itself, it was a dinosaur.

Milmine wished to "stop the world" but she couldn't. Not only was the national scenery different but the Christian Science landscape shifted right under her feet. Those she supported in her March and May 1908 installments, George Washington Glover and Ebenezer J. Foster Eddy, were losers as of September 1907, when the "Next Friends" litigation was dismissed. They both submitted, despite the fact that Milmine was partial to a "wronged, gladly abandoned son" and a naive adopted son, never entrepreneurial or opportunistic in his own right but misled and misunderstood, an ineffectual Eddy dupe. Ever the aggressor, Milmine contrasted the goodness of New Thought and its founder Walter Felt Evans with the predatory nature of Christian Science and Mary Baker Eddy. Whereas New Thought was the product of independent writers and investigators who "affirmed the power of the mind," Christian Science was idiocy, offering nothing of value to individual healing or American faith. On the practical side, however, Eddy was marvelously efficient, a dynamo, a juggernaut; at least, she was some sort of machine because she certainly acted and spoke inhumanely: "Poverty is only a form of error. It can be abolished as readily as sin . . . disease or old age; 'at-oneness with God' " was evident in prosperity and in the overcoming of infirmity. If Christian Science, concluded Milmine, were universally believed and practiced, it would be "the revolt of a species against its own physical structure; against its relation to its own physical environment, against the needs of its own physical organism, against the perpetuation of its kind."

As a "trafficker" in the Temple, Eddy was "guilty" of MAM, demonophobia, self-satisfaction and materialism. According to Milmine, there would be no need to consider the founder of Christian Science as a product of limited choices, Victorian sensibilities, unresponsive faith and creative inspiration; she was, as the story unfolded in *McClure's*, entirely premeditated, controlling, callous and disciplined, with occasional lapses for witchcraft, extraordinary rage and bad grammar. "Optimism is the cry of the times and of all the voices that declare it, this [Eddy's] is the most insistent, proclaiming the shortest of all the short roads to happiness . . . the secret of contentment is total anaesthesia."[20] By 1908, though, Milmine was dated and her name barely survived her journalism. She tried a book on Eddy in 1909, based on her *McClure's* series. Eddy and the hierarchy of her Church considered it so prejudicial that a way was found to have it withdrawn from circulation.[21]

One author whose work was never withdrawn, regardless of topic or intent, was Mark Twain. Born in Florida, Missouri and reared at Hannibal on the banks of the Mississippi, he was time's fisherman, forever casting about in his masterpieces for nostalgia, radiant moments, swirling currents of past lives whirling, forever whirling, then rushing through the sand to some deep, nearly obtainable core of memory. Twelve years old when his father died, he helped support his family as an apprentice printer but his heart yearned for the river; at age twenty-two, four years before the Civil War began, Twain was licensed as a riverboat pilot and recorded his experiences in his classic *Life on the Mississippi*.

He fought with the Confederacy just long enough to realize that he didn't like it, then took off with his brother for Nevada, where he lived the life of a wandering journalist and an author of humorous sketches, the most famous of which is "The Notorious Jumping Frog of Calaveras County." In 1864 he moved to California, where he lectured to supplement writing fees; after locating a newspaper that would finance a proposed trip abroad, he journeyed to Europe and Palestine. Originally a collection of articles, the memory of that jaunt became a book published in 1869, entitled *Innocents Abroad*; he married Olivia Langdon, the sister of one of the tour members. Following a brief period as an editor in Buffalo, New York, he settled in Hartford, Connecticut, where he enjoyed years of productivity recalling the past—his and the nation's—in the American vernacular, without condescension and with enviable exuberance, raising the level of literature to art. Emerging from those years were *A Tramp Abroad*, *The Prince and the Pauper*, *A Connecticut Yankee in King Arthur's Court* and his amazing trilogy—with last as best—*The Adventures of Tom Sawyer*, a youthful tale drawing on the Hannibal years, *Life on the Mississippi* and *The Adventures of Huckleberry Finn*, a story of white-black relationships, escape to the West and, perhaps, even flight from the present that he and co-author Charles Dudley Warner ironically named *The Gilded Age*.

Mark Twain had a dark side and it is necessary to look at it to understand the source of his engine's power. Ambivalence, failure and hatred made him the man he was as surely as did his humor and, in fact, provided an extra razor. As in the case of many creative people—writers, artists, prophets, thinkers of various types—solving individual problems takes precedence over being nice or loose. The result is what a community sees—a work of art, a religious tract, a worldview—which, when and if accepted, becomes part of its collective truth. The creator, on the other hand, may not have solved his dilemma but what does it matter? In accepting the truth, remodeling it, reshaping it to render it less personal and more universal, individuality fades. So it was with Mark Twain who was torn, whose work today is more easily recalled by students and their instructors as cultural truth; how much harder would it be and how much more veracity would a discussion have—how much harder would a teacher have to work—to recall the same masterpieces as products of guilt, conflict and eccentricity. More interesting: Would the same work, the same piece or book, the same revelation be equally acceptable to the community or would it be angrily and painfully rejected as unsatisfying, even counterfeit?

Twain, like Mary Baker Eddy, was the product of contradictory currents operative in the United States between 1820 and 1910. Though his books demonstrate an antipathy for bondage and an abiding sympathy for blacks, he joined the Confederacy and, throughout his life, detested the Pope;[22] in a way, he may be properly construed as an anti-Catholic bigot. Interestingly, Twain is hailed as a great democrat, but he swung toward the Republican party in most presidential elections. His works affirm rural, native American values, common sense on the order of Abraham Lincoln and pastoral harmony. But he did care a great deal for money, shared a utilitarian, pragmatic value system with those who had it, among them Carnegie and Rockefeller,[23] overspent grandly, gained and lost fortunes and envied the material success of others. He spent his life "plunging" (speculating), seeking a material El Dorado and finding its shadow instead. In *Connecticut Yankee*, does Hank Morgan's immolation of a medieval army with nine-teenth-century know-how speak for Twain? It seems so, until one comes to grips with the author's irresistible hunger, almost rapture, with contempo-rary technology.[24] He hoped to make a killing, but the only violence he did was on his and his family's bank account. It was destroyed in the financial panic of 1894, when he lost his shirt on a device called the Paige typesetter.

If given a choice, Twain might have dispensed with the 1890s altogether. He went bankrupt, began a worldwide lecture tour to achieve solvency leaving his family behind, entered a creative dry spell from which he never emerged and experienced the loss of his eldest daughter Susy. A young woman with a delicate constitution and an intense feeling of underachieve-ment that bred insecurity, she tended to seek some comfort in mind cure. During the winter of 1894 she lived with her mother in relatively inexpen-sive Paris quarters, while Mark Twain was forced to travel. Noting his daughter's fragility and constant illness, he consulted with Olivia through the mail and suggested that they seek a Christian Scientist. They were all right, he said, since their practice paralleled hypnotism, at least according to William James. It was a legitimate suggestion since the family dabbled in mind cure because they all thought it worked. Twain stopped wearing eyeglasses but Susy and Olivia remained nearsighted. Nevertheless, they employed mind cure for "minor stomach and headache pain where they believed it most effective." Olivia, however, did not consult a Christian Scientist at that time since she had heard rather offensive things concerning the movement's guiding spirit, Mary Baker Eddy.

Susy recovered and relapsed, waxed and waned for two more years. She continued to study and rely upon mental science during her father's enforced absence as a curative for what she believed to be a trivial and shallow existence; during this time she was generally unwell and might have suffered from anorexia too. Nevertheless, she remained steadfast in her mental healing convictions. But it didn't help. On 18 August 1896 she succumbed to spinal meningitis. A conventional doctor was in attendance, but his presence failed to lift the veil of remorse and guilt experienced by Twain.[25] His mood changed and his work was informed less by humor and hominess than by a certain grayness tinged with bitter memory, cynicism and bleakness. He had more in common with the *Mont St. Michel* outlook and that of its author Henry Adams than he ever did with Tom Sawyer. The *Mysterious Stranger*, written in 1905 but unpublished until 1916, is a lugubrious evocation of the future from a born evangelical who retained his underlying moral sensibilities[26] until he lost his personal anchor. A fortune gone in 1894, a daughter in 1896, and a wife in 1904 turned the Twain personality wintry. And it was in this turn of mind that he approached the spiritual healing ministry of Mary Baker Eddy.

The once magnificent humorist and novelist had little of the rustic in his ferocious satire of Christian Science. "For all the strange . . . frantic, uncomprehensible and uninterpretable books which the imagination of man has created, this one [*Science and Health*] is the prize. It is complacent, eloquent and meaningless." Twain scoffed at Eddy's nonmedical cure, which operated through the patient's imagination; he glibly stated that, eventually, her followers would replace Virgin Mary with Matron Mary!

In the crux of his attack, the nostalgic chronicler of Americana revealed himself as either an old-line mugwump or a late-blooming muckraker. He believed that the vitality of Christian Science was sustained by money, and plenty of it: "Next, the power and authority and capital must be concentrated in the grip of a small and irresponsible clique with nobody outside privileged to ask questions. . . . Next . . . it must bait its hook with some attractive advantages over the baits offered by its competition. . . . They offer the following benefits; health, absence of fear and anxiety in this life and a new person to worship."[27] Science, then, was viewed as a bargain, a pooling of interests so that all might profit.

The theme is developed in a manner which precludes ambiguity: "Christian Science is for sale and the terms are cash . . . in advance. Its god is Mrs. Eddy first, then the dollar." As an example, Twain used the bargain counter in Boston, which sold but never gave away spiritual wares. "There is no such thing as credit to Christian Scientists, and everything is priced so expensively that it's robbery."[28]

There were no apologies made for "the Mother Church . . . factory in Boston . . . [bearing] . . . the trademark of the trust." Included in the "trust" were the Church itself, the Metaphysical College and healing courses, together realizing an annual income of $1 million. Twain's bravado, however, yielded to a touch of Progressive, racist fear. Irrationally, he estimated that by 1920 there would be 10 million Christian Scientists in America and

3 million more in Great Britain; by 1930, "they will be a political force and by 1940 . . . the governing power of the Republic. . . . It [Christian Science] will be the most insolent, unscrupulous, tyrannical politico-religious master since the Inquisition. . . . It will divide Christendom and erect a 'Boston Pope.' . . . I think the 'trust' will be handed down like the other papacy." Augusta Stetson thought it quite a compliment when Twain's public dinner conversations included a caution against Christian Science becoming the "only religion." "And so it will," she concluded.[29]

Twain's excesses knew no limit. He contradicted visible, physical evidence to say that Christian Science did not appeal to intellectuals, its market being—in the best Anglo-Saxon superiority sense—the "unintelligent, mentally inferior . . . people who do not think." Twain blasted Protestantism for deteriorating to a level that not only permitted but encouraged the growth of dissident sects; he enjoined traditional religion to awaken before it was overrun.[30]

This tract was written in 1899, but was published with a "reevaluation," first in 1903, and again in 1907 by Harper and Brothers. In the 1903 version, Twain thought Eddy a despot, but not a benevolent one, "the most daring . . . masculine . . . woman that has appeared on the earth in centuries." He examined her rambling style of writing and compared it to the cleaner, relatively straightforward delivery of *Science and Health*, concluding that she either had a magnificent "ghost"—she did, James Henry Wiggin, a retired Unitarian minister and grammarian—or was a downright plagiarist. Twain granted that there was insufficient evidence to positively identify her ideas as Quimby's but asserted that she undoubtedly stole from the work of a dead man.[31]

Like the Pope (at the time Leo XIII), she made herself infallible to avoid schism in the Church; she "concentrated power in her own hands by electing and having the final say in the appointing of the president, treasurer and clerk." Twain dubbed Science a religious empire and bestowed upon "great Mary"—incapable of thinking on a high plane, reasoning clearly or writing trenchantly—his choicest epithets: "Ambitious . . . with a far-seeing business eye . . . organizing and executive talent . . . indifferent . . . efficient . . . opportunistic . . . sordid . . . pernicious, famishing for money . . . power, glory . . . vain, unfaithful, jealous . . . insolent, arrogant, pitiless, shallow . . . commercial." Worst of all, Twain rejected Christian Science as an instrument of reform capable of improving business and political—public—morals.[32]

Twain penned a number of articles for the *North American Review*[33] between December 1902 and April 1903, at exactly the same time as Steffens and Tarbell were featured in *McClure's*. They added little to his fundamental, though inimical, appraisal. Twain was taken to task by William McCrackan, who was sensitive to the reverential inferences that might be drawn from Christian Scientists who, as a matter of course, addressed Eddy as "Mother." Twain, he said, need not fear "that the practice implies true worship." Stirred to her own defense, Eddy responded personally and directly, denying that she sought deification and refuting any divine intent in the words "matron" or "mother."[34]

The general tone of Scientists and Science sympathizers indicated that they believed Twain to be frivolous, biased, misinformed and vindictive.[35] Given his autumnal turn of mind, this criticism was not unjust. Twain's emotional condemnation weakened rather than bolstered his argument. He was punitive in much of what he said but sardonic, searing prose often obscures objectivity, making balanced inquiry not only unnecessary but often undesirable. The Progressive antimonopoly vocabulary was used and misused: trust, centralization, concentration, monopoly, money, power, greed and profit described forms of business abuse but did not properly define the Christian Science movement and its contributions to the era of Progressivism. Words were bandied about until they lost all meaning; arguments constructed on valid premises evaporated on the wings of nebulous fancy. In its intolerance of Christian Science, Progressive hatred of unfair business practices is amply demonstrated; unfortunately, so is Progressive preachiness, moralizing and cynicism.

But the steamroller tactics worked. Obviously, Eddy underestimated her literary adversaries and the intense hatred they harbored for her. In the case of some it was, perhaps, a personal resentment[36] that drove them to settle with her; with most it was probably a fatal susceptibility to overkill. In any event, the Mother Church Board of Directors, the Pleasant View staff and Eddy heard the message. To quiet her critics, Eddy forbade her followers to address her as "Mother" since the title was not informal and could be misconstrued.[37] In 1908 she was helped to formulate an idea whose time had come, especially in light of all the anti-Christian Science activity in courtrooms, periodicals and books. On November 25 the first issue of the *Christian Science Monitor* was published. Unlike the movement's previous papers, this one was motivated by "an ambition for excellence" and was guided by "high moral" intent. Nevertheless, ever-mindful of its mission, the Board sought a professional staff whose commitment was to "consciousness of human affairs but not . . . involvement with them."[38]

Some influential Christian Science friends intervened in the faith's defense. "Morally criminal" was the *Arena*'s countercharge against Mark Twain.[39] And that magazine would discourse at some length and with a great deal of authority since its treatment of Eddy had been evenhanded. More like an *Outlook* in temper and style than a *McClure's*, *Arena* retained a pristine tone in an age of disclosure: editor Benjamin O. Flower admired transcendentalism and supported those contemporary American causes in which he detected its essence, among them temperance, feminism, slum removal and labor unionism. To him, Mary Baker Eddy was a refugee from that golden chapter in the American past and a welcome corrective to a certain variety of materialism—"sordid . . . egoistic and mammon worshipping"—which threatened to "enslave the nation." To his credit, though, he was eager to find points of view critical of Christian Science and print them for the purpose of rumination and debate. Naturally, it didn't hurt sales either. In May 1899 there appeared a long article on deceptive Christian Science and its irrational founder authored by Josephine Curtis Woodbury; in July 1907 contributor Edward C. Farnsworth found *Arena* receptive to his ten-page critique of Christian Science, which concentrated on the movement as grounded in the "doctrine of the Eastern ascetic."[40]

Flower differed from *McClure's* in his designating space for equal time and rebuttal. In the pages where Woodbury appeared so did William McCrackan; following the Farnsworth essay, John B. Willis took an opposite point of view. Of the four, none were as convincing as the editor himself, who occasionally offered his own comments on Eddy's place in American culture. He considered the phenomenon of MAM as Eddy's "delusion" but reached no conclusion on obsession save one—that personal experience played a crucial role in the development of Jesus, Luther and Wesley, and probably did the same for Mary Baker Eddy. His recommendation was a basic one: "don't throw the baby out with the bath water." There was something of value—at least something salvageable—in the religious rhetoric of Science, but he couldn't put his finger on exactly what it was. To him, it was a metaphor that lacked substance, perhaps an expression of moral idealism. Most important, it was a way for him to understand social Progressivism's spiritual contribution to American civilization. When the "Next Friends" suit against Eddy collapsed, the *Arena* offered a complete, gleeful account of "shrewd" and "reckless" counsel's failure to impugn the sanity of a formidable woman, despite the aid of "black journals" and heretical statements.[41] Eddy's triumph, though, was not the one he sought; she did not re-create Emerson, Thoreau, Fuller or any other transcendentalist. If anything, Eddy may have revived an ancient debate on metaphysics and health that Flower touched upon but never really grasped.

Eddy had another defender and she, too, emerged in 1907. She was no more credible than Milmine and her work is the mirror image of that done at *McClure's*. Sibyl Wilbur O'Brien's *Life of Mary Baker Eddy* was "subsidized by John V. Dittemore, then a Director of the Mother Church,"[42] and was published by the Christian Science Publishing Society in Boston. It was based on a series of articles favorable to Mary Baker Eddy that the author had contributed to *Human Life*[43] and was conceived as a corrective rather than an objective inquiry: "I ask the reader to refuse to accept as biography such gossip which the ephemeral press has detailed . . . the true story . . . has been ruthlessly caricatured."

Partial and patronizing, maudlin and pretentious, it excused, apologized for and venerated Eddy, who was portrayed as the victim of yellow journalism and exposés. Always in the right and roundly misunderstood, she was a democrat in thought and practice, shielding beneath her canopy all make and manner of humanity. At the 1906 ceremonies marking the dedication of the Mother Church extension, representatives from Liverpool, St. Petersburg and Paris were in attendance, "negroes as well as white men . . . French, German and Scandinavian . . . British nobility . . . teachers, clerks and day laborers." Despite the internationalization of the movement, Mrs. O'Brien was advised by Dittemore not to use her married name as author; according to the "petty prejudices of the day, O'Brien sounded too Catholic" for someone writing on the Christian Science founder.[44]

The work allayed no suspicions but gave many sufficient reason to believe Milmine.[45] Eddy wasn't much of a fan either but she authorized it grudgingly at the behest of Dittemore and the Mother Church Board. Thus, it became the only biography of which she personally approved.

'I have not had sufficient interest in the matter to read or to note from others' reading what the enemies of Christian Science are circulating regarding my history, but my friends have read Sibyl Wilbur's book . . . and request the privilege of buying, circulating and recommending it to the public. I briefly declare that nothing has occurred in my life's experience which, if correctly . . . understood, could injure me; and not a little is already reported of the good accomplished therein, the self-sacrifice . . . that has distinguished all my working years.

I thank Miss Wilbur . . . for [her] unselfish labors . . . and hereby say that [she has] my permission to publish and circulate this work.'[46]

Signed by Mary Baker Eddy, who continued to have reservations about an avalanche of publicity, the only valid conclusion is one drawn by *Current Literature*: that neither Wilbur nor Milmine are accurate; yet both attested to the unearthly influence Eddy "had and has" on her generation.[47]

3 December 1910. At 10:45 Saturday evening, Eddy no longer cared about her supporters or her critics. The physician in attendance said the cause of death was natural, with pneumonia as a contributing factor. Alfred Farlow, president of the Christian Science Publication Committee, waited a day to issue an official statement, carefully construed, which avoided the word "death." He said, in a number of ways, that Mary Baker Eddy "passed away," "departed," "left" and "is no longer with us."[48] Perhaps not as dramatic as the former disciple Augusta Stetson, who awaited her leader's imminent spiritual resurrection, nevertheless they both, in their unique ways, upheld the charming fiction that death is a dream.

The World, of course, and the *Sun* saw no dignity in Eddy's life; her death was just another exploitable commodity. In the former, Pulitzer's account was sensational, concentrating on money, MAM and a "wonderful" career that included Eddy's giving away her only child. In the latter, Charles A. Dana was nearly as bad, even though his paper had a reputation for being the "best written" in New York City; it was also as "cynical and shallow" as the *Herald*, according to Lincoln Steffens. In any event, the *Sun* refrained from editorializing and was not quite as negative as the *World*. Its focus, in a three-page life story, was to show how a woman who borrowed ideas from a mental healer could parlay them into a new American religion. In a much shorter piece, the *Herald* marveled at the abilities of Mother Church spokesmen to find euphemisms to describe Eddy's lifeless state.[49]

Authoritative, thoroughly researched, even distinguished, the *New York Times* exuded a certain honesty in its farewell editorial on Mary Baker Eddy. This was not a charitable daily—it had been recording the public career of Christian Science for years—but its byword was "all the news that's fit to print," at least from the time Adolph Ochs bought it in 1896. Choosing its words carefully in order to direct readers toward a certain point of view, the *Times* described "the triumph" of Eddy and "the cult she founded in defiance of common sense [and] . . . practical science . . . an anachronism in the age of enlightenment." Not a denomination or a sect, the "cult" of Christian Science attracted the self-deluded and ignorant who, oddly enough, created a strong, secure and wealthy Church; how they could achieve this, given their shortcomings, was left unexplained. Christian Science, noted the editorial, was representative of human weakness, a human failing "we cannot deny our fellow men, and they carry their own punishment. But they [Christian Science practitioners] must not be permitted to endanger the common welfare. . . . The law of the land must be obeyed."

Easy answers came to the *World*, the *Sun* and the *Herald* but not to the *Times* and that's what made it more interesting reading. "Founder of a Cult," the editorial's title, could be an invitation to judge or discuss and it seems the *Times* would have liked to have it both ways. In the midst of its rhetoric on an ostensibly counterfeit religion, the paper urged Science's further consideration: freed of its spiritual radicalism, there might be more to it. And the cult leader? Having exerted her influence upon Christianity for forty years, she must be considered an "extraordinary" woman.[50]

Extraordinary. An extraordinary woman whose achievement would endure. This was also the verdict of the *New York Evening Post*, a daily like the *New York Times* that was not much associated with muckraking. Founded in 1801 by Alexander Hamilton, the *Post* was known for its stability—Lincoln Steffens might have called it stodginess—and actually retained the same editor, the acclaimed romantic poet and publisher William Cullen Bryant, for forty-nine years. Following his retirement in 1868, the Social Darwinist E. L. Godkin, a "transplanted Irish liberal and founding editor of the *Nation*," assumed Bryant's post and developed the paper in consonance with his own personality. As described by National Book Award and Pulitzer Prize winner Justin Kaplan, the *Post* was factual: it excluded humor, pathos, "literary flourish and personality" as inappropriate to good journalism, was "strong on local politics, industry, culture and finance," and "shunned crime, scandal" sensationalism and yellow jour-

nalism. In sum, both the editor and the paper were "chary of party politics . . . unalterably opposed to protective tariffs . . . organized labor [and]
ignorant mobs." There was a certain chilliness about the *Post*, a "failure of
mercy," which rendered the laissez-faire philosophy attractive, even virtuous.

If papers have a personality, and this one certainly appeared to have one,
Mary Baker Eddy would feel at home reading it or reading about herself in
it, at least according to her critics. Paper and woman seemed to have similar
personalities and, in truth, it was not unkind to her at the end. In 1906 an
editorial on Christian Science printed the day before the Mother Church
rededication envisioned the faith as dying, despite its less demanding
spirituality and overarching wealth. Having peaked in the previous decade, Christian Science would bow before the newfound tolerance of Protestantism that would shortly cause the movement's demise, as would the
rise of cosmic philosophies like New Thought. Three years later, the *Post*
took an anti-Eddy position during the Augusta Stetson affair, reporting on
the order that healers could no longer maintain offices or rooms—in effect,
their practices—in Christian Science churches. The reason given for this
pronouncement was that Eddy wished to "avoid a strong material organization." A few paragraphs hence, the *Post* speculated on the real reason—
removing a rival: "In this city [New York], the new rule will especially affect
the West Ninety Sixth Street Church, with which Mrs. Augusta E. Stetson
has been most prominently identified."[51]

Sober and straightforward, the *Post* analyzed but not quite eulogized
Mary Baker Eddy. On the whole, the chronicle of her life and work verged
on complimentary, although Milmine-like jabs at her uniqueness were
evident. The article, entitled "Mary Baker Eddy's Work," contained correspondence from Eddy's Unitarian editor James Henry Wiggin, attesting to
his belief that his employer adapted a number of Quimby ideas; the other
story, "Mrs. Eddy's Career," presented some resuscitated wishful thinking
on the part of the *Post*. With the leader's death the paper anticipated a
reabsorption of Christian Scientists into traditional Protestant churches,
which were attempting to win over those who believed in the efficacy of
mental healing. Some would fall away—meaning they would never return—but the "impetus of the cult had been checked." There was a lot of
punching going on but, interestingly, the *Post* refrained from—or couldn't—
deliver a knockout blow.

Yes, this was a cult according to the *Post*, but in the United States it was
also an acceptable form of religious novelty; what occurred within it and
the founder's source of inspiration would remain problematic for students
"of religious vagaries" for years to come. It was not a superstition, the paper
continued, and it would be a mistake on the part of investigators to assume
it was merely this; rather—and in praise of Science—the work it had done
to illuminate the causes of and provide a strategy for treating mental illness

assisted in patient recovery. Whether deceased, "departed," "passed away" or "gone," Eddy was an energetic and charismatic woman,[52] aspiring to individuality in a society that prided itself on individualism.

Optimism, hope, salvation and redemption were the messages Eddy sent. Some returned, some were lost, some were wrong and many were misunderstood. Writing in September 1912, several weeks before Republican Progressivism foundered on the crags and shoals of American politics, Burton J. Hendrick of *McClure's* had the last word on Christian Science: "The Pacific Coast is Christian Science's most successful field. . . . Its dominant note harmonizes . . . with the Western atmosphere . . . of complacency; it has its face always toward the sunrise; it is constantly preaching that everything is the best in the best of all possible worlds."[53]

NOTES

1. Justin Kaplan, *Lincoln Steffens: A Biography* (New York: Simon and Schuster, 1974), 119, 141, 149–51; David Mark Chalmers, *The Muckrake Years* (New York: D. Von Nostrand, 1974), 17, 45, 61, 80, 125–30.

2. Quoted from the Spokane, Washington *Inland Herald* in *Editorial Comment on the Life and Work of Mary Baker Eddy*, 23–24.

3. Eugene Wood, "What the Public Wants to Read," *Atlantic Monthly* 88 (October 1901): 571.

4. J. Leonard Bates, *The United States 1898–1928* (New York: McGraw Hill, 1976), 52.

5. Chalmers, *Muckrake Years*, 44.

6. Harold S. Wilson, *McClure's Magazine and the Muckrakers* (Princeton, N.J.: Princeton University Press, 1970), 308–9; John Huston Finley, *A Pilgrim in Palestine* (New York: Charles Scribner's Sons, 1919), 55.

7. Kaplan, *Lincoln Steffens*, 117; Wilson, *McClure's Magazine and the Muckrakers*, 68.

8. Wilson, *McClure's Magazine and the Muckrakers*, 153, 304–9; Kaplan, *Lincoln Steffens*, 22–23, 117–18.

9. Charles S. Braden, *Christian Science Today* (Dallas: Southern Methodist University Press, 1958), 55–58.

10. Boston, Chicago and New York were the most active building sites. See "Chicago Scientists Plan Church" (editorial), *New York Times*, 19 January 1989, 6; "Topics of the Times," *New York Times*, 9 April 1901, 8; Lloyd Morris, *Postscript to Yesterday: America, The Last Fifty Years* (New York: Random House, 1947), 422.

11. "Topics of the Times," *New York Times*, 3 July 1899, 6; "Estimate Mrs. Eddy's Fortune at $7,000,000," *New York Herald*, 5 December 1910, 2; *Allegations Contained in the Bill of Equity*, Newspaper Clippings and Misc., Streeter, Eddy Litigation Papers; Mary Baker Eddy's interview before Hon. Edgar Aldrich, Hon. Hosea W. Parker and Dr. George F. Jelly at Concord, N.H. 14 August 1907. Mary Baker Eddy Litigation Papers, 1907, 1912. Steno Records, 1907, Folder 1, 100–101 under Frank Sherwin Streeter, New Hampshire Historical Society, Concord, N.H.; Streeter Testimony, 23 May 1907, 1, 3, Streeter, Eddy Litigation Papers.

12. Lyman P. Powell, *Mary Baker Eddy: A Life Size Portrait* (New York: Macmillan, 1930), 6; Morris, *Postscript to Yesterday*, 431.

13. "Christian Science Victims" (editorial), *New York Daily Tribune*, 25 September 1889, 6; "Mystified But Satisfied," *New York Times*, 16 February 1889, 2.

14. Clyde Griffen, "The Progressive Ethos," *The Development of an American Culture*, ed. Stanley Coben and Lorman Ratner, 2d ed. (New York: St. Martin's, 1983), 144, 149–50, 155–57, 170, 177–78.

15. "The Life of Mary Baker Eddy" (editorial), *McClure's Magazine* 28 (December 1906): 211–17.

16. Wilson, *McClure's Magazine and the Muckrakers*, 159, 303.

17. Georgine Milmine, "Forty Years of Obscurity," *McClure's Magazine* 28 (January 1907): 227–42, "The Encounter with Quimby," *McClure's Magazine* 28 (February 1907): 339–54; "The Quimby Controversy," *McClure's Magazine* 28 (March 1907): 506–24; "Six Years of Wandering," *McClure's Magazine*, 28 (April 1907): 608–27; "Mrs. Eddy and Her First Disciples," *McClure's Magazine* 29 (May 1907): 97–116; "The Revival of Witchcraft," *McClure's Magazine* 29 (June 1907): 333–48; "The Church and the Mesmerists," *McClure's Magazine* 29 (July 1907): 447–62; "The Massachusetts Metaphysical College and Calvin Frye," *McClure's Magazine* 29 (August 1907): 567–81, "Literary Activities," *McClure's Magazine* 29 (October 1907): 688–99; "The Schism of 1888, the Growth of Christian Science and the Apotheosis of Mrs. Eddy," *McClure's Magazine* 30 (February 1908): 387–401; "The Adopting of a Son and the Founding of the Mother Church," *McClure's Magazine* 30 (March 1908): 577–90, "Life at Pleasant View and 'War in Heaven,' " *McClure's Magazine* 30 (April 1908): 699–712; "Training the Vine: A Study of Mrs. Eddy's Prerogatives and Powers," *McClure's Magazine* 31 (May 1908): 16–31; and "Mrs. Eddy's Book and Doctrine," *McClure's Magazine* 31 (June 1908): 179–89; "How Mrs. Eddy Won Out," *Current Literature* 42 (June 1907): 652; Mark Twain [Samuel Langhorne Clemens], *Christian Science* (New York: Harper and Brothers, 1907), 289–92.

18. Robert Peel, *Mary Baker Eddy: The Years of Discovery* (New York: Holt, Rinehart and Winston, 1966), 315, 327–28, 333, 349, 352.

19. "Taft Named: First Ballot," *New York Times*, 19 June 1908, 1; "Taft, Hearing News, Turns to Mrs. Taft," *New York Times*, 19 June 1908, 1; "Roosevelt Lauds Taft," *New York Times*, 19 June 1908, 1.

20. Milmine, "Schism of 1888," 390, 392, 394, 400; Milmine, "Adopting of a Son," 577, 588–90; Milmine, "Life at Pleasant View," 704, 711; Milmine, "Training the Vine," 20, 24–31; Milmine, "Mrs. Eddy's Book and Doctrine," 186, 188–89.

21. Morris, *Postscript to Yesterday*, 447, 461.

22. Paul E. Boller, Jr., *American Thought in Transition: The Impact of Evolutionary Naturalism 1865–1900* (Chicago: Rand McNally, 1970), 206–7; David W. Noble, *The Progressive Mind 1890–1917* (Chicago: Rand McNally, 1970), 139.

23. Carl N. Degler, *The Age of Economic Revolution 1876–1900*, 2d ed. (Glenview, Ill.: Scott, Foresman, 1977), 189; Roderick Nash, *From These Beginnings: A Biographical Approach to American History*, 3d ed. (New York: Harper and Row, 1984), 1:335–37; Henry Bamford Parkes, *The American Experience* (New York: Vintage Books, 1959), 270.

24. Richard Hofstadter, *Anti-Intellectualism in American Life* (New York: Vintage Books, 1963), 241.

25. Resa Willis, *Mark and Livy* (New York: Atheneum, 1992), 172, 214–15, 230, 236–37.

26. George M. Marsden, *Religion and American Culture* (New York: Harcourt Brace Jovanovich, 1990), 174; Nash, *From These Beginnings*, 1: 354–55; Morris, *Postscript to Yesterday*, 99.

27. Twain, *Christian Science*, 51.

28. Ibid., 289–92.

29. Augusta E. Stetson, *Reminiscences, Sermons and Correspondence Proving Adherence to the Principle of Christian Science as Taught by Mary Baker Eddy* (New York: G. P. Putnam's Sons, 1913), 242; Twain, *Christian Science*, 70–83.

30. Twain, *Christian Science*, 84–93.

31. Ibid., 289–92.

32. Ibid., 106, 150, 165–66, 196–97, 229, 265–79, 285, 358–62.

33. Mark Twain, "Christian Science," *North American Review*, 175 (December 1902): 758, 760, 762; 176 (January 1903): 1–9; 176 (February 1903): 174–84; 176 (April 1903): 505–17.

34. William D. McCrackan, "Mrs. Eddy's Relationship to Christian Science," *North American Review* 176 (March 1903): 364; 176 (April 1903): 505–17.

35. Charles Klein, review of *Christian Science* by Mark Twain in *North American Review* 184 (15 March 1907): 636–41; Charles Johnston, review of *Christian Science* by Mark Twain in *North American Review* 184 (15 March 1907): 641–45; Edward A. Kimball, "Mark Twain, Mrs. Eddy and Christian Science," *Cosmopolitan* 153 (May 1908): 35–41.

36. John Milton Cooper, Jr., *Pivotal Decades: The United States 1900–1920* (New York: W. W. Norton, 1990), 88–89.

37. "Mrs. Eddy Relents," *New York Times*, 6 March 1905, 1.

38. Julius Silberger, Jr., *Mary Baker Eddy: An Interpretive Biography of the Founder of Christian Science* (Boston: Little, Brown, 1980), 232; Stephen Gottschalk, *The Emergence of Christian Science in American Religious Life* (Berkeley: University of California Press, 1975), 272.

39. Benjamin O. Flower, "Mark Twain's Attack on Christian Science," *The Arena* 38 (November 1907): 567–68.

40. Benjamin O. Flower, "The Masternote in the Message of Christian Science," *The Arena* 41 (July 1909): 460; Edward C. Farnsworth, "The Fallacies of Christian Science," *The Arena* 38 (July 1907): 60; Woodbury, "Christian Science and the Prophetess," 537–70.

41. Benjamin O. Flower, "The 7 Alleged Delusions of the Founder of Christian Science Examined in the Light of History and Present-Day Research," *The Arena* 38 (October 1907): 412–22; John B. Willis, "The Truths of Christian Science—A Reply," *The Arena* 38 (July 1907): 61–70; William D. McCrackan, "The Meaning of Christian Science," *The Arena* 37 (May 1907): 464–76; Flower, "Irresponsible Attacks on Christian Science," 60–62; "The Collapse of the Case Against the Founder of Christian Science," *The Arena* 38 (September 1907): 320.

42. Silberger, *Mary Baker Eddy*, 8.

43. Her interest in this project may have been piqued by something she heard. On 30 October 1906, a *New York World* reporter mentioned that he would not "stop until he had smashed Mrs. Eddy and the whole Christian Science Church." See

New York World abstracts, no. 4 (3 March 1907): 7, in Newspaper Clippings and Misc., Streeter, Eddy Litigation Papers.

44. Sybil Wilbur, *The Life of Mary Baker Eddy* (Boston: Christian Science, 1907), xvi, 313, 341–43; Silberger, *Mary Baker Eddy*, 228.

45. Francis Edward Marsten compared the work of Milmine to that of Ida Tarbell. See "Literature," review of *The Life of Mary Baker Eddy* by Georgine Milmine and *The Mask of Christian Science* by Francis Edward Marsten, in *The Nation* 15 (10 February 1910): 138; "Is Mrs. Eddy Sane?" *Outlook* 85 (9 March 1907), 545–46.

46. Silberger, *Mary Baker Eddy*, 228.

47. "The Enthralling Personality of Mrs. Eddy," *Current Literature* 41 (September 1907): 301.

48. "Awaiting Mrs. Eddy's Son," *New York Evening Post*, 5 December 1910, 1.

49. "Mrs. Eddy the Founder of Christian Science Is Dead of Pneumonia," "Mrs. Eddy Gives Away Only Child," and "Mrs. Eddy's Wonderful Career and Her Rise to Wealth and Power," *New York World*, 5 December 1910, 1–2, 7; "Mrs. Eddy Dies of Pneumonia" and "Mary Baker G. Eddy's Life," *New York Sun*, 5 December 1910, 1–3; "Passed from Our Sight," *New York Herald*, 5 December 1910, 4; Kaplan, *Lincoln Steffens*, 56.

50. "Founder of a Cult" (editorial), *New York Times*, 5 December 1910, 8.

51. "Christian Science Triumphant" (editorial), *New York Evening Post*, 9 June 1906, 4; "Mrs. Eddy's Latest Order," *New York Evening Post*, 6 August 1909, 2; Kaplan, *Lincoln Steffens*, 149.

52. "Mary Baker Eddy's Work," *New York Evening Post*, 5 December 1910, 6–7; "Mrs. Eddy's Career," *New York Evening Post*, 5 December 1910, 8.

53. Burton J. Hendrick, "Christian Science since Mrs. Eddy," *McClure's Magazine* 39 (September 1912): 488.

─── 7

Nobody Knows My Name

The contribution of contemporary criticism to the retreat of radicalism within the Christian Science movement was substantial but overwrought, and that was probably a product of the age. Eager to kill Science, polemicists waged war within the literary media that gave the Church invaluable publicity. The effect created was the opposite of what was intended. Thoughtful people, who otherwise would have remained in ignorance of the new religion, were enlightened. Confronted with neuroses and tensions within a dynamic American society, some chose the idealistic, assured Gospel interpretation of Mary Baker Eddy and lost themselves in a tranquil sea surrounding her "tight little island."

Christian Science settled and stabilized, but it did not disappear. Any valid inquiry into its durability should be conducted on two levels: first, the overall shift in American thought tending to inclusion rather than exclusion, which gradually afforded Science a niche within the general culture; second, the death of Mary Baker Eddy and the attendant resolution of internal conflict in favor of the Mother Church Board of Directors.

The stigma attached to Christian Science faded when its greatest heresy was absorbed by the medical establishment; by 1906 even the Episcopal Emmanuels experimented with psychotherapy. With a great deal of uncertainty medical colleges tested the embryonic system in clinics and group therapy sessions; students were introduced to psychiatry and oriented toward a physiomental or total approach. Consequently, the need to ostracize Christian Science diminished when its "radicalism" was no longer perceived as radical.

Perhaps the most important contribution Christian Science has made is in the area of health, since it equates divine understanding with healing. As the medical and scientific professions know now and accept prudently, advisedly and under controlled conditions, the equation works and is, therefore, an authorized, legitimate procedure within the framework of holistic treatment. Recently, John Maynard Smith, biologist and contributor to theoretical evolutionary understanding, posited that metaphysical responses are quite applicable to a wide range of human experience when there is no strictly scientific explanation. "This is a fairly bold use of words. The term metaphysics long had a bad name in scientific circles and the taint" has yet to disappear. But its use by respected scientists indicates a limit to their hubris and a willingness to concede, without being labeled quaint or romantic, that a part of living is impenetrable, mysterious and unknowable, governed by extant laws beyond perception.[1] Of course, some Christian Scientists wish to employ metaphysical laws as a unitary treatment, which brings the faith into direct conflict with the total approach, the civil rights of minors and the American legal system. Such issues still wind their way through the courts, are ongoing and anticipate resolution at some future date. However, it is likely that binding national law will never supersede the current case-by-case, state-by-state rulings, and that Science will remain protected by the Constitution's First Amendment religious clauses.

American Protestantism maintained—and maintains—a functional relationship with Christian Science that will hardly improve, since it is founded on "give" rather than "take": it gave all its failures or, all its "tempest tossed," to Science. In truth then, the mainstream faith was soldered to Christian Science, joined at the hip so to speak. Their common denominators were all the people who "crossed over" and, despite great exertions, traditional churches found it difficult—even painful—to disown or disavow them. Nevertheless the differences between Science and Protestantism were clearcut—too much so to ignore—although they have been blurred in the modern day.

American Protestantism—with its doctrine of the elect, Enlightenment leanings, fervent emotions, transcendental optimism, preoccupation with sin and salvation and Social Darwinist elitism—was, and perhaps still is, a tradition in the making. On this continent, the Reformation's faith was two and a half centuries old in 1900; it had emerged from a Western European milieu that developed over 1,500 years. It was a process, with its own unique internal dynamic, which included social, political and economic realities as well as spiritual. Its institutionalization and organization could be understood in terms of cultural events, political facts and storytellers, among them philosophers, playwrights, military officers, scholars, artists and clerics. For a very long time, Protestant ministers assumed a key intellectual role in the United States and it was through their eyes—Channing's, Emerson's, and Parker's, for instance—that the transcendental current can be best understood. As a matter of fact, generalized American intellectual history would be much the poorer if it lacked the discourse and contribution of ministers, priests and rabbis.

Christian Science was "Christian" but it was there that its Protestantism ended, primarily because of the founder. In some ways she aped Luther—isolated, martyrish and strangely genteel in her tastes—but she was different in one crucial respect: she was not an intellectual or professor, despite any titles she conferred upon herself. She never articulated or expounded upon a historic Christian tradition, even when she was most critical of it; instead she concentrated on the spiritual resurrection of Jesus, cared little for any devotional development either before or after, nor any scholarship related to Biblical exegesis. In certain respects, she recalls the unfortunate, albeit intuitive, sixteenth-century protagonist of Carlo Ginsburg's classic *Cheese and the Worms*. Menocchio was intelligent but expressed himself in the idiom he knew best: undercurrents of spiritual thought, insights and near-revelations, a series of impressionistic yet unalterable truths surviving millennially, resistant to change, popularly believed and coursing somewhere below contemporary culture.

Christian Science was naive or, at best, pre-Church in its assumption that the corporeal and spiritual manifestations of humanity were separate,[2] with the first a shadow of the second. Protestantism accepted the notion that such a dichotomy could not exist; only total, integrated man, shaping God's will in a brave, new world, could drink at the crystal stream of progress. The message was a worthy one but its concept of shared, community responsibility needed to be sweetened. The Science belief entertained those in need of spiritual encouragement with a more palatable concoction that was, at once, relevant to a scientific age and a confidence-builder for members of an ambivalent, sometimes guilt-ridden industrial class requiring assurances that Heaven still loved them.

The zealots of trust busting investigated oil, railroad, beef, drug, bureaucratic and human abuse. By contrast, Christian Science was hardly the villainous octopus conjured up by the muckrakers. As a group, they ignored the essence of Science, which they would have understood had they been more sensitive: it was a legitimate, middle-class movement, presumably responding to the unendurable pressure exerted by business rigidity and labor militancy upon the center stratum of society.

Science responded to the expanding society in the same fashion as Reform Darwinists and Progressives. Of the three, none can be termed innovative or inventive; all were adaptations—some less and some more so—to a system that was thought to be undesirable and objectionable. However, Progressivism brandished a two-edged sword. Unlike Christian Science, its creed was one of exuberance and faith in the American experience with the hope that scientific creativity would enable humanity to reach ever upward. Eddy, though sanguine on the fate of the soul, regarded civilization's material conquests with something less than ecstasy. The new frontier she conceived as part of a personal crisis ended just short of reality; her brand of idealistic conservatism, burdened by pre-Church roots and overlaid with popular, poetic romance, carried the torch to a given point but no farther. Eddy had little faith in the tangible, physical, objective efforts of humanity, regarding its excursions as miserable, pitiable experiments bound to end disastrously; no doubt she projected her own life into her vision, but it became a potent message for a class of Americans with a similar inclination, though perhaps not as intensely pessimistic or as enmeshed in inner conflict. Eddy never entertained the need to strive and reform materially if one could become a living spirit. In an ambiguous way, though, the spark she kindled warmed the hands of a new generation willing to step into the future, beyond the arbitrary boundary imposed by Christian Science.

Only after her death was the movement freed from the more malignant and malevolent components of her thought. In a sense, however, whether for good or ill, Eddy's mind and will were the twin dynamos powering the movement. Pursued by private fears and ambition, she solved a dilemma for tens of thousands that plagued her all her life and offered the shelter to her flock which she was only intermittently able to find for herself. Eddy has been grouped with the greatest women in history[3] because her unique temperament tended toward prophecy; also, she represented a different sort of voice for women—religious—when those of her gender designated the social arena as their most favorable entry point into public life. Eddy's obstinacy weathered all onslaughts and her integrity insisted that the faith be practiced precisely the way it had been revealed. This is, perhaps, a reason why Christian Science demonstrates only imperfect evolutionary tendencies. After 1910 it became virtually impossible to separate "the mover from the moved": all seemed to be an extension of one mind. With no disciples, interpreters or synthesizers—only formalizers and institutionalizers—timelessness rather than tradition was assured, although not necessarily desirable, within a denomination aspiring to wider significance.

It was almost a blessed release when Mary Baker Eddy died. The eccentric qualities of her religion had long been challenged by younger, entrepreneurial and more socially astute male leaders. Eddy was a woman with a large, occasionally shrewd, insightful but vague and disorganized mind.[4] Like the prophets of old—and some of more recent vintage—she did what she had to do but was not altogether attractive or consistent while doing it. Childlike, she wished Science to be the ultimate, absolute cure; until her death, compelled by the leader's blueprint, it was. It had been discredited as a sole medical cure for organically ill patients before 1910, and would achieve a greater respectability in a holistic curative environment. It would likewise prosper once its demonic aspect withered and detached itself from the spiritual religion. To peruse a current *Christian Science Monitor*, with one column of each twenty-page issue devoted to the religion and its metaphysical healing qualities,[5] one would hardly believe that Malicious Animal Magnetism (MAM) or health were ever—sometimes still are—legal and social issues.

Personal and cultural anxieties intersected during the lifetime of Mary Baker Eddy, creating the phenomenon of Christian Science. "Mrs. Eddy was not a material reformer in the usual acceptance of the term. She did not uplift humanity through human ethics . . . but through the ethics of truth. . . . She was not the founder of a sect, but was the 'scribe of Spirit.' "[6] Perhaps that is why biographers of Mary Baker Eddy either suffer from motivational indefinition or cringe upon finding their subject to be merely human. In an unguarded moment, Eddy lifted the veil of spirituality to reveal a mortal and quite human thought revelatory of the woman: "let us be wise today. Tomorrow is not ours. When we reach it, it is gone."[7] There are altogether too few of these insights in a life informed by "Principle" and divine metaphysics. But it is, of course, an easier task to deal with the facts and motivations of culture than with the creative chemistry and driven individuality of a "spiritual scribe." Thankfully, the founder's obsessions died with her and, like some great wave whose fury is spent upon the shore, only her legacy remains.

NOTES

1. Robert Wright, "Science, God and Man," *Time* 140 (28 December 1992): 43–44.

2. J. H. Bates, *Christian Science and Its Problems* (New York: Eaton and Mains, 1898), 6–7.

3. Harford Powell, Jr., "Are Women Losing Their Hold?" *Collier's Magazine* 76 (5 December 1925): 6.

4. Will Irwin, "The Mystery of a Personality," *Collier's Magazine* 46 (24 December 1910): 16.

5. See, for example, "Friendship," *The Christian Science Monitor*, 6 January 1993, 17; "Pure Love Satisfies," *The Christian Science Monitor*, 7 January 1993, 17.

6. Augusta E. Stetson, *Reminiscences, Sermons and Correspondence Proving Adherence to the Principle of Christian Science as Taught by Mary Baker Eddy* (New York: G. P. Putnam's Sons, 1913), 1075.

7. *Letters of Mary Baker Eddy to Augusta E. Stetson, C.S.D. 1889–1909*, reproduced from the manuscript collection in the Huntington Library, San Marino, Calif. (Cuyahoga Falls, Ohio: Emma, 1990), 41–42.

Bibliography

ARCHIVAL AND MANUSCRIPT SOURCES

Eddy, Mary Morse Baker Glover. Personal Miscellaneous Papers—Mary Baker Eddy, Rare Books and Manuscripts Division, The New York Public Library, Astor, Lennox and Tilden Foundations, New York City.

Streeter, Frank Sherwin. Mary Baker Eddy Litigation Papers, 1907, 1912. New Hampshire Historical Society, Concord, N.H.

PUBLIC DOCUMENTS, COLLECTIONS AND LETTERS

Letters of Mary Baker Eddy to Augusta E. Stetson, C.S.D. 1889–1909. Reproduced from the manuscript collection in the Huntington Library, San Marino, California. Cuyahoga Falls, OH: Emma, 1990.

Messages and Papers of the Presidents. 20 vols. New York: Bureau of National Literature, 1914.

Stetson, Augusta E. *Reminiscences, Sermons and Correspondence Proving Adherence to the Principle of Christian Science as Taught by Mary Baker Eddy*. New York: G. P. Putnam's Sons, 1913.

UNPUBLISHED WORK

Mellard, Douglas. "The Religious Dispute over Slavery." Bachelor's Essay, College of Charleston, 1992.

NEWSPAPERS

Brooklyn Daily Eagle (1892, 1898–1902)
The Christian Science Monitor (1992–93)
The Jewish Review and Observer (1922)
The New York Daily Tribune (1889, 1893, 1897–98, 1900–1903, 1906)

The New York Evening Post (1901, 1905–7, 1909–10)
The New York Herald (1910)
The New York Sun (1910)
The New York Times (1887, 1889–90, 1892, 1894–95, 1897–1905, 1908, 1910, 1991)
The New York World (1910)

MAGAZINES AND PERIODICALS

American Catholic Quarterly Review 30 (January 1905): 132–42.
The Arena 7 (April 1893): 554–67; 21 (May 1899): 537–70; 37 (January 1907): 47–67;
        38 (July 1907): 52–61, (September 1907): 320, (October 1907): 408–32, (November 1907): 567–74; 41 (July 1909): 452–60.
Atlantic Monthly 88 (October 1901): 566–71; 93 (April 1904): 433–48.
Bibliotheca Sacra 59 (October 1902): 682–95; 85 (October 1928): 417–23.
Blackwood's Edinburgh Magazine 165 (April 1899): 659–68, (May 1899): 845–52.
Business Week (1974)
Canadian Magazine 6 (December 1895): 183–87.
Catholic Mind, no. 24 (22 December 1906): 487–502.
Catholic World 80 (February 1905): 638–52; 96 (November 1912): 180–90, (December
        1912): 360–69, (January 1913): 466–76, (February 1913): 655–60.
Chautauquan 10 (March 1890): 715–21.
Collier's Magazine 46 (24 December 1910): 16–17; 76 (5 December 1925): 6.
Congress Monthly 59 (November–December 1992): 3–4.
Cosmopolitan 43 (July 1908): 330–34; 45 (August 1908): 319–23.
Current Literature 41 (August 1906): 202–4, 43 (September 1907): 301–5; (December
        1907): 651–52; 45 (August 1908): 184–87; 46 (January 1909): 65–68, (April
        1909): 408–10; 47 (July 1909): 70–74; 50 (January 1911): 58–61.
Current Opinion 63 (June 1919): 382–83.
Dublin Review 143 (July 1908): 61–71.
Hibbert Journal 57 (January 1959): 161–70.
Homiletic Review 37 (January 1899): 15–20.
The Independent 55 (19 March 1903): 776–79.
Literary Digest 44 (4 May 1912): 940.
London Quarterly Review 136 (July 1921): 58–71.
McClure's Magazine 28 (December 1906): 211–17, (January 1907): 227–42, (February
        1907): 339–54, (March 1907): 506–24, (April 1907): 608–27; 29 (May 1907):
        97–116, (June 1907): 333–48, (July 1907): 447–62, (August 1907): 567–81,
        (October 1907): 688–99; 30 (February 1908): 387–401, (March 1908): 577–
        90, (April 1908), 699–712; 31 (May 1908): 16–31, (June 1908): 179–89; 39
        (September 1912): 481–94.
Methodist Review 80 (March 1898): 281–91.
The Monist 17 (April 1907): 161–72, 186–99.
Montreal Medical Journal (August 1904): 1–16.
The Nation 86 (25 June 1908): 572–75; 90 (10 February 1910): 138–39.
New Church Review 3 (January 1896): 10–36.
New England Magazine 51 (April 1914): 56–66.
New York Medical Times (December 1888): 1–64.
Nineteenth Century and After 98 (October 1925): 560–80.

North American Review 169 (August 1899): 190–209; 173 (July 1901): 22–34; 176 (January 1903): 1–9, (February 1903): 174–84, (March 1903): 349–64, (April 1903): 505–17; 184 (15 March 1907): 636–45.

Open Court 1 (21 July 1887): 320–23.

Outlook 49 (24 March 1894): 526–27; 62 (15 July 1899): 606–7; 68 (6 July 1901): 606–7; 83 (23 June 1906): 404–6; 85 (9 March 1907): 545–46; 93 (23 October 1909): 363; 96 (17 December 1910): 843–44.

Overland Monthly 53 (February 1909): 147–52.

Popular Science Monthly 34 (April 1889): 798–809; 67 (September 1900): 461–72; 72 (March 1908): 211–23.

Psychological Review 10 (November 1903): 593–614.

Spectator 81 (12 November 1898): 680–81; 86 (25 May 1901): 760–61.

Time 140 (28 December 1992): 36–44.

Westminster Review 167 (February 1907): 159–69.

World To-Day 7 (April 1905): 403–6.

Yankee 56 (July 1992): 76–93, 112–24.

SCHOLARLY ARTICLES, MONOGRAPHS, PAMPHLETS, ADDRESSES, SERMONS AND SECONDARY WORKS

Adams, Henry. *The Education of Henry Adams*. Boston: Houghton Mifflin, 1961.

Auchincloss, W. S. *The Mask of Eddyism*. New York: n.p., 1907.

Bailey, Thomas A., and David M. Kennedy. *The American Pageant*. 9th ed. 2 vols. Lexington, Mass.: D. C. Heath, 1991.

Ballard, Frank. *Eddyism Miscalled Christian Science: A Delusion and a Snare*. London: Robert Culley, 1909.

Baltzell, E. Digby. *The Protestant Establishment*. New York: Vintage Books, 1964.

Banner, Lois W. *Elizabeth Cady Stanton*. Boston: Little, Brown, 1980.

Barrington, A. H. *Anti-Christian Cults*. Milwaukee: The Young Churchman, 1898.

Bates, J. H. *Christian Science and Its Problems*. New York: Eaton and Mains, 1898.

Bates, J. Leonard. *The United States 1898–1928*. New York: McGraw Hill, 1976.

Beasley, Norman. *The Cross and the Crown*. New York: Duell, Sloan and Pearce, 1953.

Bernheim, Isaac W. *The Reform Church of American Israelites*. n.p., 1921.

———. *An Open Letter to Rabbi Stephen S. Wise*. Louisville: n.p., 1922.

Boller, Paul E., Jr. *American Thought in Transition: The Impact of Evolutionary Naturalism 1865–1900*. Chicago: Rand McNally, 1970.

Braden, Charles S. *Christian Science Today*. Dallas: Southern Methodist University Press, 1958.

Bronson, S. C. *Delusions*. Burlington, Iowa: Acres, Blackman, 1895.

Buckley, James Monroe. *Christian Science and Other Superstitions*. New York: Century, 1899.

———. *Faith Healing, Christian Science and Kindred Phenomena*. New York: Century, 1892.

Calvert, B. *Science and Health*. n.p.: n.d.

Canham, Erwin D. *Commitment to Freedom*. Boston: Houghton Mifflin, 1958.

Chalmers, David Mark. *The Muckrake Years*. New York: D. Von Nostrand, 1974.

Clark, Gordon. *The Church of St. Bunco*. New York: Abbey Press, 1901.

Cooper, John Milton, Jr. *Pivotal Decades: The United States 1900–1920*. New York: W. W. Norton, 1990.

Cornford, Francis MacDonald. ed. and trans. *The Republic of Plato*. New York: Oxford University Press, 1967.

Cross, Robert D. *The Emergence of Liberal Catholicism in America*. Chicago: Quadrangle Books, 1968.

Cunningham, Raymond J. "The Impact of Christian Science on American Churches, 1880–1910." *American Historical Review* 72 (April 1967): 885–905.

Current, Richard N. *The Lincoln Nobody Knows*. New York: Hill and Wang, 1969.

Dakin, Edwin Franden. *Mrs. Eddy: The Biography of a Virginal Mind*. New York: Charles Scribner's Sons, 1930.

Davis, Allen F. *American Heroine: The Life and Legend of Jane Addams*. New York: Oxford University Press, 1973.

Degler, Carl N. *The Age of the Economic Revolution 1876–1900*. 2d ed. Glenview, Ill.: Scott, Foresman, 1977.

Dixon, Amzi Clarence. *The Christian Science Delusion*. London: Marshall Brothers, 1918.

———. *Is Christian Science A Humbug?* Boston: James H. Earle, 1901.

Dollar, Charles M., Joan R. Gundersen, Ronald N. Satz, H. Viscount Nelson, Jr., and Gary W. Reichard. *America: Changing Times*. 2d ed. New York: John Wiley and Sons, 1982.

Dresser, Horatio, ed. *The Quimby Manuscripts*. New York: Thomas Y. Crowell, 1921.

Dresser, Julius A. *The True History of Mental Healing*. Boston: Alfred Mudge and Son, 1887.

Eddy, Mary Baker. *Miscellaneous Writings 1883–1896*. Boston: Trustees under the Will of Mary Baker Eddy, 1896.

———. *Science and Health with Key to the Scriptures*. 11th ed. Boston: Trustees under the Will of Mary Baker Eddy, 1934.

Editorial Comments on the Life and Work of Mary Baker Eddy. Boston: Christian Science, 1911.

Erikson, Erik H. *Young Man Luther: A Study in Psychoanalysis and History*. New York: W. W. Norton, 1962.

Finley, John Huston. *A Pilgrim in Palestine*. New York: Charles Scribner's Sons, 1919.

Fisher, Herbert Albert Laurens. *Our New Religion*. London: Ernest Benn, 1929.

Fleming, Donald. *William H. Welch and the Rise of Modern Medicine*. Boston: Little, Brown, 1954.

Gordon, Adoniram J. *Christian Science Not Scriptural*. Boston: n.p., 187_.

Gottschalk, Stephen. *The Emergence of Christian Science in American Religious Life*. Berkeley: University of California Press, 1975.

Gray, James M. *The Antidote to Christian Science*. New York: Fleming H. Revell, 1907.

Greene, Reverend George Francis. *Christian Science and the Gospel of Jesus Christ*. Cranford, N.J.: Chronicle, 1902.

Griffen, Clyde. "The Progressive Ethos." In *The Development of an American Culture*. Edited by Stanley Coben and Lorman Ratner. 2d ed. New York: St. Martin's, 1983.

Haldeman, Isaac Massey. *An Analysis of Christian Science: Based on Its Own Statements.* Philadelphia: Bible, 1909.

_____ . *Christian Science in the Light of Holy Scripture.* New York: Fleming H. Revell, 1909.

_____ . *Christian Science Unveiled in Its Own Words.* New York: n.p., 192_.

_____ . *Mental Assassination or Christian Science.* New York: n.p., 192_.

Handlin, Oscar. *Boston's Immigrants.* New York: Atheneum, 1977.

Hart, Dean. *A Way That Seemeth Right: An Examination of Christian Science.* New York: James Pott, 1897.

Harwood, Ann. *An English View of Christian Science: An Exposure.* New York: Fleming H. Revell, 1899.

Hayes, Carlton J. H. *A Generation of Materialism 1871–1900.* New York: Harper and Row, 1963.

Hegeman, J. Winthrop. *Must Protestantism Adopt Christian Science?* New York: Harper and Row, 1914.

Higham, John. *Strangers in the Land.* New York: Atheneum, 1970.

Hirshson, Stanley P. *Farewell to the Bloody Shirt.* Bloomington: Indiana University Press, 1966.

Hofstadter, Richard. *The Age of Reform.* New York: Vintage Books, 1955.

_____ . *Anti-Intellectualism in American Life.* New York: Vintage Books, 1963.

Hollifield, A. Nelson. *Christian Science or Mind Cure.* Newark: Advertiser, 1889.

Hopkins, Henry Reed. "The Progress of Eddyism." *American Medical Quarterly.* Reprint, 1900.

Hughes, H. Stuart. *The Obstructed Path.* New York: Harper and Row, 1968.

Jones, F. D., and W. H. Mills. *History of the Presbyterian Church in South Carolina.* Columbia, S.C.: R. L. Bryan, 1926.

Kaplan, Justin. *Lincoln Steffens: A Biography.* New York: Simon and Schuster, 1974.

Kimball, Gayle. *The Religious Ideas of Harriet Beecher Stowe: Her Gospel of Womanhood.* New York: Edwin Mellen, 1982.

Knee, Stuart E. *The Concept of Zionist Dissent in the American Mind.* New York: Robert Speller and Sons, 1979.

_____ . "John Brown and the Abolitionist Ministry." *Negro History Bulletin* 45 (April–June 1982): 36–37, 42.

Kraus, Michael. *The United States to 1865.* Ann Arbor: The University of Michigan Press, 1959.

Kraut, Benny. "Not So Strange Bedfellows: Felix Adler and Ahad Ha'am." *American Jewish Archives* 37 (November 1985): 305–8.

Krull, Virgilius Herman. *A Common Sense View of Christian Science.* Collegeville, Ind.: St. Joseph's Printing Office, 1908.

Lawson, Albert G. *A Short Method with Christian Science.* Philadelphia: American Baptist Association, 1902.

Leech, Margaret. *In the Days of McKinley.* New York: Harper and Brothers, 1959.

Locke, Charles Edward. *Eddyism—Is It Christian? Is It Scientific? How Long Will It Last?* Los Angeles: Grafton, 1911.

Mackey, Albert G., ed. *Encyclopedia of Freemasonry and Kindred Sciences Comprising the Whole Range of the Arts, Sciences and Literature of the Masonic Institutions.* 2 vols. Chicago: Masonic History, 1929.

Malone, Dumas, and Basil Rauch. *The New Nation 1865–1917*. New York: Appleton-Century-Crofts, 1960.

Marsden, George M. *Religion and American Culture*. New York: Harcourt Brace Jovanovich, 1990.

Marshall, Dorothy. *Eighteenth-Century England*. New York: David McKay, 1966.

Matthews, F. H. "The Americanization of Sigmund Freud: Adaptations of Psychoanalysis before 1917." *Journal of American Studies* (April 1967): 39–62. In *Builders of American Institutions*. Edited by Frank Freidel, Norman Pollack and Robert Crunden. 2d ed. 2 vols. Chicago: Rand McNally, 1972.

May, Henry F. *Ideas, Faiths and Feelings*. New York: Oxford University Press, 1983.

McHenry, Robert, ed. *A Documentary History of Conservation in America*. New York: Praeger, 1972.

McLoughlin, William G. *Revivals, Awakenings and Reforms*. Chicago: University of Chicago Press, 1978.

McPherson, James M. *Abraham Lincoln and the Second American Revolution*. New York: Oxford University Press, 1990.

Medicare Handbook. Baltimore: U.S. Department of Health and Human Services, 1989.

Meyer, Donald. *The Positive Thinkers: A Study of the American Quest for Health, Wealth and Personal Power from Mary Baker Eddy to Norman Vincent Peale*. New York: Doubleday, 1965.

Miller, Kerby A. *Emigrants and Exiles*. New York: Oxford University Press, 1985.

Moore, A. Lincoln. *Christian Science: Its Manifold Attractions*. Harrisburg, Pa.: Star Independent, 1906.

Moore, R. Laurence. *Religious Outsiders and the Making of Americans*. New York: Oxford University Press, 1986.

Morris, Lloyd. *Postscript to Yesterday: America, The Last Fifty Years*. New York: Random House, 1947.

Moulton, T. G. *An Exposure of Christian Science*. London: James Nisbet, 1906.

Mowry, George E. *The Era of Theodore Roosevelt and the Birth of Modern America 1900–1912*. New York: Harper and Row, 1958.

Nash, Roderick. *From These Beginnings: A Biographical Approach to American History*. 3d ed. 2 vols. New York: Harper and Row, 1984.

Noble, David W. *The Progressive Mind 1890–1917*. Chicago: Rand McNally, 1970.

Norton, Carol. *Legal Aspects of Christian Science*. Boston: Christian Science, 1899.

Oates, Stephen B. *With Malice toward None*. New York: New American Library, 1978.

O'Dell, Reverend Willis P. *A Sermon on the Theology of Christian Science*. New York: n.p., 1904.

Olitzky, Kerry M. "The Sunday-Sabbath Movement in American Reform Judaism: Strategy or Evolution?" *American Jewish Archives* 34 (April 1982): 75–88.

Parkes, Henry Bamford. *The American Experience*. New York: Vintage Books, 1959.

Parmele, Mary Platt. *Christian Science: Is It Christian? Is It Scientific?* New York: J. F. Taylor, 1904.

Patten, A. W. *Facts and Fallacies of Christian Science*. Chicago: n.p., 188_.

Peabody, Frederick W. *A Complete Expose of Eddyism or Christian Science and the Plain Truth in Plain Terms Regarding Mary Baker Glover Eddy*. n.p., 1901.

_____. *The Religio-Medical Masquerade*. New York: Fleming H. Revell, 1910.

Peabody, William B. O. *An Address Delivered at Springfield before the Hampden Colonization Society, July 4, 1828*. Springfield: S. Bowles, 1828.

Peel, Robert. *Christian Science: Its Encounter with American Culture*. New York: Henry Holt, 1958.

_____ . *Mary Baker Eddy: The Years of Discovery*. New York: Holt, Rinehart and Winston, 1966.

Peterson, Merrill D. *The Great Triumvirate: Webster, Clay and Calhoun*. New York: Oxford University Press, 1987.

Podmore, Frank. *From Mesmer to Christian Science*. 2d ed. New York: University Books, 1963.

Powell, Lyman P. *Mary Baker Eddy: A Life Size Portrait*. New York: Macmillan, 1930.

Purrington, William A. *Christian Science: An Exposition*. New York: E. B. Treat, 1900.

Ramsay, E. Mary. *Christian Science and Its Discoverer*. Boston: Christian Science, 1935.

Rausch, David A., and Carl Hermann Voss. *Protestantism—Its Modern Meaning*. Philadelphia: Fortress, 1987.

Schaad, J. A. *Only a Mask: A Comparison of the Teachings of Christ and of Christian Science*. Kansas City, Mo.: M. C. Long, 1910.

Silberger, Julius, Jr. *Mary Baker Eddy: An Interpretive Biography of the Founder of Christian Science*. Boston: Little, Brown, 1980.

Smith, Clifford P. *Christian Science and Legislation*. Boston: Christian Science, 1905.

_____ . *Historical Sketches*. Boston: Christian Science, 1941.

Sorin, Gerald. *Abolitionism: A New Perspective*. New York: Praeger, 1972.

Spencer, William. *The Middle East*. 4th ed. Guilford, Conn.: Dushkin, 1992.

Stampp, Kenneth M. *America in 1857: A Nation on the Brink*. New York: Oxford University Press, 1990.

Susman, Warren I. *Culture as History*. New York: Pantheon Books, 1984.

Twain, Mark [Samuel Langhorne Clemens]. *Christian Science*. New York: Harper and Brothers, 1907.

Tyler, Alice Felt. *Freedom's Ferment*. New York: Harper and Row, 1962.

Underhill, Andrew F. *Some Valid Objections to So-Called Christian Science*. Yonkers, N.Y.: Arlington Chemical Co., 1902.

Walker, Reverend J. R. *Eddyism*. Nashville: Cumberland, 1899.

Walters, Ronald G. *American Reformers 1815–1860*. New York: Hill and Wang, 1978.

Whitehead, John. *Illusions of Christian Science*. Boston: Garden, 1907.

Wilbur, Sybil. *The Life of Mary Baker Eddy*. Boston: Christian Science, 1907.

Willis, Resa. *Mark and Livy*. New York: Atheneum, 1992.

Wilson, Harold S. *McClure's Magazine and the Muckrakers*. Princeton, N.J.: Princeton University Press, 1970.

Wilson, John F., ed. *Church and State in American History*. Boston: D. C. Heath, 1965.

Winbigler, Charles F. *Christian Science and Kindred Superstitions*. London: Abbey Press, 1900.

Wood, Ezra Morgan. *Schools for Spirits*. Pittsburgh: Joseph Horner, 1903.

Woodbury, Josephine Curtis. *War in Heaven*. Boston: Press of Samuel Usher, 1897.

Index

About the Author

STUART E. KNEE is Professor of History at the College of Charleston in Charleston, South Carolina. He is the author of *The Concept of Zionist Dissent in the American Mind* and *Hervey Allen: A Literary Historian in America.*